VARIETIES
OF LITERARY
THEMATICS

Varieties

OF LITERARY THEMATICS

by
Theodore Ziolkowski

PRINCETON UNIVERSITY PRESS
PRINCETON, NEW JERSEY

Published by Princeton University Press, Princeton, New Jersey
In the United Kingdom: Princeton University Press, Guildford, Surrey

Library of Congress Cataloging in Publication Data will be
found on the last printed page of this book

ISBN 0-691-06577-2

Publication of this book has been aided by a grant
from the Whitney Darrow Publication Reserve Fund
of Princeton University Press

This book has been composed in Linotron Sabon

Clothbound editions of Princeton University Press books
are printed on acid-free paper, and binding materials are
chosen for strength and durability

Printed in the United States of America by Princeton
University Press, Princeton, New Jersey

For Pauline and Howard Behrman
with admiration and affection

CONTENTS

Contents

PREFACE

How one longs for the satisfactions of Monsieur Jourdain! That *bourgeois gentilhomme* was able to savor the simple certainty of learning a name for the prose he had been speaking all his life. I have been pursuing research of the sort represented in this volume for over twenty years, but I still know of no generally accepted term to designate the activity. Is it that much-maligned *Stoffgeschichte*? an anthropologically legitimated *Motivforschung*? a chic *thématologie*? a learned symbology? or—heaven forbid!—an awesome imagology? For a time I toyed with the notion of calling the book "Six Essays in Search of a Title." But I finally settled for the sober—though associatively resonant and, I hope, accurate—label that now adorns the title-page.

The past ten to fifteen years have witnessed an encouraging rehabilitation of the thematic approach to literary studies, which for several decades in Europe and the United States was treated with a certain condescension by literary scholars committed to the so-called *werkimmanent* forms of criticism. Increasingly, however, many have begun to appreciate that themes, motifs, and images constitute an important link between the literary work and the social, cultural, and historical contexts in which a post-formalist age now again insists on apprehending the work of art. In addition, we have come to understand that the sensible application of thematic analysis can expose aspects of the work itself that would otherwise remain inaccessible. In this volume I have assembled a group of essays that exemplify some of the varieties of literary thematics. Each essay represents an attempt to use the same basic procedures to explore

ix

different implications of the thematic material. I hope that the essays substantiate my conviction that the thematic approach alerts us in every instance to significant dimensions of the literary work ranging from the existential and socio-political to the religious and ethical.

Because several generations of literary scholars largely neglected the tools and methods of thematic research, students now attracted by this approach find little practical guidance, especially in English. In my own work I have learned principally, apart from a few such classic models as E. M. Butler's *The Fortunes of Faust* (1952) and W. B. Stanford's *The Ulysses Theme* (1954), from the example of art historians—notably Erwin Panofsky, Wolfgang Stechow, and Kenneth Clark—who have refined the techniques of iconography into sensitive procedures for analysis, interpretation, and historical explication. I have also profited from Ernst Robert Curtius' study of topoi as well as the practice of historians of ideas like Arthur O. Lovejoy. Although their subject matter is less tangible, their methods are often applicable, *mutatis mutandis*, to the study of themes, motifs, and images in literature.

As an aid to students and to colleagues interested in the kind of study represented by these essays I decided to try my hand at a practical guide to literary thematics in the form of a personal essay. I made that decision, I must confess, with certain misgivings. I am reluctant to have construed as "methodology" a set of procedures for which I claim at most a certain pragmatic validity and to have evaluated as "bibliography" a working list of reference tools that—no matter how helpful I have found them—would make many a librarian shudder. Yet the six essays do in fact display a similarity of approach and organization that prompted me to bring them together as a volume.

To keep matters in perspective, I must stress my wholehearted agreement with Harry Levin, who in his 1968 Presidential Address before the American Comparative Literature Association, chided us because "we spend too much of our energy talking—as I am now—about comparative literature, and not enough of it comparing the literature. . . . In short, the substance of our common pursuit is jeopardized by an overemphasis on organization and methodology" ("Comparing the literature," in *Yearbook of Comparative and General Literature*, 17 [1968], 5-16). I want to compare the literature—not talk about theory and methodology. Accordingly the heart of this book should be sought in the thematic essays themselves, which generated the methodological appendix, and not vice versa. I prefer to persuade and teach by example rather than by precept.

Although the six essays are topically independent, they turned out to a gratifying extent to be complementary. As I revised and collated essays written over a period of more than twenty years, I was pleased to note how often the same writers and texts kept recurring in thematically different contexts. In part, of course, this emphasis emerges from my own area of specialization. If the six pieces betray in almost every instance their origin in works of German literature, that is consistent with my conviction that thematic study properly begins with a critical question thrust upon us by a particular text and, following the cycle of investigation, should end with an act of interpretation and enhanced understanding. Since my base is German literature, works from that language, and specifically from the periods of romantic and modern literature, usually provide the *terminus a quo* for my explorations. But in my experience thematic research almost always leads beyond national and historical boundaries as soon as the scholar looks past the initial text. The thematic study of literature inevitably becomes a comparative study of literature. The appendix attempts to suggest a few means of exploring those comparative aspects in a bibliographically and procedurally systematic way. If the essays attract a few more students to the thematic approach, and if the appendix helps them to get started on their own, this book will have fulfilled its mission.

ALL THE ESSAYS but "Talking Dogs" and the "Practical Guide to Literary Thematics" have previously appeared in one form or another. "The Telltale Teeth"—originally published in *PMLA*, 91 (1976), 9-22—has been slightly expanded to accommodate several additional examples suggested by readers who were kind enough to communicate with me. I first wrote about "Der Karfunkelstein" in *Euphorion*, 55 (1961), 297-326; for this collection that piece has been wholly rewritten in English with a more comparative focus and a corresponding number of different examples. "Figures on Loan" is the full-length English text of a shorter lecture version published in German under the title "Figuren auf Pump: Zur Fiktionalität des sprachlichen Kunstwerks" in Akten des VI. Internationalen Germanisten-Kongresses: Basel 1980, *Jahrbuch für Internationale Germanistik*, Reihe A, Bd. 8/1 (Bern: Peter Lang, 1981), pp. 166-76. "The Resurrection" is the original English version of a paper (written some ten years ago) that was contributed in German as "Die Auferstehung: Ein geistesgeschichtliches Motiv des 19. Jahrhunderts im Roman des 20. Jahrhunderts," to *Literaturwissenschaft und Geistesgeschichte*. Festschrift für Richard Brinkmann, ed. Jürgen Brummack (Tübingen: Niemeyer, 1981), pp. 616-34. The essay "The Ethics of Science" is reprinted in essentially the same form in which it appeared in *Sewanee Review*, 89 (1981), 34-56, under the title "Science, Frankenstein, and Myth"; only the notes have been added. These papers are included here with the kind permission of the publishers and editors. All translations, unless otherwise indicated, are my own.

For permission to include the lines of poetry quoted in Chapter One, I am grateful to acknowledge the following:

From *Times Three* by Phyllis McGinley. Copyright 1954 by Phyllis McGinley. Originally published in *The New Yorker*. Reprinted by permission of Viking Penguin Inc.

Anyone who pursues a set of thematic topics for more than twenty years incurs a number of obligations along the way. I am appreciative for the suggestions I have received from the graduate students who worked through some of the material with me in seminars here at Princeton; from the audiences who initially heard most of the following chapters presented as lectures; and above all from my family, who have brought me treasures untold from their various worlds of art, religion, Slavics, and medieval studies. The National Endowment for the Humanities supported the preparation of the Practical Guide to Literary Thematics with a Summer Stipend in 1978. I am grateful to my Executive Assistant, Mary Gutbrodt, not just for typing an immaculate manuscript but also for managing my office so efficiently that a dean can continue to be a scholar. I remain fortunate in my associations with Princeton University Press. As readers, Lillian Feder brought to the manuscript the unique combination of graceful erudition and literary sensibility known to us from her own works of scholarship; Horst Daemmrich appraised it with the special understanding derived from his own studies of themes and motifs. Laury Egan has again enhanced a book of mine with her tasteful design. And in Jerry Sherwood I continue to benefit from a friend skilled in the art of ironic dialogue that characterizes the productive drama of author and editor.

My wife Yetta joins me in the expression of friendship intended in the dedication.

Theodore Ziolkowski
Princeton, New Jersey
Ada's Day
10 December 1982

VARIETIES
OF LITERARY
THEMATICS

Chapter One

THE TELLTALE TEETH:
PSYCHODONTIA TO
SOCIODONTIA

I

IT WOULD BE DIFFICULT to find a more appropriate graduation present for a new dentist than Günter Grass's novel *Local Anaesthetic* (1969). This is not to suggest that the plot revolves around odontology. In fact, the action of the novel can be recapitulated with no mention of teeth or dentists. The story takes place in West Berlin of 1967, where a seventeen-year-old high-school student named Philipp Scherbaum has devised a plan to publicize his opposition to violence in general and, specifically, to the use of napalm in the Vietnam war. He intends to pour gas over his pet dachshund, Max, and to set him on fire in front of the Hotel Kempinski on the Kurfürstendamm. Scherbaum reasons that the prosperous customers spooning their rich pastries in the fashionable café would hardly be impressed by merely another self-immolation of a human being. But in Berlin, the most dog-loving city in the world, the incineration of a dog is sure to create a furor. Philipp anticipates that he may well be mobbed and beaten to death by the incensed matrons of Berlin.

Several other people are intensely concerned with Scherbaum's plot. His radically politicized girlfriend, Vero Lewand, who is always armed with quotations from "Marxengels" and Chairman Mao, urges him to disregard any danger to his person and to act quickly. But his forty-year-old teacher, Eberhard Starusch, attempts in various ways to dissuade him. Drawing on examples from history and from his own past, Starusch argues that revolution always consumes its own children and that any direct political action is inevitably compromised. The novel turns into a struggle between youthful radicalism and middle-aged liberalism for the soul of the wavering intellectual. In the end the teacher seems to win: Scherbaum compromises by accepting the editorship of the student newspaper, where it is argued that he can do the most good; and the school administration appeases the student agitators by agreeing to let them have a smoking area on the school grounds. But the compromise has an ironic implication. Scherbaum has not failed to notice that his teachers invariably divert any discussion of present evil to reminiscences about their past. His real reason for forsaking the protest action, we learn, is so that he may not also be obsessed, when he is forty years old, by the memory of a single memorable incident from his youth.

Now this largely allegorical action has little to do with dentistry. But Grass has come up with a unique narrative device. Starusch suffers from a prognathous lower jaw, and during the weeks of Scherbaum's indecision he is undergoing a long and involved treatment for the condition. Most of the story gets told in the form of conversations that Starusch invents between himself and his dentist. It is never absolutely clear how much of the dialogue actually takes place and how much is merely imagined. Most of the time no talk is possible since Starusch's mouth is filled with aspirators, cotton swabs, casts, and the fingers of the dentist's assistant. We must even assume that many of the telephone conversations between Starusch and his dentist, in the weeks between the treatments of the upper and the lower jaws, are simply a product of his imagination. To complicate the situation even more, the dentist has a television set in his office. As Starusch watches the set, his imagination is stimulated by the blank screen, the ads, the news

4

reports, and the shows—e.g., reruns of "Lassie" or cooking lessons—to think about his own past, which becomes weirdly blended with the events on the television screen. As a result, even though during most of the novel Starusch is sitting immobile in the dentist's automated chair, undergoing painful operations and unable to utter a word, we obtain a great deal of information about his life and fantasies as well as the affairs of his student, Philipp Scherbaum.

In the course of all this we also learn much about the history, theory, and practice of dentistry. First, we get a detailed and graphic description of the cleaning of Starusch's teeth as well as the measures undertaken for the adjustment of his prognathous bite. (The novel also turns out to be a catalog of dental technology with rhapsodies on saliva ejectors, air-turbine drills, ultrasonic scalers, and water piks.) Second, the book contains a thumbnail sketch of the history of dentistry. It begins with a threefold invocation of St. Apollonia, the patron saint of dentists and those who suffer from toothache, since as part of her martyrdom in third-century Alexandria her teeth were torn out. We hear about dental practices among the Romans as well as the brutal methods of extraction before the invention of anesthetics. There are speculations, finally, about the possible effects of toothache in world history. Could it be, we are asked, that Nero set fire to Rome simply because he was suffering from a severe toothache? (p. 76, p. 217).[1]

All this might be considered irrelevant and even distracting were it not for the fact that Grass develops the odontological material into a consistent image for society as a whole.[2] Starusch, whose prognathous bite suggests a certain brutality and who now submits to a treatment that will give him normal human articulation, is not merely an individual; this teacher of German literature and history represents an entire generation of Germans trying to come to terms with past illness and present moral discomfort. "I regard pain as an instrument of knowledge," he concedes (p. 175). The dentist to

whose treatment he submits remains nameless and face-
less—we know him only from the tennis shoes he wears—
because he represents the anonymous and impersonal
social engineer of the modern welfare state that promises
to cure all ills through technology. The dentist has developed a veritable philosophy of odontology. He gives
lectures at a local community college on tooth decay,
which he abhors with moral fervor as "a by-product of
civilization" (p. 134). Tartar is explained psychologically as "calcified hate" (p. 31) and capitalism is likened
politically to the tartar on the teeth of society (p. 139).
As a rationalist, the dentist is opposed to drastic revolutionary acts and advocates preventive measures instead, in dentistry as well as politics. When Starusch
outlines his plan for dissuading Scherbaum, the dentist
gives him some sober practical advice, "as though speaking of a root treatment" (p. 132). Politics, the dentist
argues, must be put on the rational basis of science and
preventive medicine. "In contrast to politics, modern
medicine can point to achievements which show con-
clusively that progress is possible if we confine ourselves
strictly and exclusively to the findings of natural science
and the results of empirical research" (p. 179).[3]

In the course of his treatment Starusch permits himself
to succumb for a time to this vision of an "age of pro-
phylaxis" (p. 188), in which preventive measures will
be taken against every evil. He dreams of a society in
which religions and ideologies will disappear because
"the question of being is answered . . . by hygiene and
enlightenment" (p. 188). And yet, as Starusch realizes
by the end of the book, any such sanitized society must
inevitably fail because it involves too many compromises
of the sort that Scherbaum is forced to make. The local
anesthetic upon which dentistry and the welfare state
pride themselves diverts our attention from causes to
symptoms. It eases the pain for a time, but it does not
do away with the problem. Whenever aggressive impulses—like the war in Vietnam—burst out they are
momentarily stilled or, in the idiom of the novel, locally

anesthetized. But the anesthetic never lasts. In the last paragraph we learn that a new infection has undermined Starusch's bridgework. The bland solutions of social engineering cannot eradicate the deep pains of existence.

Grass's dentist exposes his feelings long enough at one point to complain that there are so few dentists in literature, even in comedies. (The only exceptions, he notes, are certain spy stories in which microfilm is hidden in bridgework.) He believes that dentists are condemned to secondary roles because their work has become too painless and inconspicuous to be interesting. "Local anaesthesia prevents us from being weirdies" (p. 124). But if Grass's orthodontist had put aside his professional journals long enough to keep up with contemporary literature, he would have known that an entire fictional branch of the American Dental Association could be established by the dentists who people American novels of the sixties alone. The forerunner of all these contemporary literary dentists is of course the hulking, slow-witted hero of Frank Norris's naturalistic novel *McTeague* (1899), who operates a Dental Parlor in San Francisco even though he has no training or degree but only a shelf-full of books. Norris describes dental procedures in careful realistic detail, cribbing many passages directly from Thomas Fillebrown's *A Text-book of Operative Dentistry*.[4] But McTeague himself is concerned not with teeth so much as with gold. This *idée fixe* is stated on the first page of the novel, when we hear of McTeague's ambition to have "a huge gilded tooth, a molar with enormous prongs, something gorgeous and attractive" to advertise his office. And it continues to the end when, forced to abandon dentistry to work in the gold mines, he notes in the drills and bits "a queer counterpart of his old-time dental machines" (Ch. 20). The narrator-hero of Saul Bellow's *Henderson the Rain King* (1959), in contrast, is as much obsessed with his teeth as is Grass's Starusch, although for the American the aching in his gums is not a symptom of conscience, but a sensation that accompanies the experience of beauty.

7

After he breaks his acrylic bridge on a hard biscuit, he devotes the better part of a chapter (Ch. 10) to an account of his dental history. Henderson speaks at length of Doctor Spohr, the New York dentist who made the bridge he has just broken. But more colorful by far is his first dentist in Paris, a women endowed with such a large bust that she smothered her patients as she worked and who objected to American dentistry "on artistic grounds." When Henderson sits down in her chair, "she starts to stifle me as she extracts the nerve from a tooth in order to anchor the bridge. And while fitting the same she puts a stick in my mouth and says, 'Grincez! Grincez les dents! Fâchez-vous.' And so I grince and fâche for all I'm worth and eat the wood. She grinds her own teeth to show me how." Whereas these two dentists occupy only one vivid chapter in Bellow's novel, a colleague of theirs plays one of the major roles in John Updike's *Couples* (1968). Freddy Thorne, a competent dentist "obsessed with decay," is an insecure man who uses his bedside collection of pornography and his lewd conversation to conceal his inadequacies. When Freddy helps Piet Hanema to arrange an abortion for his mistress (a "little pelvic orthodonture," as he calls it), he demands in return a night in bed with Piet's wife—and turns out to be impotent.

Norris's McTeague, Bellow's Mlle Montecuccoli, and Updike's Freddy Thorne, though memorable as characters, are not true philosophers of odontology in comparison with such figures as Dudley Eigenvalue, D.D.S., in Thomas Pynchon's *V.* (1963). Eigenvalue, whose Park Avenue office houses a museum of dental history, propounds a theory that he calls "psychodontia"; just as psychoanalysis once usurped the role of father-confessor from the priesthood, now "the analyst in his turn was about to be deposed by, of all people, the dentist" (Ch. 7). According to Eigenvalue's theory, the soft pulp of the tooth is the warm pulsing id that is protected and sheltered by the "enamel" of the superego; neurosis is equated with "malocclusion"; and so forth. Whereas

Pynchon's psychodontist regards teeth as a clue to the patient's emotional state, other fictional dentists practice what might more fittingly be called sociodontia. Consider the Reverend Doctor Lionel Jason David Jones, D.D.S. and D.D., in Kurt Vonnegut's *Mother Night* (1966), a bigot and racial agitator who has a "political interpretation of teeth" according to which "the teeth of Jews and Negroes proved beyond question that both groups were degenerate" (Ch. 13). As his investigations proceed, he even begins "to detect proof of degeneracy in the teeth of Catholics and Unitarians."

But it is not enough merely to establish the presence of these dentists—psychodontists and sociodontists alike—who drill away in contemporary German and American fiction. In order to appreciate these philosophers of decay, who assign psychological and political significance to tartar and caries and who gaze into their patients' mouths as raptly as any soothsayer into a crystal ball, we need to consider the history of human attitudes toward teeth.

II

WHEN TEETH OCCUR in cultural contexts, as opposed to specifically odontological ones, they tend to be characterized by one of three attributes: potency, beauty, or pain. In myth and folklore, teeth have long symbolized sexual vigor as well as wisdom. In Greek mythology Cadmus brought forth a race of warriors by sowing upon a plain the teeth of a dragon he had slain, a motif exploited by C. L. Sulzberger in his political satire *The Tooth Merchant* (1973), in which an Armenian agent stumbles upon the still potent dragon's teeth and tries to sell the troops to Stalin, Roosevelt, and other leaders of contemporary world powers. In the age of Chaucer, to have a "coltes tooth" was a proverbial expression implying youthful sexual vigor (Reeve's Tale, Wife of Bath's Prologue).⁵ In Egyptian iconography the god Horus is often depicted with his thumb in his mouth during moments of deliberation; and according to Celtic legend, Fionn places his thumb under his tooth whenever he requires magical guidance.

Because of their symbolic potency it is imperative to guard against the loss of teeth. In the Old Testament one of the most terrible curses involves the appeal to God to break the teeth of the enemy (Job iv:10; Psalms iii:7; Psalms lviii:6). Sir James Frazer tells of African tribes in which the king cannot be crowned if he is symbolically emasculated by having a broken tooth; and in another tribe the ruler is put to death if he loses a tooth.[6] Because of the virtue inherent in teeth, they must not be allowed to fall into the hands of one's enemies; extracted teeth should be buried or hidden, a superstition still evident in the practice of mothers who carefully save their children's baby teeth. Another popular belief has it that teeth should be salted and burned in order to keep them away from witches. Of course, the sexual implications of teeth are familiar to Freud, who interprets the pulling of teeth in dreams as castration.[7] By the same token, when Anse Bundren finally acquires his false teeth at the end of William Faulkner's *As I Lay Dying* (1930), the spiritual boost "made him look a foot taller," giving him the confidence he needs to acquire a new wife.

For these reasons, teeth make potent charms and relics.[8] At Kandy, in Ceylon, a tooth of the Buddha is preserved in the Temple of the Holy Tooth; in *The Song of Roland* (St. 173) the hero has a tooth of St. Peter set in the pommel of his sword Durendel; and when Robert Guiscard laid siege to Salerno in 1076, he demanded as part of the surrender terms the tooth of St. Matthew that was owned by the ruler of the city. Among many peoples, a tooth set as a jewel is considered a good-luck charm of considerable virtue, a superstition still evident in the lodge emblem worn by members of the Order of Elks. In F. Scott Fitzgerald's *The Great Gatsby* (1925) the gangster Meyer Wolfsheim wears cuff-links made of "the finest specimens of human molars" (Ch. 4). The view of teeth as a symbol of potency is preserved, finally, in language, which in its metaphors constitutes a vast repository of ancient beliefs. Thus, if something sets our teeth on edge or if someone casts an insult in our teeth, we can gnash our teeth in anger, show our teeth belligerently, grit our teeth resolutely, take the bit in our teeth, arm ourselves to the teeth, then fight tooth and nail in the teeth of great danger and, with luck, escape by the skin of our teeth.

The attribution of magical significance to teeth helps to account for the ancient practice of dental ablation, which has been observed in skulls dating from the neolithic period in many parts of the world. In some societies one or two incisors are removed during the rites of passage as a test of manhood or to provide an exit through which evil spirits may escape from the body. On the Sandwich Islands, young men sacrificed their front teeth to the gods, and among certain tribes of southwest China girls had two of their incisors knocked out on their wedding day to mark them as married women. In Japan, through the nineteenth century, married women resorted to a less violent surrogate: they stained their teeth with a solution of urine, iron, and saki to achieve the black gleam (resembling a gap in the teeth) that distinguished them from unmarried maidens. Although most of these practices—including filing, notching, and staining of the teeth—originated as religious rituals with sexual connotations, the magical origins were gradually lost sight of, and mutilated or darkened teeth came to be regarded as a mark of beauty, as in Japanese geisha culture. To cite a contemporary example, the inlaying of teeth with precious stones among Central American Indian tribes originally had religious meaning; but when two stars of the Baltimore Bullets basketball team had diamond stars embedded in their teeth, they were presumably motivated by purely decorative impulses.[9]

These oddities of dental lore are worth noting for at least two reasons. First, they provide dramatic evidence for the shift from the superstitious view of teeth to the cosmetic view: many modern beliefs concerning teeth have their origin in religious or cultic practices. Second, they suggest the extent to which the current Western ideal of shining white teeth is culturally determined since in some societies mutilated or darkened teeth are considered comme il faut.

The Old Testament mentions teeth with notable frequency, so often that dental historians cite it as evidence for the surmise that the Hebrews, in contrast to the Egyptians, were blessed with unusually sound teeth.[10] Yet most of the biblical references to teeth betray that the Hebrews are still close to the superstitious view. Virtually all the teeth occur in contexts involving potency (e.g., the teeth of the enemy that are to be shattered) or in such pronouncedly sexual contexts as the Song of Solomon (iv:2 and vi:6): "Thy teeth are like a flock of sheep that are even shorn, which came up from the washing."

But teeth do not belong to the standard canon of attributes—such as hair, eyes, cheeks, lips—normally cited in classical and medieval literature. The reasons seem fairly obvious. In the first place, the grinning face that is considered socially de rigueur in the mid-twentieth century is a product of our image-conscious culture. The Romans had a highly developed art of dentistry, as we know from a variety of texts ranging from Pliny's *Natural History* to Martial's epigrams, and they set great store by healthy teeth. Yet it was not consistent with Roman *gravitas* to expose the teeth in smiles. Thus Catullus (*Carmina*, no. xxxix, ll. 1-7) pokes fun at a young man named Egnatius, who was so vain of his perfect white teeth that he went around with a huge grin on his face, like a Hollywood matinee idol:

> Egnatius, quod candidos habet dentes,
> renidet usquequaque. . . .
> . . . quicquid est, ubicumquest,
> quodcumque agit, renidet.

To take an example of a different kind: among the 330 illustrations in John Pope-Hennessy's magisterial study

The Portrait in the Renaissance[11] fewer than ten show even the slightest glint of teeth; and not a single face displays a toothy smile. By contrast, in the 1970-71 picture book of the Princeton University faculty, well over a hundred of the 660 photographs reveal teeth, most of them in full glittering grins.

In the second place, given the precarious state of dental hygiene during what Henry James once called the "undentisted ages,"[12] an otherwise beautiful girl might display far less than flattering teeth if she opened her lovely lips. As a result, in medieval literature we hear much more about toothaches than about pearly teeth. Fredegard of St. Riquier (fl. 825) composed twenty-four Latin hexameters to tell how the song of a thrush charmed away his toothache;[13] Heinrich Kaufringer relates a *märe* in which a young wife uses toothache as an excuse to meet her lover;[14] and the *Roman de la Rose* (ll. 1075-76) draws on the popular lapidaries of the period for its allusion to a magical stone that cures toothache. To be sure, lovely teeth are cited from time to time. In his work *On Christian Doctrine* (*De Doctrina Christiana*, Bk. II, Ch. vi), Augustine interprets the quoted passage from the Song of Solomon allegorically, likening the saints to the healthy teeth of the Church (*quasi dentes ecclesiae*): "They bite men off from their heresies and carry them over to the body of the Church when their hardness of heart has been softened as if by being bitten off and chewed." Wolfram von Eschenbach praises a lady's kissable mouth by saying:

> von snêwîzem beine
> nâhe bî ein ander kleine,
> sus stuonden ir die liechten zene.
> (*Parzival*, Sec. 130, ll. 11-13)

And the pretty heroine of *Aucassin et Nicolette* is characterized by "les dens blans et menus" (xii, 22). Yet in these fairly infrequent cases we sense that the attribute is singled out precisely because of its rarity: lovely teeth amount to a literary topos inasmuch as they belong to a conventional vision of the ideal that seldom finds a

counterpart in reality. Indeed, it was regarded as so un-
likely that anti-Petrarchan poets in seventeenth-century
England often inverted the topos in such "deformed mistress" poems as John Collop's "On Dentipicta: A Lady
with Enamell'd Teeth, Black, White and Yellow."[15]

The image of lovely teeth, admired because they are
so rare, reaches its weird culmination in Poe's "Berenice"
(1835), in which a young man named Egaeus tells of his
fateful love for his cousin, who suffers from a kind of
epilepsy that frequently terminates in a deathlike cata-
tonic trance. Egaeus, for his part, is afflicted by a psychological disorder that he calls "monomania": an "un-
due, earnest, and morbid attention . . . excited by objects
in their own nature frivolous" (p. 86).[16] One day, when
Berenice parts her lips in a smile, Egaeus fixes his attention upon her teeth. From that moment forth he is unable
to rid his mind of its obsession with "the white and
ghastly spectrum of the teeth. Not a speck on their surface—not a shade on their enamel—not an indenture in
their edges . . . long, narrow, and excessively white, with
the pale lips writhing about them" (p. 88). Unable to
think of anything else, Egaeus longs for the teeth "with
a phrenzied desire" (p. 89) and convinces himself that
he could be restored to health and reason if only he
could possess them. As this distraught fetishist sits en-
tertaining his morbid lust for his cousin's teeth, a servant
bursts in with the news that Berenice has died of an
epileptic fit. After the interment, in a state of shock,
Egaeus cowers in his library, trying to decipher some
"dim, and hideous, and unintelligible recollections" (p.
90) when again a servant enters with the horrendous
report that the grave has been desecrated and the in-
truder has removed all of Berenice's teeth. It turns out
that Egaeus himself, in one of his seizures, has violated
the grave in order to obtain the coveted teeth, which
now repose in a box on his desk.

Poe's tale was allegedly inspired by a report he read
in the *Baltimore Saturday Visitor* (23 Feb. 1835) concerning grave robbers who stole teeth for dentists, a

ghoulish practice that can be explained by the fact that the first adequate porcelain teeth were not made available to the public on a commercial scale until 1844. (Recall Fantine in Hugo's *Les Misérables*, who sells her two front teeth to a dentist for forty francs.) Poe's obsession with teeth has been interpreted psychoanalytically as a product of his fear of being destroyed by women (the motif of the *vagina dentata*) or as a surrogate for his obsessional attachment to the womb.[17] In both cases the associations are clearly sexual. But as a literary image—as distinct from Poe's subjective psychological motivation—Berenice's teeth are quite conventional: they represent an intensification of the topos of beautiful teeth that goes back by way of the Old Testament to the primitive identification of teeth with potency.

Egaeus' obsession with Berenice's teeth makes sense only in an age when lovely teeth are still the exception rather than the rule. With the advent of modern dental science along with advertising, enlarged photographs, and close-ups on television, the situation has changed. The glistening white teeth that were formerly an exceptional attribute to be singled out in song or coveted by an obsessed odontomaniac have now become commonplace.

> How pure, how beautiful, how fine
> Do teeth on television shine![18]

Everyone—from clowns and announcers to masters of ceremony and weather girls—comes equipped with "miles of smiles," each one an orthodontist's dream. As a result, many people can sympathize with Phyllis McGinley, who longs for the sight of plain, unadorned, uncapped natural teeth.

> 'Twould please my eye as gold a miser's—
> One charmer with uncapped incisors.

In literature the inevitable inversion of the image took place among many writers at the beginning of our century. In his diaries and letters Franz Kafka returns obsessively to his fiancée's (Felice Bauer) deteriorating and eventually gold-capped teeth. In his volume *Morgue* (1912) the expressionist poet Gottfried Benn frequently refers to rotting or defective teeth in contexts that would formerly have required the topos of glittering white teeth. The poem "Nachtcafé" depicts the encounter between a young man and woman in a bar:

> Grüne Zähne, Pickel im Gesicht
> Winkt einer Lidrandentzündung.
> (Green teeth, pimply face
> Waves to a case of infected eyelids.)

In another poem ("Kreislauf") Benn describes the cadaver of a prostitute, which contains only a single molar—and it has a gold filling. The morgue attendant knocks out the tooth, pawns the filling, and goes dancing for the money he receives, the "circulation" of the title.

The most familiar inversions of the topos occur in the works of Thomas Mann. In "Tristan" (1903) the image is used for an ironic effect. The "carious teeth" of the writer Detlev Spinell contrast not only with his own pretensions to a life of pure beauty but also with the robust health of Herr Klöterjahn, with whose wife Spinell carries on his ineffectual dalliance. In *Death in Venice* (1912) the image shows up in a more serious context. As Gustav von Aschenbach becomes increasingly infatuated with the Polish boy Tadzio, whom he regards as an ideal of male beauty, he notices that Tadzio's teeth are not attractive: "rather jagged and pale, without the glitter of health and with a peculiarly brittle translucency" (Ch. 3). This ironic inversion of the topos is expounded theoretically in *Doctor Faustus* (1947), which introduces the images of "the dead tooth" and "root treatment" to designate conventional esthetic forms that have outlived their time but are resurrected parodistically for modern purposes (Ch. 18).

Finally, Poe's tale provided the inspiration and motto for a story by the American writer Richard G. Stern. His story "Teeth" deals with an old-maid instructor of English history in Chicago who falls in love with her dentist.[19] In her infatuation she reads up on teeth and dentistry in the encyclopedia, thinks constantly in tooth metaphors, and "felt the root tremble in her heart whenever Dr. Hobbie leaned over to pass a steel shaft beneath her strong, white crowns" (p. 17). Her obsession reaches its climax during a nighttime emergency treatment while the dentist is lancing an abscess. In her pain and intoxication, Miss Wilmott recalls Poe's "Berenice" and translates the operation on her teeth into an act of sexual violation—from Berenice's point of view! "And out, out they came one by one, her thirty glorious crowns, roots, rapt from her yielding jaws. Oh it was over. She lay back, vacant, depleted, fulfilled" (p. 28). Stern's story, with its explicit inversion of Poe's tale, represents the ultimate parody of the tooth as an image of sex and beauty, which goes back through Poe and the Bible to primitive myth and folklore.

III

THE POTENT AND BEAUTIFUL TEETH that concern folklore have little need of dentists; as a result dentists do not often figure in literature before the twentieth century. (Stern's Dr. Hobbie is of course a colleague of the dentists who appear so frequently in novels of the sixties.) It was left to the visual arts to deal more realistically with the third attribute, the pain of toothache and the related art of dentistry. The activities of dentists and the symptoms of tooth disease have been portrayed in so many drawings, paintings, and sculptures that the history of dentistry has routinely drawn on examples from the plastic arts for documentary evidence.[20] A Scythian vase from the third or fourth century B.C. depicts in realistic detail one of the earliest recorded dental treatments. The main door to the cathedral of St. Mark's in Venice includes a panel representing a medieval dentist at work on an extraction. Wells Cathedral in Somerset contains a column whose capital depicts a man swollen with toothache, a work that enjoyed considerable fame in the Middle Ages because it was rumored that a toothache would disappear if one said the appropriate prayer while visualizing that carving. And St. Apollonia with her attributes—a pair of pincers clasping a gigantic molar—provided one of the most popular subjects of medieval art.

The Dutch artists, with their realism and faintly malicious humor, found a gratifying subject in dentistry. Lukas van Leyden produced a copperplate engraving showing a contemporary dental treatment. One of Rembrandt's etchings shows a charlatan hawking remedies for toothache. Jan Steen's painting "The Tooth Master" depicts an extraction so painful that the patient must be tied down to his chair while a throng of onlookers grins in amusement. Several of Daumier's cartoons contain dental motifs, notably a picture of a fierce female dentist ("She Stands Her Ground") in action in an office strewn with huge extracted molars—a treatment with clear sexual implications. In 1862 the German humorist Wilhelm Busch published a series of twenty-five drawings accompanied by rhymed couplets entitled "The Hollow Tooth."[21] It tells the story of a man named Friedrich Kracke, who bites down on a rotten tooth during his supper. After trying all sorts of home remedies to relieve his pain—smoking, drinking, soaking his head in a bucket of cold water, bandages, sweating—he finally goes to the dentist, who removes the offending tooth. In the fourth chapter of *À rebours* (1884) J.-K. Huysmans is inspired by the traditions of his Dutch ancestors when he describes in graphic detail a painful visit to the dentist. When Des Esseintes has an abscessed molar that needs to be removed quickly, he goes to a quack whose office is advertised by two cases of artificial teeth in gums of pink composition and wired together with brass. Terrified by the screams and blotches of expectorated blood on the stairs, he almost flees. The huge dentist first breaks off his tooth, then pulls it out, "a blue tooth with a red thread hanging from it."

In *Much Ado about Nothing* Shakespeare observes that "there was never yet philosopher / That could endure the toothache patiently" (V.i). And the history of art bears this out. The paintings, drawings, and sculptures make it clear that men through the ages, for all their reverence before the magical potency of teeth and all their admiration for the beauty of teeth, still find something grotesque, ridiculous, and degrading about toothache. The patient with the swollen and bandaged jaw, with fearful eyes and gaping mouth, groveling in abject helplessness before a dentist who is usually portrayed as a charlatan or brute, provides unusual and challenging poses for the visual arts. But in literature it was considered unsuitable for anything but the sadistic comedy of Wilhelm Busch or the grim ironies of Huysmans. Then suddenly, in the second half of the nineteenth century, authors began to emerge who made a virtue of the very agony of toothache.

IV

THE NARRATOR of Dostoevsky's *Notes from Underground* (1864) devotes a short chapter to teeth, which differs notably from all the other examples that we have considered: toothache is cited here as an example of the narrator's ability to derive edification from his own self-degradation. "Even in toothache there is enjoyment," he insists. "I had toothache for a whole month and I know there is" (Ch. 4; Garnett trans.). The narrator makes the point that man derives pleasure from the utter humiliation of pain represented by toothache: aware that there is no enemy to punish for his pain, he is in complete bondage to his teeth and conscious of his own all-too-human condition. "In all these recognitions and disgraces it is that there lies a voluptious pleasure," he argues. As a result, the educated men of the nineteenth century, who are intelligent enough to understand the meaning of their pain, take a positive pleasure in their own moans, which represent an advance of human consciousness. We have come a long way indeed from the malicious humor of Dostoevsky's contemporaries, Wilhelm Busch and Huysmans.

From Dostoevsky it is only a short step to Hans Christian Andersen, who was similarly obsessed with the agony of toothache, from which he suffered excruciatingly toward the end of his life. But instead of reveling in his agony, like his Russian contemporary, Andersen sought to sublimate his pain through art. The last story he wrote is called "Auntie Toothache" (1872), a reference to the narrator's elderly friend who had endured much pain from her teeth during her youth.[22] This Aunt Mille, who stuffed children with sweets, first suggested to the narrator that he should become a poet; so from his earliest days the agonies of poetic creation are associated in his mind with the toothaches caused by Auntie Mille's candies. One night, while he and Auntie Toothache sit up chatting about old times, she recalls the day when he got his first tooth, "the tooth of innocence." When he goes to bed, he is disturbed by a violent storm outside and by the throbbing that announces the onset of a severe toothache. Suddenly in the moonlit room the shadows seem to assume a vague shape. Becoming more and more corporeal, the shadow reveals itself as Old Mother Toothache, who is pleased to have found such a cozy refuge. " 'So you're a poet,' she said; 'just wait, I'll teach you to write poems, to write in all the meters of pain,' " Telling him that his mouth is "a splendid organ on which I intend to play," she threatens him by saying that the greater the poet, the greater the toothache. The narrator objects that he is no poet at all, that he had merely suffered a passing attack of "poetitis." After forcing the poet to acknowledge that she is mightier than poetry, philosophy, mathematics, and music, Old Mother Toothache boasts that she is older than all other feelings and emotions. Born in the garden of Paradise, it was none other than she who prompted Adam and Eve to get dressed because of the cold. She promises to depart only if the narrator will swear never again to write verses. When the young man wakes up in the morning, he still confuses dream and reality, seeing Old Mother Toothache in the person of Aunt Mille. But he remains true to his promise. Although he has written down the present account, he concedes, it is prose, not verse, and not intended for publication.

Andersen's melancholy tale, written only three years before his death, is clearly an attempt to conquer his own suffering through humor and esthetic form. Yet, in the combination of toothache (i.e., suffering) and art, he belongs to a romantic tradition that culminates in such authors as Thomas Mann. It is well known that Mann inherited the belief prevalent in German thought at least since romanticism that art and beauty are somehow related to, even a product of, disease. The Magic Mountain is "magic" in large measure because it is a tuberculosis sanatorium with the feverish consciousness generated by that affliction; the growth of Adrian Leverkühn's music, in *Doctor Faustus*, is accompanied by the worsening of the syphilis that ravages his body. It is perfectly consistent with this attitude, therefore, that Mann's figures are often characterized by the state of their dental health: we have already noted two examples. But in the 800 pages of the novel *Buddenbrooks* (1901) Mann has the time and space to develop more fully the implications of his odontological images.

Buddenbrooks bears the subtitle "The Decline of a Family." But the German (*Verfall*) also permits the translation "The Decay of a Family," a translation that brings out the parallel between the deterioration of the prosperous North German family in the course of four generations and the decaying teeth that both characterize and ultimately precipitate the deaths of the last two males of the family line. Within the first few pages we are told of the "small and yellowish teeth" that ominously mar the appearance of the otherwise handsome and elegant Thomas Buddenbrook. These teeth, plus a certain fastidiousness of manner, are the first indications that Thomas has lost some of the robust vigor that brought the two preceding generations of Buddenbrooks to a position of wealth and prominence. So it is appropriate that Thomas' death, some forty years later, is signaled by a violent toothache that forces him to leave a meeting of the Municipal Senate and, in his agony, to seek out the dentist. When the dentist attempts to extract the rotten molar, the crown breaks off. Unable to endure the pain of a root extraction, Thomas leaves the dentist's office; but just outside he collapses in a puddle of mud and blood and dies—as rumor puts it—"because of a tooth."

The description of Thomas Buddenbrook's agony in the dentist's office (Bk. IX, Ch. 7) is a small naturalistic masterpiece, and because of the prominence of the scene the dentist himself assumes an important role in the novel. It is said of Dr. Brecht that his very name suggests the noise one hears in the jaws when the roots of teeth are being forcibly removed (Bk. VIII, Ch. 7). Dr. Brecht has no television set in his office, but his waiting room is attended by a parrot named Josephus, who invites patients to "Have a Seat." Otherwise, Dr. Brecht bears little resemblance to Grass's self-confident dental technologist in tennis shoes. Corrupted by the pain and fear of his own art, he breaks into a sweat whenever he has to extract a tooth and then collapses afterward in an exhaustion equal to that of his patient.

Dr. Brecht's office is the common ground where Thomas Buddenbrook and his son Hanno meet in their suffering. Hanno, to be sure, dies of typhus, not from his teeth. But as a true son of the family, with a fateful talent for music, he has inherited his father's bad teeth: although in appearance white and lovely like his mother's, they are soft and vulnerable underneath. In the many pages between the first mention of Thomas Buddenbrook's yellowish teeth and his death outside the dentist's office, Hanno's agonies serve to remind us of the poor teeth that symbolize the decaying family. Hanno almost dies as a result of the fever and cramps attending the cutting of his baby teeth. When he begins to get his permanent teeth, he falls into a fever and suffers nights of torment. His teeth grow so badly that Dr. Brecht has to remove four molars to make room for the wisdom teeth; this operation, which takes four weeks, is followed by a week of illness during which Hanno is too weak to get out of bed. The condition of his teeth, which are repeatedly mentioned throughout the novel, is so deplorable that it not only affects his emotional state; it also produces gastric disturbances, dizziness, and palpitations of the heart.

In Thomas Mann's works the dental images are still largely personal and "psychodontic"; they are attached as a symptom of disease and weakness to individuals who, according to Mann's conception, have been debilitated by art or beauty. Only the fact that Hanno Buddenbrook inherits his father's poor teeth suggests that Mann is using the decay of teeth for a larger purpose, to signify the decay of an entire family and, by implication, of civilized European society as a whole. Forty years later two other novelists developed these implications more elaborately.

V

In Arthur Koestler's *Darkness at Noon* (1940) the throbbing toothache that plagues Rubashov through the weeks of his interrogation is no longer a sign of esthetic degeneration, as it was for Hans Christian Andersen and Thomas Mann. It has become, in a very literal sense, a reification of the word "remorse," which refers etymologically to teeth and biting (*re-mordere*, "to bite again"; cf. Middle English "the agenbite of inwit"). N. S. Rubashov, a chief Party functionary, is being tried for his life on trumped-up charges of plotting against the life of the Party leader. Both the accused and his interrogators know that the charges are false, but the trial revolves around the question of motivation and plausibility. Given his defection from strict Party ideology, would such an attempt be consistent with Rubashov's beliefs? When he finally confesses, Rubashov is shot in the back of the neck and the novel ends.

Rubashov's tooth trouble—stemming from a defective eyetooth broken off at the root while he was being tortured by the Fascists—dates back to 1933 when for the first time he felt stirrings of personal concern for a Party agent in Germany. During his interrogation the tooth begins to throb every time the discussion turns to people from his past with whom he had felt any involvement going beyond legitimate Party commitments: the young agent in Germany, a Party organizer in Belgium, the secretary with whom he had had an affair. These intrusions of personal memory always occur "without visible cause and, strangely enough, always accompanied by a sharp attack of toothache" (p. 110).[23]

References to toothache occur several dozen times in the course of the novel. On the first day of his imprisonment Rubashov reports sick because of toothache, and several days later he is taken to see the doctor, who offers to remove the root of the broken eyetooth. But Rubashov refuses, hoping that the abscess will open by itself. On days when he is afflicted deeply by memories of betrayed friends, the toothache flares up so violently that his whole cheek becomes swollen. At other times, when he develops a new theory of historical necessity that enables him to justify his past behavior, the toothache goes away for a time. All indications make it absolutely clear that the toothache symbolizes individual conscience, which refuses to be consoled by the Party doctrine that the end justifies any means.

However, the odontological image is even more complex. For it is rooted in a broader organismic metaphor that depicts the Party as a living body. In reference to the situation in Germany after 1933, for instance, Rubashov reflects: "The Party was no longer a political organization; it was nothing but a thousand-armed and thousand-headed mass of bleeding flesh. As a man's hair and nails continue to grow after his death, so movement still occurred in individual cells, muscles and limbs of the dead Party" (pp. 31-32). When he thinks of the corrupt Party of the present, "The Party's warm, breathing body appeared to him to be covered with sores—festering sores, bleeding stigmata" (pp. 57-58).

It is only in the context of the organismic conception of the Party that the consistency of the toothache image becomes apparent. Just as conscience, like toothache, pains the individual, so the questioning individual becomes the rotten tooth that torments the body of the Party. Fittingly, it was in the disguise of a salesman of dental equipment that Rubashov went to Germany in 1933 to heal the ailing Party organ. When he compiled his list of reliable Party members, he wrote down their names and addresses in his order book in spaces left between the names of actual local dentists. What Rubashov only slowly realizes is that by developing an individual conscience, he has himself become a rotten tooth in the body of the Party. Rubashov with his aching tooth of conscience therefore becomes the infected tooth that must be removed. Appropriately, his executioner is twice described with dental images. As he speculates on the procedure of execution, Rubashov wonders if "perhaps he hid the revolver in his sleeve, as the dentist hides his forceps" (p. 137, p. 265).

One of the secondary motifs connected with the odontological image in *Darkness at Noon* is pain. As Rubashov contemplates the possibility of torture during his interrogation, he reminds himself that "every *known* physical pain was bearable; if one knew beforehand exactly what was going to happen to one, one stood it as a surgical operation—for instance, the extraction of a tooth" (p. 51). In Graham Greene's *The Power and the Glory* (1940) this motif becomes a central theme. Greene's "whiskey priest," the last representative of the Church in a Marxist state, confesses that he has "always been afraid of pain" (p. 278);[24] he is obsessed with the thought of the death that awaits him when the government police catch up with him. When others try to reassure him about the pain of being shot, they tell him that "toothache is worse" (p. 170). Appropriately, it is a representative of this dental pain through whose consciousness we enter the world of the novel. Mr. Tench, the dentist, is an expert in pain: "it was his profession" (p. 62).

In this novel, which begins with the dentist going down to the docks to locate his cylinder of ether—the painkiller!—the author develops a veritable rhetoric of odontological images. Unlike Koestler, Greene does not fasten his dental images principally on the hero and his conscience. The whiskey priest, who has broken his vows by becoming a drunkard and sleeping with a woman, is characterized by the bad teeth of decay. Mr. Tench notices that "one canine had gone, and the front teeth were yellow with tartar and carious" (p. 18). Almost as in a story by Thomas Mann, he concludes that "death was in his carious mouth already." It would be possible to set up an elaborate scale of tooth decay in this novel, for virtually every figure is characterized by the state of his dental health. Almost the only person with sound teeth is a pious woman whom the priest encounters in jail. "He saw the pious woman a few feet away—uneasily dreaming with her prim mouth open, showing strong teeth like tombs" (p. 180). Ranging down from this pinnacle of health—that is, intact faith—we find varied stages of decay. The simple soldiers and policemen, who have deserted their faith and sold themselves to the government, invariably have gold teeth. On the first page, for instance, as Mr. Tench walks down to the pier, he meets a guard who "stared malevolently up at Mr. Tench . . . as if Mr. Tench were not responsible for his two gold bicuspid teeth" (p. 9).

If those who have unthinkingly switched their allegiance from Church to State are characterized by gold teeth, those motivated by more opportunistic impulses are not so fortunate. When Mr. Tench reaches the warehouse, the customs agent is complaining about his teeth.

"The man had none: that was why he couldn't talk clearly: Mr. Tench had removed them all" (p. 11). One of the worst cases is the corrupt Chief of Police, whose moans punctuate the novel from start to finish. When we first meet him, he is holding a handerchief to his mouth. " 'Toothache again,' he said, 'toothache' " (p. 28). Later he complains about his tooth, saying that "It poisons the whole of life" (p. 30). Mr. Tench tells him, in fact, that "I've never seen a mouth as bad as yours— except once" (p. 292). (We are told nothing about the teeth of the police lieutenant who relentlessly pursues the whiskey priest. But to judge from the explicit contempt with which he greets the laments of his superior, this priestlike young Marxist must have a perfect set of teeth, like the pious woman.) Even more formidable are the teeth of the villain—the half-caste who betrays the priest and lures him back across the border to his capture and execution. "He had only two teeth left—canines which stuck yellowly out at either end of his mouth like the teeth of long-extinct animals which you find enclosed in clay" (p. 114). On almost every occasion when he is mentioned, the mestizo's yellow, fanglike teeth are cited as a leitmotif of identification and characterization. It needs to be stressed again that the elaborate rhetoric of dental images is meaningful only in the larger context of the novel: for Greene is portraying a society that is falling apart with corruption and decay. The Church driven out, a moral vacuum has been created that is not yet filled by the new regime, which in itself is corrupt.

VI

IF WE LOOK for the common denominators that link these various fictions using odontological images, it is conspicuous that many of them deal with the notion of pain: the spiritual agony that accompanies artistic creation or social conscience. Now the toothache is an apt image for this kind of pain, as Ogden Nash puts it,

> Because some tortures are physical and some
>   are mental,
> But the one that is both is dental.[25]

Dostoevsky's "underground man" uses toothache as an occasion to expatiate on the degradation of pain. Hans Christian Andersen sublimates his own pain in a story about Auntie Toothache. When Rubashov contemplates physical pain, he thinks first of toothache. Greene's whiskey priest is obsessed with pain, which nevertheless he manages finally to bear with a certain degree of human dignity. The aching gums of Bellow's Henderson announce the presence of something beautiful. And Grass's novel ends with the words: *immer neue Schmerzen*—"there will always be pain."

But the characteristic that distinguishes most twentieth-century dental images from earlier ones is the shift in emphasis from psychodontia to sociodontia: decaying teeth now represent with increasing frequency society as a whole and not just the esthetic or moral agony of the individual. G. B. Shaw once remarked (1909) that "the nation's morals are like its teeth: the more decayed they are the more it hurts to touch them."[26] Ezra Pound, speaking of the generation of young men who perished in World War I, exclaimed:

> There died a myriad,
> And of the best, among them,
> For an old bitch gone in the teeth,
> For a botched civilization.[27]

And in *Fantasia of the Unconscious* (1923) D. H. Lawrence expanded the image in his indictment of a debilitated Western world:

> And we, in our age, have no rest with our teeth.
> Our mouths are too small. For many ages we have
> been suppressing the avid, negroid, sensual will. . . .
> Our mouth has contracted, our teeth have become
> soft and unquickened. Where in us are the sharp
> and vivid teeth of the wolf, keen to defend and

devour? If we had them more, we should be happier.
Where are the white negroid teeth? Where? In our
little pinched mouths they have no room. We are
sympathy-rotten, and spirit-rotten, and idea-rotten.
We have forfeited our flashing sensual power. And
we have false teeth in our mouths (Ch. 5).[28]

This is essentially the sentiment underlying *Buddenbrooks*, where the "decay" of the family finds its analogy
in the decaying teeth that torment Thomas Buddenbrook
and his son Hanno. The same thought is implicit in
Darkness at Noon, where the incapacitating remorse of
conscience must be extracted from the body of the Party
if it is to remain socially healthy. The various degrees
of rotten teeth among the denizens of Greene's world
symbolize the corruption and decay of the society itself.
Eberhard Starusch's agonies in the dentist's chair correspond to the agonies of an entire people trying to come
to terms with its past. All these writers share with Vonnegut's Reverend Doctor Lionel Jason David Jones an
explicitly "political interpretation of teeth."

Various diseases and afflictions have been singled out
from time to time to symbolize the state of society. One
German cultural historian was led by his findings to the
conclusion that "civilization is syphilization."[29] And other
critics have sought less drastic analogues in tuberculosis,
leprosy, limping, madness, and defective vision.[30] An
equally good case could be made for paralysis (e.g., Joyce's
Dubliners), cancer (e.g., Solzhenitsyn's *Cancer Ward* or
Bernanos' *Diary of a Country Priest*), or meningitis (e.g.,
Hesse's *Rosshalde*, Huxley's *Point Counter Point*, and
Mann's *Doctor Faustus*). Yet of all these symbolic afflictions none is more appropriate than tooth decay. For
dental history demonstrates statistically that the incidence of tooth decay varies in a direct proportion to the
level of civilization. Of all the Stone Age skulls recovered
in Denmark, for instance, only fourteen percent reveal
any evidence of caries; the incidence of tooth decay among
citizens of modern Copenhagen is close to ninety-five

percent. By the same token, caries, almost wholly absent in the earliest Egyptian mummies, occurs with increasing frequency in later ones. So it is not just a catchy conceit when a writer suggests that tooth decay symbolizes the decay of a society. As a matter of fact, the decay of a society—to the extent that contemporary development is regarded as deterioration—in all probability does involve a significantly higher incidence of tooth decay.

Now we have seen—notably in the novels of Koestler, Greene, and Grass—that the odontological images are justified within the text by an organismic view of society. How, we might inquire in conclusion, did this view arise? Today we have become so inured by the rhetoric of social critics to the notion of a "sick" society that we no longer examine the implications of the metaphor, which has been trivialized through thoughtless use into a cliché. But literary images do not arise fortuitously and at random; they are usually consistent with, and an expression of, fundamental assumptions shared by the society that produces them. The images of social disease and decay go back to the organismic conceptions of the state that arose in the late eighteenth century as a response to specific historical circumstances.

Political thinkers of the seventeenth and eighteenth centuries generally believed in the "natural rights" of the individual, and they assumed that individuals established governments by "social contract" to suit their needs.[31] According to these rationalist theories, in other words, government is a man-made institution created in line with ideal principles of reason. The language of the Declaration of Independence makes it clear that our Founding Fathers regarded the state in this light as a human construct of convenience and prudence, to be modified at will. (E.g., governments are "instituted"; political bands can be "dissolved"; and so forth.) This generally "mechanistic" view of government and the state can be detected in the rhetoric of most revolutionary societies. For it is inherent in the nature of revolution that established government be regarded as a temporary institution of convenience rather than as an eternal form with any claim to higher sanction.

It was in reaction against these revolutionary doctrines that the organismic conceptions of the State first arose.[32] There had of course been earlier use of biological analogies in political writings. Under the influence of biblical allegoresis various medieval thinkers, like John of Salisbury, constructed schemes according to which each segment of the State could be equated with a specific part of the human body. But his thinking was purely analogical. When Rousseau wrote in *Le Contrat social* that the legislative power is the heart of the State and the executive branch its brain, he did not believe for an instant that the State had actually grown organically, like a living body. It was among conservative thinkers, principally in Germany, that the State began to be viewed as an organism in explicit opposition to the mechanistic theories of the Enlightenment. The metaphorical organicism so conspicuous in the works of Herder and Goethe, for instance, expressed their hostility to the mechanistic view of man and his institutions.[33] Fichte, in his theory of natural law (*Grundlage des Naturrechts*, 1796), presented the State as a product of nature, not as man-made; hence it cannot be tampered with or discarded in favor of a new State, as the revolutionaries were doing on the other side of the Rhine.

In the hands of such publicists as Adam Müller and Joseph Görres the organismic theory of the State became one of the most familiar weapons in the rhetorical arsenal of nationalistic propaganda. At the same time, organicism was rapidly applied to other areas of human society and its institutions. Karl Friedrich Eichhorn and Friedrich Carl von Savigny put the study of jurisprudence on a wholly new basis by presenting the law as an organic growth.[34] Romantic philologists like Wilhelm von Humboldt and Jakob Grimm taught that language itself is the product of organic growth, and not a static absolute.

In the mid-nineteenth century, under the impact of

this romantic historicism and the emerging science of biology, the organismic metaphor was gradually adapted to society as a whole. As early as the 1830's Comte had argued that the maladies of the social organism are accessible to pathological analysis.[35] But it was Herbert Spencer, in his *Principles of Sociology* (1878-80), who made the first consistent use of the biological analogy, speaking of the growth, development, differentiation, and evolution of social bodies in precise parallel to the evolution of plants and animals. By the nineties the organismic metaphor for society had become commonplace. Paul von Lilienfeld insisted in *La Pathologie sociale* (1896) that the analogy is not merely rhetorical. The social organism has cellular substance, social tissues, anatomical elements, and progressive evolution. But like all organisms it is subject to political decay. Therefore a science of social therapeutics is required to correct the pathological state, and the statesman becomes the doctor of society. (At this point we can already hear the familiar cadences of Grass's dentist.) In the same year René Worms published a book on *Organisme et société* (1896), which concludes with a chapter on the "Pathology, Therapeutics, and Hygiene" of society.

It was during this period that Max Nordau wrote his notorious attack on the "degenerate" literature of the *fin de siècle* under the telling title *Entartung* (1893). In his preface Nordau pointed out that the idea of organismic degeneration had already been applied fruitfully in the fields of penal code, politics, and sociology, but that no one had yet considered literary culture in that light.[36] Accordingly, his book opens with chapters on the symptoms, diagnosis, and etiology of the degeneration that he detected in contemporary cultural life. In Thomas Mann's early works we find a direct echo of this controversy concerning healthy and unhealthy art, which reached its peak around the turn of the century. But at the same time, among historians and sociologists, opposition to the organismic theory of state and society was beginning to make itself felt.[37] In all likelihood the organismic analogy would have been relegated permanently to the intellectual dustbin as an oddity of nineteenth-century philosophy of history had it not been revived in one of the most influential works of the twentieth century: Spengler's so-called "morphological" interpretation of history, which popularized the view that cultures *are* (and not: *are like*) organisms.[38]

To recapitulate: by the end of the nineteenth century the conventional image of the tooth with its attributes of potency and beauty had been exhausted. It still sufficed for "psychodontic" analysis as long as its implications were restricted to the individual who is debilitated by his art. But the works of Poe, Andersen, Benn, Mann, and others reveal that it was an overwhelmingly great temptation for the writer to invert the overworked image into parody. Just at this point, when the popular tooth image had been liberated by parody from its traditional associations, various social thinkers revitalized the organismic theory of society. It seems plausible to assume that writers like Koestler and Greene, who perceived society as an organism and were obsessed by their vision of its decay, found in teeth a familiar literary image that was now free to accommodate new and timely organismic associations. In other words, Grass's sociodontist can peer into his patient's mouth and see society largely because so many generations of post-romantic sociologists and cultural historians have looked at society and seen an organism.

Chapter Two

THE MYSTIC CARBUNCLE:
TRANSMUTATIONS OF AN IMAGE

I

SHORTLY AFTER Dorian Gray, in Oscar Wilde's fiction of 1891, has locked away his fatal portrait in the old attic schoolroom, he becomes fascinated by a plotless novel whose author is left unnamed but which is said to be written in the "curious jewelled style" of the French school of *Symbolistes*. Inspired by that work, in which "the life of the senses was described in the terms of mystical philosophy," he devotes himself systematically and passionately for several years to "the search for sensations" (Chap. 11). An interest in Roman Catholicism gives way to an obsession with mysticism and then with "the materialistic doctrines of the *Darwinismus* movement in Germany." He dedicates himself successively to the olfactory delectations of perfumes, to the auditory satisfactions of music, and to the tactile gratifications of embroideries. On one occasion he takes up the study of precious stones. "This taste enthralled him for years, and, indeed, may be said never to have left him." He spends whole days fondling and arranging the stones he has collected, and he tracks down wonderful stories about jewels in Alphonso's *Disciplina clericalis*, the legends surrounding Alexander the Great, the lapidary treatise of Leonardus Camillus, and other exotic sources. From an account describing the palace of John the Priest he learns among other things that "over the gable were 'two golden apples, in which were two carbuncles,' so that the gold might shine by day, and the carbuncles by night."

Another allusion to the legend of the carbuncle that glows in the dark and illuminates its surroundings occurs in an untitled poem at the end of the cycle *Das Jahr der Seele* (1897) by Stefan George:

> Wie in der gruft die alte
> Lebendige ampel glüht!
> Wie ihr karfunkel sprüht
> Um schauernde basalte!
>
> Vom runden fenster droben
> Entfliesst der ganze glanz·
> Von feuriger monstranz
> Mit goldumreiften globen
>
> Und einem weissen lamme—
> Und wenn die ampel glüht
> Und wenn ihr kleinod sprüht
> Ist es von eigner flamme?

The first strophe, describing a crypt illuminated by the reddish glow cast upon dark stones by a hanging lamp, gives the impression that the ornamental carbuncle does no more than disperse the light generated within the lamp. The next five lines make it clear that the monstrance, decorated with golden globes and an *agnus dei*, glitters wholly from the reflected light that enters through the single small high window of the crypt. This contrast suggests to the observer the possibility expressed in the concluding question: that perhaps the jewel in the lamp is after all a mystic carbuncle that glows with the power of its own flame.

Wilde hinted to friends, and readers have long assumed, that the book by which Dorian Gray is so profoundly affected was none other than that classic of French *décadence*, J.-K. Huysmans' *À rebours* (1884). Certainly Dorian's "search for sensations" seems to have been inspired by the systematic sensualism of Huysmans' Des Esseintes. It is appropriate, therefore, that our third example comes from a work by the French master. In his autobiographical novel *La Cathédrale* (1898) the hero Durtal, who in his earlier appearance in *Là-bas* (1891) was still a complete Decadent, has undergone a radical transformation. Having retired from an administrative position in the civil service, he has come to Chartres to pursue his meditations on medieval art and architecture. (The novel remains even today an excellent, if wearyingly thorough, guide to the great basilica of Chartres.) In Chapter 7 Durtal engages his friends, the Abbé Plomb and the Abbé Gévresin, in a lengthy discussion on the science of Catholic symbolism. Following an exhaustive analysis of the "palette of symbols" employed by the Primitive painters of the early Church, the conversation moves abruptly to the "hermeneutics of precious stones," that vague and imprecise subject developed by the "jewelers of the Bible" to aid them in their interpretation of such passages as those describing the breastplate of the high priest in Exodus or the foundations of the New Jerusalem in Revelation. They allude in passing to ecclesiastical writers from Bishop Marbodus to the celebrated seventeenth-century Spanish abbess, Maria d'Agréda, and enumerate the qualities attached to various gems. Among these we hear again of "the carbuncle, this eye that shines in the night and proclaims the eternity of her [the Virgin's] glory." The concordances they cite extol the carbuncle as the image of *Virgo praedicanda*, and other commentaries attribute to the stone the virtue of truth.

At first glance these passages from representative English, German, and French works of the *fin de siècle* might seem to do little more than confirm the well-documented obsession of the age with precious materials of every sort, including specifically jewels.[1] Jewels constitute an important material in the interior decor of those *paradis artificiels*, often subterranean, that the writers and painters of the period lovingly constructed in their works as a retreat from the ugly industrial reality they perceived to be taking over the world. In the use of precious stones, whose brilliance ranges over the entire spectrum, various meanings can be ascertained. Their hardness sometimes exemplifies the permanence that men living at the end of a spiritual epoch oppose to the transience they sense around them. At·other times the stones symbolize the frigid beauty as well as the emasculating barrenness of the *femmes fatales* they adorn in many poems and paintings of the period. This lithophilia accounts for the catalogues of jewels featured frequently in the literature of the age; it inspired Mallarmé's plan to write a treatise on "pierres précieuses";[2] and it helps to explain the popularity of the numerous books on precious stones published in the later nineteenth century: e.g., Harry Emanuel's *Diamonds and Precious Stones* (London, 1867) and Charles William King's *Natural History of Precious Stones* (London, 1870), as well as the important scholarly editions (cited in the notes below) of ancient and medieval lapidaries, notably by such French experts as M. Berthelot, Fernand de Mély, and Léopold Pannier.

Yet the generational obsession with jewels in all their glittering ambiguity cannot adequately account for the appearance of the carbuncle in the three works just cited. For the carbuncle, unlike the gems in Dorian Gray's collection or the stones that decorate the underground palace in George's poem-cycle *Algabal* (1892) or the unusual jewels that Des Esseintes has inlaid in the gilded shell of his pet tortoise, is not a real mineral but a mystic stone. Put most bluntly, nature does not produce minerals that glow in the dark and that are capable of illuminating dark spaces, either the palace of Prester John or the crypt described by George. Such wonders occur only in literary texts, whether lapidary, theological, or poetic in kind. Indeed, Huysmans subsequently observed that the chapter on the symbolism of gems in *La Cathédrale* was a conscious attempt to animate the "dead stones" of his earlier novel.[3] We must therefore pose a different set of questions. How did the carbuncle acquire its glow? How did it receive its symbolic associations? How did it come by its legendary characteristics? How did it find its way into literary works of the *fin de siècle?* To determine the answers to these questions we must go back through the Middle Ages into classical antiquity. From the first glimmer of the mystic carbuncle to its last flickers we can trace a history that covers some two thousand years.

II

IN THEOPHRASTUS' TREATISE *On Stones* (c. 315 B.C.) we can say for the first time with linguistic confidence that we are dealing with that bright red hard transparent mineral that subsequently became known to the entire Western world variously as *carbunculus, carbuncle, Karfunkel, carbonchio, escarboucle,* and other variations of the Latin root *carbo, carbonis,* signifying burning wood or coal. Theophrastus, of course, calls the stone by its Greek name ἄνθραξ ("charcoal" or "stone-coal"), a generic term comprising various red-colored precious or semiprecious stones: particularly the ruby, the spinel, the pyrope, the almandine, the garnet, and the red jacinth.[4] (The vocable seem to have been used first by Aristotle in his *Meteorologica,* IV, 9, 387b, to designate a stone.) But the Latin lapidarists routinely refer to the etymological significance of the term to establish the identity of Greek *anthrax* and Latin *carbunculus.*

This first extant lapidary, which constituted part of a larger mineralogical work, is an eminently practical handbook containing none of the magical-medical lore about stones that was soon to become popular in the Hellenistic world. (Only at one or two points has an irrational element crept into Theophrastus' text, and his discussion of the carbuncle contains no trace of magic or lithotherapy.) Theophrastus' division of stones into male and female, as well as his explanation of their origin from the four elements, is consistent with the scientific principles enunciated by his teacher Aristotle. (The sexual distinction almost certainly was understood in a purely metaphorical sense; neither Aristotle nor Theophrastus

considered stones to be capable of actual sexual reproduction, as did many medieval mineralogists.) The sober
manual is based primarily on the practical experiences
of miners and on Theophrastus' firsthand observation
of the phenomena he describes.

Theophrastus takes up *anthrax* in Paragraph 18 under
the category of incombustible stones. Noting that it is
characterized by its reddish hue, he points out that the
stone is frequently used for signets. (This fact leads scholars to assume that Theophrastus must have had the garnet in mind since the ruby is too hard for engraving with
the techniques available in Theophrastus' time.) He spec-
ifies the regions (actually, the ports of export: Carthage
and Marseilles) from which the stones are obtained, and
reports that they are the most valuable of gems. Finally—
and this is what matters in the present context—he states
that the stone, when it is *held up to the light of the sun*
(πρὸς δὲ τὸν ἥλιον τιθέμενον), sparkles like a glowing coal. We find here, in sum, no properties that cannot
be explained rationally; the resplendence of a stone in
the sunlight is entirely natural. Yet precisely this property provided the basis for a mystical interpretation as
soon as the effulgence began to be regarded, or mis-
understood, as being endogenous.

We know from a variety of sources that Theophrastus'
treatise was only one of numerous Greek lapidaries with
which classical antiquity was familiar.[5] Theophrastus'
work, the only one that survived, remained for centuries
the authoritative source for factual information concerning stones. Methodologically, however, Theophrastus' effort to categorize and describe stones systematically was not influential until the sixteenth century, when
such Renaissance mineralogists as Agricola took it up
again. Within a century the scientific approach to mineralogy began to be displaced by the pharmacological
lapidaries of the Hellenistic period and by the magical
stone-lore of the Orient.

The next extant lapidary, which occupies Book 37 of
the *Naturalis Historia* of the Elder Pliny (23-79 A.D.),

is on the whole—notwithstanding many assertions that would today have to be classed as superstitious—a reasonably rational document—what might be described as an exercise in popular science. We know from many allusions in the text that Pliny was acquainted with the magical traditions that were rapidly emerging in the East, and he repeatedly finds occasion to jeer at the credulity of the Hellenistic lithotherapists. Other passages attest his (not always successful) attempt to distance himself critically from the *vanitas* and exaggerations of the Eastern charlatans.

Following an explanation of the name (like coals, incombustible stones do not feel the flames), Pliny enumerates twelve different *genera* of the carbuncle,[6] which in agreement with Aristotelean theory are divided into male and female according to their refulgence, and characterizes each according to subtleties of color and brilliance. The finest varieties are said to glow with an inner radiance—*ex alto lucidos; (p)innato fulgore radiantes; convoluto igne flagrare; stellam intus ardere*—but this characteristic does not yet imply that the stones glow endogenously. It simply means, as Theophrastus had already pointed out and as Pliny makes amply clear, that they glitter in the light of the sun (*contra radios solis scintillare*). Rejecting various reports that the stones shine with their own power, he offers a rational explanation for the phenomenon. There are many methods, he says, whereby the appearance of luminosity can be produced—among others, by steeping the stones in vinegar for fourteen days, following which they glow for as many months. Finally, Pliny mentions India as a source for the finest stones, as did Strabo before him in his *Geography* (XV, i, 67). At this point the reference is meant simply as a geographical specification; but, as we shall see, associations with the mystical East emerged in the following centuries as the Western tradition began to be blended with the entirely different beliefs current in the Orient.

Although Pliny was aware of a magical stone-lore in the East, the earliest extant documents of that tradition date back no further than the second century of the Christian era.[7] This magical stone-lore was based for its facts on the scientific tradition of Aristotle and Theophrastus, to which were joined influences from Eastern *mageia*, from the Hermetic and Gnostic arts, and from other esoteric sources. The most famous evidences are two remarkable Hellenistic works from the third or fourth century: the first book of the so-called *Cyranides* (reputedly the work of Hermes Trismegistus), a litteromantic treatise of twenty-four chapters, of which each is devoted to a plant, a bird, a stone, and a fish; and the so-called *Lapidary of Damigeron*, the first stone-book to include a fully developed astrological system and one that profoundly influenced the stone-lore of the European Middle Ages. The *carbunculus* or *anthrax* occurs in neither of these texts. But in the so-called *Nautical Lapidary* from the same period we learn that the carbuncle protects the bearer against drowning—the first extant case in which a magical-apotropaic effect is unmistakably attributed to the carbuncle. In the lapidary ascribed to Socrates and Dionysos other magical powers are mentioned; but the stone possesses them only when the sigil of Athene is engraved upon it: in such cases it has the power to ward off enemies and to make its owner popular and articulate.

The fact that the carbuncle does not belong among those stones frequently cited in the early magical stone-books—e.g., the bezoar, the draconites, or the rhinoceros[8]—reinforces the assumption that it was originally a Western stone, unrelated to the magical stones familiar in the East, which usually have different names and a different history or lore.[9] But that very absence can help us to understand how the carbuncle subsequently acquired the power of endogenous luminosity. Among the many wonders known to the Orient were also stones, usually nameless, that allegedly glowed in the dark. According to ancient Brahman traditions the abode of the gods was lighted by luminous stones. Near Eastern legends report that Noah's ark was illuminated by a stone suspended inside.[10] Lucian writes that a statue of the goddess Astarte wore on its head a lampstone (*lychnis*) so radiant that it lighted up the whole temple.[11] Although we can reconstruct the process only hypothetically, it seems plausible that the story of the Western carbuncle was contaminated by these legends when the Eastern and Western traditions mingled. The expectation was already present, produced by Theophrastus' and Pliny's statements that the carbuncle is the most radiant of stones (when held up to the rays of the sun). If any stone from the Western tradition could be said to glow endogenously and to provide a convenient name to which to link the Oriental lore, then it was obviously the carbuncle. Given the expectation in the West and the mysteries reported from the East, it is understandable that early alchemists should have helped nature to imitate art by causing the stones to glow by artificial means. We have already noted that, as early as the first century, Pliny told of macerating the stones in vinegar in order to produce the effect of luminescence. His example is not isolated. According to a Greek alchemistic treatise from the third century certain priests treated stones— and especially the garnet seems to have been suitable for the purpose—with the bioluminescent organs of various sea creatures.[12] The luminescence produced by this process lasted several hours, even several days, and could of course be touched up at any time. Evidence of this sort helps us to understand how the mystified visitors, without necessarily believing in magic, might well attest as eyewitnesses to the endogenous luminosity of the carbuncle. Indeed, no less reliable a witness than Albertus Magnus, in his *Liber mineralium*, assures us twelve hundred years after Pliny that he has seen with his own eyes a splendid carbuncle shining in the dark.[13]

In short, within the first few centuries of the Christian era the carbuncle, a stone known originally to the Western scientific or pragmatic tradition for the splendor of its reflected radiance, had become known *par excellence* for the property of endogenous luminosity. That this development took place on the Eastern fringes of the Christian realm indicates the influence of tales of Oriental wonders, assisted by the craft of magi, priests, and alchemists. But that the legend persisted in the West despite the objections of scientists like Pliny or the ridicule of churchmen who opposed magic attests to the inherent power of the legend.[14] It needs to be stressed that from this point on—from the moment when the stone is said to glow of its own power—we are dealing no longer with the real stone known to Theophrastus but with a fictional gem to which the name *carbunculus* was henceforth attributed.

III

THE FIRST explicitly Christian lapidary, Epiphanius' *De Gemmis* (c. 394 A.D.) accepts the carbuncle's endogenous luminosity as a given.[15] Epiphanius, the bishop of Constantia in Cyprus, is writing to Diodorus, the bishop of Tyre, to expound the meaning of the twelve stones of the high priest's breastplate. Describing the properties of the stones, Epiphanius tells us that the carbuncle glows so brightly that its light even penetrates clothing, making it impossible for the bearer to conceal the stone. Indeed, the bishop explains that owing to its glow it is better to look for the stone by night than by day. The second section of the treatise undertakes an allegorical exegesis of the described stones. "The hue of this stone glows like a glowing coal, for from this tribe there shone forth He, Whom Isaiah reveals to us through the Holy Spirit."[16] In color the stone resembles blood because mankind was redeemed by the blood of Christ, and it is likened to fire and hot coals because Jesus will judge the quick and the dead at His coming. The stone also recalls the glowing coal that purified the lips of the prophet Isaiah (Isaiah vi:6-7). We learn, moreover, that the carbuncle occupies the first place in the second row of Aaron's pectoral and that the name of the tribe of Judah is engraved upon it.

(In the last section, which need not concern us, the bishop discusses the sequence of the tribes of Israel.)

Epiphanius' treatise perfectly exemplifies the methods of Christian lapidology. Whereas the Western tradition sought to arrange all known stones according to various pragmatic categories (e.g., combustible and incombustible) and whereas the magical-pharmacological lapidaries usually organized their stones alphabetically according to some numerological principle (e.g., the twenty-four letters of the Greek alphabet), the Christian lapidaries are interested only in those stones that show up in crucial biblical contexts: the twelve stones of the breastplate, the twelve stones in the foundations of the New Jerusalem, the twelve stones of the Virgin's corona, and so forth. Accordingly, the carbuncle plays an important role in some of these lapidaries (notably those based on the pectoral) but not in others (e.g., the stones of the New Jerusalem). It should be stressed that the allegorical interpretation of the breastplate of the high priest (as well as the other stones mentioned in the Old Testament) was left to the Christian exegetes. There seems to have been in the Hebrew tradition no independent stone-lore; for this reason even the translation of the names of the stones is problematical. The earliest Jewish lapidaries, which appear in the thirteenth century, are based wholly on foreign sources: Latin and Arabic stone-books, which in turn go back to Greek texts. The Hebrew authorities sometimes cited by earlier Christian lapidaries are demonstrably fictitious.[17]

The Christian lapidarists were interested not in the science of stones *per se* but in the interpretation of existing knowledge. In general, they simply took over the properties of stones from classical lithology, including any magical properties that had succeeded in making their way into the accepted canon. (For example, Epiphanius relied principally on Pliny for his material.) What the exegetes added was essentially the exhaustive interpretation of those properties according to the accepted methods of biblical hermeneutics.[18] In his work *On*

Christian Doctrine (*De Doctrina Christiana*, Bk. II, Ch. xvi, 24) Augustine argued that any proper exegesis of Scripture was impossible without an appreciation of the allegorical significance of such natural things as plants, animals, and minerals. Specifically, he continues, "a knowledge of the carbuncle, which shines in the darkness, also illuminates many obscure places in books, where it is used for comparisons." Christian exegetes rapidly developed that elaborate "tropology of jewels" admired centuries later by Huysmans. According to a well-known formula, any object was deemed to have as many allegorical meanings as it possessed properties: *res autem tot possunt habere significationes, quot habent proprietates.*

Various properties are cited by the medieval allegorists in connection with the carbuncle. Even its fragrance and magnetic attraction are mentioned from time to time. But the property by which the carbuncle was mainly known was its luminosity, which thanks to the process suggested earlier had been deemed wholly endogenous by the end of the fourth century. Indeed, among the various stones to which different degrees of luminosity were sometimes attributed—e.g., topaz, lychnites, selenite, chrysophase—the carbuncle is invariably cited as the principal and foremost.[19] It is this property of radiance that informs most of the allegorical analogies because it makes possible the contrast of light and dark, day and night. Just as Christ is the light that glows in the shadows, so too faith is radiant in the darkness of heresy, *caritas* turns the night of tribulation into the day of consolation, wisdom lights up the gloom of ignorance, the saints are illuminated by the radiance of the Holy Spirit, the apostles bring the lamp of Christianity to the darkness of the pagans, and so forth. The possibilities are limited only by the ingenuity of the exegete. The fact that the carbuncle is said to lose its color when placed among glowing coals and to flare up again when sprinkled with water suggests Christ's love, which was extinguished in the fire of the Passion, only to rise up again through divine grace in the resurrection.

The first Western work that brought together the scientific tradition of classical antiquity and the Eastern Christian tradition was Isidore of Seville's seventh-century *Etymologiae*.[20] In the sixteenth book of his compendium Isidore appropriates most of his material directly from Pliny: he tells us that the carbuncle has twelve *genera*, that it is called *anthrax* by the Greeks, and that it is found in Libya among the Troglodytes. But he also includes Eastern lore concerning the luminosity of the carbuncle, which is said to occupy first place among luminescent stones, glowing like a coal with an effulgence that cannot be vanquished by the night. Isidore contributes nothing new to our knowledge of the carbuncle or to its interpretation: his work is an encyclopedic compilation. Yet here for the first time we encounter a formulation that, in the history of this mystical stone, resounds again and again through the following centuries. The radiance of the carbuncle, which shines at night, suggests to Isidore the words from the Gospel of John (i:5) that Jesus is "the light [that] shineth in darkness." Indeed, the carbuncle is so radiant that it hurls its flames into the eyes of the beholder: *Lucet enim in tenebris, adeo ut flammas ad oculos vibret.*

The stability of lapidaries as a genre is astonishing even by medieval standards.[21] By the time of Isidore the properties of the most important stones were for all practical purposes firmly established. To be sure, scholastic ingenuity added a few subtleties of allegoresis. But the descriptions of the stones—including details of vocabulary and phraseology—were fixed in a form that remained recognizable down to the great compendia of the seventeenth century. This tendency is evident in the first medieval text devoted wholly to stones, the famous *Liber de Gemmis* that Marbodus, bishop of Rennes, composed in Latin hexameters sometime between 1061 and 1081. The fact that it is a largely pagan work, based mainly upon the magical-medical traditions of the East, suggests that Marbodus may have written his lapidary as a school exercise.[22] The framework points clearly to the Hellenistic *Lapidary of Damigeron* as its source, for it employs the same fiction: that Evax, king of the Arabs, is writing to the emperor Nero to set forth the types, names, colors, provenance, and virtues of sixty stones. But since, as we noted, the carbuncle is absent in the Eastern tradition, Marbodus must rely in this instance on Western authorities. The description of the carbuncle amounts to little more than a versification of Isidore's prose text, in which we recognize certain code words. The carbuncle, supreme among glowing gems, emits rays like a fiery coal, whence it gets its name (which in Greek is called *anthrax*). Its light cannot be quenched by the dark: indeed, its radiance sparkles in the eyes of the beholder. Brought forth in Libya in the region of the Troglodytes, it is said to have twelve varieties:

> Ardentes gemmas superat carbunculus omnes,
> Nam velut ignitus radios jacit undique carbo,
> Nominis unde sui causam traxisse videtur.
> Sed graeca lingua lapis idem dicitur anthrax.
> Hujus nec tenebrae possunt exstinguere lucem,
> Quin flammas vibrans, oculis micet aspicientum.
> Nascitur in Lybia Tragoditarum regione,
> Et species ejus ter ternae, tresque feruntur.[23]

Marbodus' *Liber de Gemmis*, which was rapidly translated into at least seven vernacular languages, dominated medieval stone lore for several centuries. A standard manual for pharmacists until the end of the sixteenth century, its importance is suggested by the fact that well over a hundred manuscripts of the text and its translations are extant. And we encounter its influence not only in the translations: often we hear verbatim echoes of Marbodus' phrases in later works, such as Arnoldus Saxo's thirteenth-century *De Virtutibus Lapidum*, which writes of the carbuncle: *hic omnes ardentes gemmas superat colore et virtutibus.*[24]

Given the conservative tendency of the genre, it is unnecessary to recapitulate the lapidaries that, like bestiaries and herbaries, succeed one another with increasing frequency beginning in the thirteenth century—partly in response to a new influx of Oriental lore by way of the Crusades and the Arabic presence in Spain.[25] The *Liber Mineralium* of Albertus Magnus is an exemplary *summa* of Christian allegoresis enhanced by the magical-pharmacological lore available in the mid-thirteenth century.[26] The carbuncle, called *anthrax* in Greek and—most recently—*rubinus* by some, is the most radiant and the reddest and the most solid of stones, standing in the same relationship to other minerals as does gold to the other metals. It possesses more virtues than all other stones, but its special power is to ward off poisonous vapors. When the stone is truly good, he concludes, it shines in the dark like a fiery coal, "and I have seen such a one myself": *quando vere bonus est, lucet in tenebris sicut carbo, et talem vidi ego.*

Because it is so representative Albertus' lapidary raises two questions that ought to be considered at this point. In the first place, it is difficult to know precisely what degree of credibility the sophisticated thirteenth-century mind attached to such wonders as the endogenous luminosity of the carbuncle. Certainly most writers of the period, and for centuries to come, accepted luminosity at least as a working hypothesis in order to use it as a basis for allegoresis. Albertus Magnus, as we have noted, said that he had seen a luminous carbuncle with his own eyes. At the same time, there is also evidence for a pronounced skepticism, as in the short poem written around 1230 by the Middle High German moralist known as *Der Stricker*, which attacks the increasingly popular magical-mystical lapidaries. Speaking of the mystic carbuncle, he points out that even though a piece of rotting wood also has the ability to glow in the dark, no one pays it any heed or regards it as special:

Sô hât der edel rubîn
von sîner art solhen schîn,
daz man in wol siht in der naht.
ein fûles holz hât ouch die maht,
daz man ez nahtes wol siht
unt enahtet dar ûf niemen niht.[27]

In the second place, the poem by *Der Stricker* as well
as the passage from Albertus Magnus alert us to the fact
that, in the course of the thirteenth century, a new word—
cognate with the English form "ruby"—was beginning
to assert itself, especially in the vernacular, as a designation for the familiar red translucent stone. The precise
etymology of the word is problematical, but a few facts
can be established.[28] The word, derived from Latin *ru-
beus* (meaning, therefore, "the reddish stone") first shows
up in twelfth-century Provençal in the form *robi* or *ro-
bina* and soon thereafter appears in Old French as *rubin*.
From Old French the word makes its way around 1200
into Middle High German in the form *rubîn*, and in the
course of the thirteenth century the vocable is taken over
by the other European vernacular languages. Middle
Latin *rubius, rubium, rubinus* as synonyms for *carbunculus* do not become current until the late thirteenth
century, no doubt under the retro-influence of the vernacular terms. Among educated Latinists the various
formations based on the root *rub-* were long considered
less elegant. Since the royal and ecclesiastical inventories
of the fourteenth and fifteenth centuries do not employ
the word "carbuncle,"[29] it can be concluded that the
older word gradually absorbed the various magical, mystical, and legendary associations attached to the familiar
red stone while in the more practical realm of gold-
smiths, jewelers, and artisans the more homely words
"ruby" and "garnet" began to establish themselves. The
word "carbuncle" becomes increasingly a code-word for
mystery and exoticism. This is apparent if we single out
from the mass of late medieval lapidaries two works in
the tradition that influenced Huysmans and Wilde.

In Konrad von Megenburg's famous *Book of Nature* (1349-1350), the first scientific work in the vernacular addressed to a lay audience, we learn nothing new about the properties of the carbuncle: as usual, it is said to be the noblest among stones, possessing all their virtues as well as great healing powers. Repeating information familiar since Isidore, Konrad tells us that the stone shines more brightly at night than by day, that it is found in Libya, and that it has three (not twelve) principal types. But Konrad concludes his discussion with a *moralisatio* that goes beyond the customary allegorizations in which the stone is likened to Jesus as a light shining in the darkness. No doubt in response to the powerful Marianic impulses of his age, he compares the carbuncle to the Virgin's wisdom, which is capable of comprehending the mystery of the Trinity as well as the nature of God itself: "den stain hân ich geleicht unserr frawen weisheit, dâ mit si die götleichen drivaltichait und daz götleich wesen durchschawt."[30]

If Konrad von Megenburg exemplifies the German Marianic works cited by Huysmans, the lapidary consulted by Dorian Gray is specified as the *Speculum Lapidum* of Camillus Leonardus or Camillo Leonardi (Venice, 1502), the physician to Cesare Borgia, to whom it is dedicated.[31] The last of the great medieval lapidaries, following Marbodus in its alphabetical organization and recapitulating the standard information passed along from Pliny and Isidore by way of Albertus Magnus and other later sources, it functioned as a handbook for the Renaissance, transmitting its lore in many editions. Following a list of properties that go back to the classical tradition and of "virtues" accumulated from Arabic medicine and Christian allegoresis, the author points out that the stone not only drives away poisonous vapors and preserves the health of the bearer; it also represses tendencies toward dissipation, suppresses vain thoughts, reconciles differences among friends, and increases the prosperity of the owner.

At the beginning of the seventeenth century, however,

we begin to sense a difference. The great compilations of the age assemble, to be sure, all available lore. But in every case the author's encyclopedic compulsion is qualified by a rationalistic skepticism, with the result that an amusing tension emerges with respect to the luminosity of the carbuncle. In his widely consulted *Gemmarum et Lapidum Historia* (1609) Anselm Boetius de Boot first reminds us of the *magna fama* that attends the carbuncle. But Boetius, after citing a few travel accounts, notes that no responsible authority maintained that he had witnessed the phenomenon with his own eyes. (Curiously, he fails to mention the conspicuous example of Albertus Magnus.) "If nature should produce a gem that glows at night, then truly it would be the Carbuncle, and accordingly it would be distinguished from other gems and would exceed all others in its worth."[32] Boetius concludes his discussion by disagreeing with those who say absolutely that it would be impossible for nature to bring forth stones that shine in the dark. It is possible, he concedes. But it is still not clear whether or not it has ever happened: *An itaque habeatur, aut non, incertum adhuc est.*

It requires Ulisse Aldrovandi a chapter of five long pages in his *Musaeum Metallicum* (1648) to rehearse all the information he has compiled from Pliny, "Evax," Marbodus, and Albertus Magnus regarding the carbuncle.[33] We hear again about its names and synonyms, its sources, its different types, its sigils. Like Boetius, Aldrovandus concedes that, though it is theoretically possible for a stone to shine in the dark—just as rotting wood and luminescent fish do—it is *incertum* whether or not any such stones have been found. Nevertheless, in his *Mystica et Moralia* he repeats all the by now familiar allegorical meanings based on the assumption of endogenous luminosity. It signifies Christ the Redeemer; it is an image of *caritas*, the greatest of all virtues; it is radiant in the night of calamities, it dispels the poison of sin, and it preserves all other virtues. Thomas Nicols' chapter on the carbuncle, or ruby, in his English *Lapi-*

dary (1652) amounts to a recapitulation of Boetius and Aldrovandus.[34] In systematic presentation he expounds the Description, Tincture or Foyl, Adulteration, Names, Places Found, Properties, and Value & Dignity of the stone, which is said to be good against poison, plague, sadness, and even bad dreams.

By the middle of the eighteenth century this ambivalence in the lapidaries and encyclopedias has given way to a sober skepticism regarding any magical qualities, largely under the influence of a scientific mineralogical study developing ever since the publication of Georgius Agricola's *De Natura Fossilium* (1546). The traditional lore gets conveyed; it still constitutes part of the cultural heritage. But the authorities make it amply clear that they no longer accept the ancient legends. Thus Giacinto Gimma in his *Storia Naturale delle Gemme* (1730) draws upon Aldrovandus, Nicols, and Agricola to describe the names, varieties, colors, sources, sizes, and symbolic meanings of the *rubino* or *carbonchio*. Although he repeats, for the sake of completeness, the legends concerning the stone's *Virtù e Favole*, he insists that he does not believe them.[35] Similarly, the English translator of Camillo's *Speculum Lapidum* (London, 1750) renders the text literally enough but warns the reader in his preface (p. ix) that the author lived in an age of superstition that assigned virtues to particular stones: such "odd Whimsies" and "extravagant Fancies," he cautions us, are now "entirely out of use." In Germany, meanwhile, the standard encyclopedia of the age laughs condescendingly at these stories. The author of the rubric *Carbunckel* repeats the various legends as a concession to those interested in the history of literature and culture, remarking that this stone, which is supposed to shine in the dark, "is worshipped by some Americans as a God, and stands in close connection to the Urim and Thumin of the Hebrews." He fiercely concludes, however, that no such fiery stone is to be found and that all reports to that effect are "fabulous" and "smack of a tradition."[36]

To recapitulate: during the first centuries of the Christian era the stone(s) known to the Western pragmatic tradition as *anthrax* or *carbunculus,* through contamination by Eastern legend and priestly-alchemistic manipulation, acquired the reputation of endogenous luminosity. This property was exploited by Christian exegetes in their allegorical lapidaries as an image for an assortment of religious meanings. At the same time, the renowned stone was co-opted by magical-medical lapidaries, based for the most part on Oriental sources, and given a variety of therapeutic and apotropaic powers. The belief in the magic-mystic carbuncle grew in popularity through the Middle Ages and survived well into modern times until it began to be undermined in the seventeenth century by scientific mineralogy and rationalism and finally disappeared entirely in the ridicule of the Enlightenment.

IV

IT IS hardly surprising that a stone so fabled should have won for itself a prominent place in the literary imagination during the period of its greatest brilliance. With the notable exception of Dante, who alludes to few precious stones in the *Divine Comedy* and to none with magical or medical properties,[37] writers in every European language from the thirteenth century through the seventeenth refer with casual familiarity to the wondrous stone that glows in the dark. In the *Decameron* (X, 9) Boccaccio describes a ring set with a carbuncle so luminous that it resembles a lighted torch. In the Low German account of *Reinke de Vos* we hear of a ring set with "eyn karbunckel, lycht unde klar," that is visible at night and that possesses a number of healing and apotropaic virtues.[38] In *Hamlet* (II, 2) Shakespeare tells how "With eyes like carbuncles, the hellish Pyrrhus / Old grandsire Priam seeks." In *The Lamentations of Jeremy* (l. 295) John Donne says of the daughters of Sion before the fall of Jerusalem that "As carbuncles did their pure bodies shine." In *Paradise Lost* (III, 596-98) Milton speaks of the twelve stones—"carbuncle most or chrysolite, / Ruby or topaz"—that shone in Aaron's breastplate. And among German poets of the Baroque the stone was frequently adduced as an image for the eye of the beloved, as in Philipp von Zesen's "An sein liebes Leben, Die übermenschliche Rosemund":

> Dein Äuglein, heller als die Sonn und heller als Karfunkeln,
> Seind mir so tief ins Herz gesenkt, daß ich auch hier im Dunkeln
> Von ihnen Glanz und Licht erlang. . . .[39]

Indeed, as an image for luminosity the carbuncle constitutes such a standard requisite in the poetic repertory that its incidence in that capacity is hardly worth recording.

However, the carbuncle as an image for the eye brings up a special case that deserves particular emphasis: the association between *lux* and *vita*. The passage from the Gospel of John (*Et lux in tenebris lucet*), which at least since Isidore has been inextricably associated with the legend of the luminous carbuncle, is preceded directly by a line in which the association between light and life is established: *Et vita erat lux hominum* (John i:4). From that association it was an easy step to the carbuncle as a symbol of life itself, of the radiant human spirit. As early as the fourth century St. Ambrose had reported that the river Phison, flowing out of Paradise, produces the splendid stone carbuncle, in which resides the spark of our soul: *in quo quidam animae nostrae vivit igniculus*.[40] This association between the light of the stone and the soul of man, which occurs frequently in theological interpretations, no doubt helped to account for the many passages in which the carbuncle is used as an image for the human eye as the traditional window of the soul. It also underlies the various medical powers attributed to the carbuncle—notable the power of becoming dark when the bearer's health is threatened.

Often in medieval accounts an implicit relationship is established between the man and the stone. Perhaps the most widely cited case occurs in Ludovico de Varthema's report of the king of Pegu (in present-day Burma), who is described as being virtually a walking carbuncle, for he adorns his person with rubies worth more than the value of a large city. They sparkle on all his fingers and toes; his arms and legs glitter with gold bands filled with rubies; his ears hang down "half a palm" from the weight of the rubies—indeed, "seeing the person of the king by a light at night, he shines so much that he appears to be a sun."[41] Varthema, while establishing an analogical relationship between the king and his *rubini*, knows perfectly well that they glow not of their own power but in the reflected light: . . . *per modo tale, che vedendo la persona del Re al lume la nocte, luce che pare un sole.* As a result of an error in translation, however, the rumor arose that the king and his carbuncles shone in the dark endogenously. Most of the vernacular translations of this popular travel account were based not on the Italian original but on the Latin translation that was published in Simon Grynaeus' *Novus Orbis Regionum ac Insularum veteribus incognitarum* (Basel, 1537). And there the qualifying phrase *al lume* is symptomatically suppressed: *propterea fit, ut si quis pium tenebricosa nocte regem conspicatus fuerit, non aliter illi lumen clarissimum illuceat, quam si phoebus ipse radios suos uibrauisset* (p. 262). Accordingly in the six German translations of Varthema's work that were made in the following century the king of Pegu and his carbuncles shine miraculously on their own.[42]

Passages of this sort, in which the relationship between the man and his stones is analogical, are frequent. In the Middle High German *Lay of Roland*, for instance, Charlemagne dreams of a throne decorated with carbuncles.[43] But another passage in that same *chanson de geste* makes explicit a closer relationship between *lux* and *vita*. Both the Christians and the Saracens possess many carbuncles—on the hilts of their swords and on their helmets.

But when the Christian warriors are slain at the battle of Ronceval, the carbuncles that adorn their helmets are extinguished:

> Si erslugen manigen christen man.
> ouch was iz ir pan.
> sie riefen selbe nach dem tode.
> die ir charfunckel scone.
> uerluren gar ir schim.[44]

The association of the stone with nobility and with the secret of life is evident in two further areas that appropriated the increasingly popular carbuncle as the Middle Ages gave way to the Renaissance: heraldry and alchemy. In heraldry the carbuncle is generally represented as having eight rays, although stones with six and twelve rays also occur from time to time. Originally these rays were simply a practical reinforcement for the boss on the shield. Only retrospectively—that is, after the carbuncle had become such a popular stone—was the figure interpreted as a representation of the carbuncle.[45] An early evidence for this use occurs in Juliana Berners' *The Boke of Saint Albans* (1486), which elucidates the nine stones of heraldry according to the nine troops of angels. Each stone represents a social class, from the topaz (the gentlemen) up to the carbuncle (the prince). "The IX. stone is calde Carbuncle a shynyng stone. . . . The vertue therof is: What gentilman in his Cotearmur this stone berith, full dowghti glorious & shynyng in his kyngys batayll he shall be."[46] The same quality of unbridled courage is attributed to the carbuncle in Nicholas Upton's *De Studio Militari Libri Quattuor* (London, 1654) which is otherwise based wholly on Isidore: *Et ille color attribuitur principi, & specialiter Duci exercitus, quia signet ferocitatem* (p. 110). And in Henricus Spielmann's *Aspilogia*, a handbook of heraldry that appeared in London in the same year, it is said that a carbuncle was found in the shield of Charlemagne, which the king of Navarre had seized from the Saracens (p. 117). The carbuncle so thoroughly established its fame

as one of the favorite emblems in heraldry that by the
end of the nineteenth century the most exhaustive dictionary of heraldry was able to list seventy-five families
that included the stone in their coat-of-arms.[47]

Another realm that attests to the fame of the carbuncle
in the late Middle Ages is alchemy. The history of this
mysterious pursuit is confused.[48] Many scholars believe
that it reached the West through a purely literary transmission by way of the Arabs from the Alexandrine Greeks
and those "temple factories" that mystified their visitors
by preparing such miracles as stones that glowed in the
dark. Others have argued that the secrets of alchemy
were transmitted within the Western tradition through
the recipes of jewelers, painters, glassworkers, and other
craftsmen who needed chemical processes for their work.
In either case, by the thirteenth century the practice of
alchemy had attained in the Latin West a central importance that it retained until the seventeenth century,
when finally philosophical alchemy and practical chem-
istry went their separate ways.

That medieval lapidary lore, along with much other
learning, was co-opted by alchemy for its purposes, is
evident from such representative works as Martin Ru-
land's *Lexicon Alchemiae sive dictionarium alchemis-
ticum* (1612), which contains a summary of existing
knowledge regarding the carbuncle based mainly on Pliny
and Albertus Magnus. But the carbuncle was not merely
an ingredient to be used in alchemistical experiments.
By the end of the Middle Ages, as C. G. Jung has shown
in various writings on alchemy, the carbuncle had emerged
as one of the important synonyms for the *lapis philosophorum*. It is still not fully understood what the alchemists meant by this central term.[49] In some accounts the
lapis is the catalyst in the hermetic process by which
metals are transmuted from baser into nobler ones. In
other accounts the *lapis* is itself the product and the
sublime goal of the *opus magnum*. Thomas Aquinas
discovered a carbuncle in which he saw resolved the
forms of the various elements and their contraries: *In-*

*veni quendam lapidem rubeum, clarissimum, dia-
phanum et lucidum et in eo conspexi omnes formas
elementorum et etiam eorum contrarietates.*[50] From another text we learn that the *opus magnum* is complete
when the king emerges, crowned with his diadem and
as resplendent as a carbuncle: *In fine exibit tibi Rex suo
diademate coronatus ... clarus ut carbunculus.*[51] The
fifteenth-century Latin tract *Donum dei* describes a twelve-
stage process that culminates when the *materia* is transmuted from white into an elixir that is "red like a carbuncle."[52] And even Paracelsus outlines an experiment
that brings forth the carbuncle, first among gems.[53] We
shall return in another connection to the significance of
the alchemistic carbuncle for certain romantic and contemporary writers and thinkers. For the moment, however, let us simply stress the fact that the alchemistic
appropriation of the carbuncle was due in no small
measure to the widespread association of this stone with
the principle of life itself.

Before going on we should pause to note a final example—so drastic that it amounts to an inversion—of
the association of *lux et vita* that endeared the stone to
the medieval mind. In Greek and Latin the words *anthrax* and *carbunculus* could already serve to designate
pustules, pimples, sores, tumors, and other malignant
inflammations of the skin and subcutaneous tissue that
resembled burning coals both in appearance and in effect. (In the strict medical sense carbuncles differ from
boils and furuncles in having no central core.) Pliny,
Celsus, Galen, and other medical authorities of late classical antiquity were acquainted with both words in this
sense. But durng most of the Latin Middle Ages the
dermatological implications remained distinctly secondary to the more familiar lapidary definition with its
Christian-allegorical connotations.

In the fourteenth century, however, a conspicuous se-
mantic shift took place as, in various vernacular languages, "carbuncle" and its cognates began to occur
with increasing frequency in contexts resembling the one

when Shakespeare's Lear calls his daughter "a boil, / A plague-sore, an embossed carbuncle, / In my corrupted blood" (II, iv, 226-28). Several reasons may be adduced to account for this new emphasis on the secondary meaning of the ancient word. In the late thirteenth century, as we noted earlier, vernacular forms based on the root *rub-* were beginning to displace older forms based on *carbo-* in practical lapidary contexts, a shift that liberated the latter to accommodate more easily the medical definition.

Mainly, however, I suspect that the satisfactions of ironic inversion, so appealing to the late Middle Ages, stimulated the new usage. The stone known for centuries for its therapeutic powers lends its name to a painful ailment. The lofty allegorical *lux* is reduced to a reddish inflammation that reminds the sufferer at every moment of the frailty of his all too human *vita*. The identity of man and stone, still analogical in the cases of Charlemagne or the king of Pegu, is suddenly reified in the form of a visible pustule on the body. In any case, the growing use of the word to designate ugliness as well as beauty, illness as well as therapy, physical anguish as well as spiritual fortitude, underscores the striking ambivalence that increasingly characterizes the mystic carbuncle from the late Middle Ages on.

V

ALTHOUGH the general literary allusions, including notably the association of *lux* and *vita*, as well as its appropriation by heraldry, alchemy, and medicine attest to the popularity of the carbuncle during the late Middle Ages, two further aspects need to be singled out for special attention: the carbuncle as a means of interior illumination and the legends regarding its source. In both cases we see evidence of the ambiguity attached to the meaning of the stone as a result of its mysterious Eastern origins.

It seems inevitable that any stone reputed to shine so

brightly would eventually be appropriated to illuminate outer space as well as the human soul—a possibility implicit in the biblical *lux in tenebris*. The passage cited by Dorian Gray occurs in the famous letter of Prester John, which was probably composed sometime before 1177 by a Crusader in the Middle East.[54] The Latin original purports to be a document written by the Oriental potentate to the Byzantine Emperor Emanuel in order to answer the latter's questions concerning the extent, the nature, and the riches of his lands. In Paragraph 57 he comes to describe the external appearance of his palace, which culminates in a ridge-beam decorated at either end by a golden apple, each of which bears a carbuncle that shines in the night: *In extremitatibus vero super culmen palacii sunt duo poma aurea et in unuquoque sunt duo carbunculi, ut aurum splendeat in die et carbunculi luceant in nocte.*[55] Here the stones are attached outside and function in their traditional Christian capacity as beacons for travelers who have gone astray. In a second palace, which Prester John's father, Quasideus, caused to be built at the command of an angel, the carbuncles are used for interior illumination in a manner described in precise detail.[56] In each corner stands a column containing relics in its base. The columns, sixty cubits high and as large in circumference as the arm-span of two men, are tapered from bottom to top. Each one is capped by a carbuncle the size of a large amphora, which casts upon the room a light so bright that even the smallest object can be seen on the floor. The hall has neither windows nor any other opening that would detract from the brilliance of the stones.

It is probably no accident that the legend of the illuminating carbuncle shows up in a work attributed to an Eastern author because this use of the carbuncle seems to have been inspired initially by Oriental stories, of which we have already noted several above (e.g., the abode of the gods in Brahmanic legend, Noah's ark, the temple of Astarte). In general, the use of carbuncles as a source for illumination is frequently attributed in Western literature to Saracens. In the *Chanson de Roland* (c. 1100), for instance, the Saracens attach carbuncles to the masts of their fleet in order to light the seas at night:

> En sum ces maz e en ces haltes vernes
> Asez i ad caruncles e laternes,
> Là sus amunt partegent tel luiserne
> Que par la noit la mer en est plus bele.[57]

Several other *chansons de geste* provide equally persuasive examples.[58] In the *Aimeri de Narbonne*, as Charlemagne returns from Spain following Roland's death, he passes a city occupied by the Saracens. Even though he remains at a distance of four leagues, he is able to inspect the fortifications in detail by the blazing light that emanates from a carbuncle on the walls. Similarly, in the so-called *Pelerinage de Charlemagne* a spy employed by the king of Constantinople observes Charlemagne and his men by the light of a carbuncle set in a column much like those in the legends of Prester John.

Rapidly, however, this originally Oriental source of light—*ex oriente lux!*—was appropriated in the West for architectural illumination. An interesting example occurs a few years after the original letter of Prester John in a travel account allegedly written by a cleric named Elyseus, who was born and raised in India.[59] For some reason, when he describes the palace of Prester John, he completely misreads the passage concerning the tapered columns. Here, following a reasonably faithful recapitulation, we find to our astonishment an arrangement that approaches the principle of modern indirect lighting. Elyseus understands that the columns are tapered; but he envisages them as being small at the bottom and large at the top. The superimposed carbuncle provides enough light so that ten thousand men can dine at the table of the king. The column is constructed this way, he notes with pedantic precision, because otherwise the width at the bottom would detract from the splendor of the stone, which would not illuminate the entire room.

In the Middle High German poem known as the *Younger Titurel* (c. 1270) we find what amounts to a free versification of the Latin passages when Parzival's brother describes the palace of Prester John.[60] The carbuncles cast a light so bright that it would be possible to find on the floor a hair plucked from a young beard! In another passage the same method of illumination is transposed from the Oriental palace to the Temple of the Grail itself.[61] On the tower outside a carbuncle acts as a beacon for templars who are overtaken by night in the wilderness; inside, the vaulted ceiling is covered with carbuncles, which are as radiant as the sun even when it is night, or cloudy, or dark. In the celestial park described toward the end of Jean de Meun's *Roman de la Rose*, written around the same time (c. 1280), the fountain of life, beneath the olive tree that bears the fruit of salvation, contains a carbuncle admirable beyond all stones (ll. 20495-548).[62] Glowing with a radiance dulled neither by wind nor rain nor cloud, it illuminates the entire park more magnificently than the sun itself, creating eternal day and filling the air with its sweet fragrance.

In such clearly religious settings as these—the palace of Prester John, the Grail Temple, the celestial park—the carbuncle has taken on still another meaning of *lux*: it has become a beacon that lights the erring Christian's way to salvation in the dark night of pagan idolatry and perfectly exemplifies the process by which Christianity coopted originally pagan images for its own purposes. Yet the carbuncle's frequent occurrence as the source of light in places of danger and temptation never permits us to forget that the stone as a source of light was originally pagan in origin. In his twelfth-century *Gesta Regum Anglorum* (Bk. II, Ch. x, § 169) William of Malmesbury tells a story about an episode involving Pope Gerbert, or Sylvester II, which allegedly took place in the year 1002. In Rome there stood a bronze statue extending the forefinger of its right hand, and on its forehead was written: "Strike here." Many men had sought unsuccessfully to solve the riddle when it occurred to Gerbert to mark the spot indicated by the finger's shadow at midday. That night he returned to the place with a page and opened a passage in the earth, through which they descended into a vast palace constructed wholly of gold. In a recess was a carbuncle, whose luster illuminated the entire palace; and opposite the carbuncle stood a figure with a bended bow. When they attempted to touch the riches, the gold images in the palace threatened to rush upon them. Gerbert was too wise to attempt this a second time, but the page snatched up from the table a golden knife of exquisite workmanship. At that moment all the images rose up with a dreadful clangor; the figure with the bow shot at the carbuncle, plunging the palace into darkness. The page replaced the knife, whereupon the light was restored and they were both saved from a cruel death. The same story is told at greater length in the *Gesta Romanorum* (Tale CVII), where the explorer is a certain "subtle clerk," who descends into the underground chamber by himself and attempts to steal several items. He perishes in the greatest misery when the building is plunged into eternal darkness. The appended *moralisatio* leaves no doubt concerning the interpretation of the tale: "My beloved, the image is the devil; the clerk is any covetous man, who sacrifices himself to the passions. The archer is death, the carbuncle is human life, and the cup and knife are worldly possessions."[63] In the Christian exegesis the carbuncle is given its traditional significance according to the formula *lux et vita*. It is evident, however, that the story goes back to a pagan source in which the carbuncle serves as the illumination of a place of temptation. A clear example occurs in Matteo Boiardo's *Orlando Innamorato* (1496), in which the underwater realm of the temptress Fata Morgana is illuminated by a great carbuncle that casts a light as bright as the sun:

> Non vi ha fenestra e d'ogni luce è priva,
> Se non che è dal carbone aluminata,

Qual rendeva là quì tanto splendore,
Che a pene il sole al giorno l'ha maggiore.
(Bk. II, viii, 28)

From literary examples of this sort it is but a short step to the countless fairy tales and legends in which carbuncles illuminate the chambers inhabited by mountain sprites and dwarves.[64] The Carinthian peasants tell of a race of giants who live in dark caves lit by carbuncles, which they present to human beings in return for good deeds.[65] In a Swiss folktale three men find a carbuncle that causes them to become arrogant and blasphemous: they boast that they no longer need God's light because their carbuncle is better.[66]

What we have seen appears to be a two-wave process. When early Christianity co-opted the carbuncle, which had received its endogenous luminosity as a result of various Eastern influences, the exegetes saw in the glowing stone nothing but an image of Christian *lux*, which assumed a variety of symbolic forms. When the Crusades mediated a second wave of stories regarding luminous stones, these stones were routinely called "carbuncles," and very often their properties—e.g., the capacity to light vast edifices—were simply translated into Christian terms. However, not all the pagan associations could be discarded: the carbuncle was too closely identified with the Saracens, for instance, and with the temptation of good Christians by evil powers. As a result, a certain ambivalence arose regarding the symbolic value of the carbuncle. The stone that had become known *par excellence* as the image of Christ and the Christian soul could suddenly take on the appearance of evil. We can test this hypothesis if we now turn to theories regarding its source. It seems inevitable that medieval thinkers should have wondered about the origins of a stone that appealed so powerfully to their imaginations.

According to Genesis (ii:11-12) the first of the four rivers flowing out of Eden was called Pison and encompassed the land of Havilah. "And the gold of that land is good; there is bdellium and the onyx stone." From earliest times the obscure term *bdellium* was often translated as "carbuncle." (In the Septuagint it is rendered as *anthrax*.) Ambrose, as we have noted, reports in his treatise *De Paradiso*, that the river Pison *habet etiam splendidum . . . carbunculum*. In the letter of Prester John the river is called Ydonus, but it flows out of Paradise through the entire province of the potentate and bears a variety of stones, including the carbuncle. In connection with this fluvial motif the travel account of Elyseus reports an interesting method by which the natives gather carbuncles.[67] In the kingdom of Prester John the carbuncles are deposited in a chasm which is inaccessible both because of its depth and because of the griffons that guard it. To obtain the jewels, the inhabitants kill sheep and throw their carcasses into the chasm, where the carbuncles become embedded in them. When the griffons seize the carcasses and fly away with them, the carbuncles fall out and can be safely collected in the fields above. A similar episode is related in the adventures of Sinbad the Sailor in the *Arabian Nights*, as well as in the fifth-century Latin translation of Epiphanius.[68]

As the carbuncle grew in legendary acclaim, its provenience in rivers, even if they flowed out of Paradise, must have seemed tame. Soon, in any case, a much more wondrous source was discovered for the mystic stone. Many writers of classical antiquity—e.g., Aristotle in his *Historia Animalium* as well as Pliny in his *Naturalis Historia*—were acquainted with stories about stones that grow in the bodies of various animals.[69] These stories, which persisted despite scientific skepticism, were expanded through the advent of Arabic learning in medieval Europe. Camillus Leonardus was familiar with fifteen such stones, which he describes in his *Speculum Lapidum* of 1505. Among the better-known examples were the alectoria from the intestines of capons, the bezoar from the intestines of mountain goats, the bufonites from the heads of frogs, the draconites from the heads of dragons, the lyncurius from the urine of lynx, and the margarita from the secretions of the oyster. Now the carbuncle is clearly out of place among these stones. Etymologically it does not belong among stones whose very names suggest their animal origins, and for many centuries it does not show up in the same contexts. Yet once again we are able to observe one—actually two—of those remarkable transmutations that characterize the history of this mystic stone.

In the Far East, from Japan to India, there had existed since oldest times the belief that the dragon bears—on its forehead, under its chin, in its ear—a precious pear-shaped stone, which possesses supernatural as well as therapeutic powers.[70] (This so-called dragon pearl is evident in many depictions of Chinese dragons.) The legend eventually made its way West in the form of the stone known as *dracon(t)ites*. Pliny, referring to an older authority named Sotacus, describes the stone in his lapidary. Draconites, he reports, is obtained from the heads of "dragons" or "serpents." But the gem does not materialize unless it is taken from the head of a living dragon, and so men cut off the heads of sleeping dragons to obtain it (XXXVII, 57). Draconites does not occur in the magical stone-books, apart from a brief mention in the so-called *Orphic Lapidary*, where we are told that is is effective against blindness.[71] But that this stone was well known in Hellenistic times emerges from various sources. According to one legend, the stone in Gyges' famous ring came from the head of a dragon.[72] Like much Hellenistic lore, however, this knowledge about draconites and its magical-medical properties was lost. In Isidore's *Etymologiae* we find nothing but a recapitulation of Pliny's sober account with the rather adventurous addition that certain daring men venture into caves where they sprinkle medicated grains that put the dragons to sleep. Then they cut off the heads of the sleeping dragons and obtain the precious stones, which are radiant and particularly cherished by the kings of the Orient. (Note the property of radiance and the association with royalty.)

Draconites seems to have aroused no particular enthusiasm in the West, for Marbodus and the early medieval lapidaries are acquainted with no such stone—
partly, of course, because it had no biblical associations
from the breastplate or the foundations of the New Jerusalem. Not until the so-called *Alphabetical Lapidarium*
of the twelfth century, which goes back to Isidore and
Damigeron, do we again encounter the dragon stone.
But here, suddenly and without motivation, an astonishing transmutation has taken place; for the stone in
the dragon's head is now identified with the carbuncle.

> Draconitides ço est un nom
> De pere qui vient de dragon;
> Draconitides est nomee
> Pur le dragon dunt est trovee;
> Escharboucle ad nom en franceis,
> Pur sa clarté l'aiment li rais.[73]

The dependence upon Isidore is evident from the lines
that follow, which describe how "enchanteûrs" put the
dragons to sleep in order to obtain the glittering stones.
But the identification with the carbuncle is a wholly new
element, prompted no doubt by Isidore's suggestion that
the dragon stone is radiant and beloved by Oriental
potentates. In sum: a familiar stone, which had by now
become quite popular, is substituted for the hitherto
unnamed stone, since ancient times reputedly found in
the head of dragons.

From this point on the carbuncle is routinely associated with dragons. We can see an amusing case of conflation in the *Mirabilia Descripta* (1330) of Jordanus
Catalani.[74] In his account of India Tertia Jordanus as-
serts there are dragons that in true Oriental fashion have
carbuncles on their heads (*super caput*). Glutting themselves so grossly that they can no longer fly, they fall
into a certain river, where they drown. The natives—no
longer so bold as the intrepid adventurers described by
Pliny and Isidore—wait for seventy days before they dare
to recover the carbuncles from the heads of the dragons'

skeletons. They then bear the precious stones to the court of the Ethiopian emperor, who is of course none other than Prester John. According to other legends dragons carry in their teeth a carbuncle to light the dark caverns they inhabit and never lay it down except to eat or drink. A late summary of these various legends was provided by Jean B. Panthot, doyen of the Collège des Médecins at Lyons, in his *Traité des Dragons et des Escarboucles* (1691). Another association shows up in Milton's description of Satan when he assumes the form of the serpent, "his head / Crested aloft, and carbuncle his eyes" (*Paradise Lost*, IX, 499-500). This association of the carbuncle with evil reminds us once again of the ambivalence that marked the stone in the Middle Ages. How could the stone that symbolized Jesus and the Virgin Mary and the Christian virtue of *caritas* have its origin in a beast as vile as the serpent or dragon? Medieval ingenuity resolved this dilemma by transplanting the carbuncle from the head of a satanic beast into the head of a holy one. Again we must go back to Hellenistic sources.

In the magical *Cyranides* the carbuncle is not cited. But the rhinoceros appears twice, and on both occasions it is related that the animal bears beneath his horn, or on its tip, an unnamed stone.[75] Here we find the association of a stone, to which the theurgic power of warding off spirits is attributed, with the animal that was also known as *monoceros* or, in its later Latin translation, as unicorn.[76] For several centuries this legend survived quietly in the East; neither Isidore nor Marbodus knows anything about the association, in connection with the carbuncle or with the rhinoceros: monoceros: unicorn. Then between 1150 and 1250, several more or less clear allusions appear to the carbuncle that is said to grow beneath the horn of the unicorn. In Lamprecht's *Lay of Alexander*, which was translated from the French into German around the middle of the twelfth century, we read of the rich gifts that Queen Candacis bestows upon the returning King Alexander: among others a rare and noble animal called monosceros, which bears the carbuncle and which lies down before virgins:

> di kuninginne rîche
> sante mir ouh ein tier,
> daz was edele unde hêr,
> daz den carbunkel treget
> und daz sih vor die magit leget.
> Monosceros ist iz genant.
> der ist luzzil in diz lant.[77]

We are confronted here with a branch of the legend of the carbuncle that apparently occurs only in Germany because the Latin Alexander, the *Historia de preliis*, contains apart from the simple naming of the beast *rhinocerotas* no trace whatsoever of this lapidary motif. Moreover, the comprehensive and exhaustive compendium of the seventeenth century, Thomas Bartholinus' *De Unicornu Observationes Novae* (Amsterdam, 1678), in which the entire accessible lore of antiquity, the Middle Ages, and the Renaissance is systematically summarized, knows nothing about a carbuncle or any other stone beneath the horn of the wondrous beast. Yet over a period of a century we encounter the association with remarkable frequency in German-speaking lands.[78]

The most familiar example occurs in Book IX of Wolfram von Eschenbach's *Parzival*, where Trevrizent enumerates the various medicaments that were unsuccessfully applied to decrease the pain of Anfortas' wound. After listing several magical drugs, Trevrizent goes on to describe the beast monicirus, which has such respect for maidenly virtue that it falls asleep on the lap of virgins. They first applied the animal's heart to the king's wound. Then they took the carbuncle from the beast's brow and stroked the wounds with it and then put the whole stone into the wound. (This operation also turns out to have been unsuccessful.)

> ein tier heizt monicirus:
> daz erkennet der megede reine sô grôz,

daz es slaefet ûf der megede schôz.
wir gewunnen stieres herzen
über des küneges smerzen.
wir nâmen den karfunkelstein
ûf des selben tieres hirnbein,
der dâ wehset under sînem horne.
wir bestrichen die wunden vorne
und besouften den stein drinne gar.
(482, 24-483, 3)

We can now express a conjecture about the manner
in which the carbuncle got under the horn of the unicorn,
at least in Germany during the twelfth and thirteenth
centuries. The unicorn had by this time become one of
the familiar symbols for Christ: the animal of great fe-
rocity and purity that could be caught only by a virgin.
It was known from Oriental lore, moreover, that the
unicorn was reputed to bear a wondrous stone beneath
its horn. This horn, finally, was reputed to have miraculous healing and apotropaic powers. As the notion became intolerable that the most precious stone of the
Middle Ages should be produced by the evil dragon,
what was more appropriate than to shift the mineral
image of Christ into the head of his principal animal
image? In the long run the dragon persisted over the
unicorn. Again we are reminded of the ambiguity that
surrounded this precious stone in the Middle Ages, where
it could be at once the image of Christ or the eye of
Satan, where it could be used to illuminate the sacred
precincts of the Holy Grail or the underground and underwater caverns of sin and temptation. And this ambiguity, as we have seen, stems ultimately from the carbuncle's ambiguous origin as a stone from the Western
pragmatic tradition contaminated by Eastern magical
influences.

VI

THE LUMINOSITY of the mystic carbuncle, which had
served since the beginnings of Christianity as a beacon

to illuminate the shadows of paganism, doubt, and evil, was finally eclipsed by the radiance of the Enlightenment. Indeed, so bright was the light of reason that for most of the eighteenth century the once-popular stone hardly gleams even as a simple literary image. By the end of the century, however, its glow was rekindled in Germany. In Goethe's works the carbuncle occurs on several occasions. In the masque *Amor* the deity springs forth from a huge sparkling carbuncle—the implied source of poetry and love—to offer the duchess Luise the text of the poem.[79] Toward the beginning of the drama *Die natürliche Tochter* (1803) the duke tells the king that his daughter Eugenie irradiates his life just as, in the dark caverns of fairy tales, carbuncles illuminate the mysteries of desolate night:

> Und wie in dunklen Grüften,
> Das Märchen sagt's, Karfunkelsteine leuchten,
> Mit herrlich mildem Schein der öden Nacht
> Geheimnisvolle Schauer hold beleben,
> So ward auch mir ein Wundergut beschert,
> Mir glücklichem![80]

In the Oriental atmosphere of the *West-östlicher Divan* the carbuncle sparkles several times, as when the lover senses sympathy in the radiant light of the beloved's gaze:

> Doch ich fühle schon Erbarmen
> Im Karfunkel deines Blicks. . . .[81]

In the tale "The New Melusine" the stone again fulfills its traditional fairy-tale role when the barber discovers that the mysterious chest he must carry around is in reality the abode of his beloved. When he notices that light penetrates through a crack in the ceiling, he assumes that it is illuminated within by a carbuncle.[82] Finally, in *Faust II*, as Wagner contemplates the flask in which he is creating Homunculus, he notes that the phial glows like a coal, sending rays of light through the darkness:

Schon hellen sich die Finsternisse;
Schon in der innersten Phiole
Erglüht es wie lebendige Kohle,
Ja wie der herrlichste Karfunkel,
Verstrahlend Blitze durch das Dunkel.[83]

It is worth noting here how etymology has contributed to the shaping of poetic language: the last three verses recapitulate in concentrated form the familiar lapidary lore concerning the carbuncle from Isidore on. In general, as the examples show, Goethe alludes to conventional associations: the carbuncle that illuminates the dark in fairy tales, the carbuncle of the beloved's eyes, and the carbuncle as the image of *lux et vita*. Goethe's acquaintance with legends concerning the carbuncle could have come from a variety of sources: from his study of mineralogy, from his readings in alchemy, from his perusal of literary works in which the carbuncle occurs. Yet in none of Goethe's works does the carbuncle play what could be called a major symbolic role. With his allusions to the famous stone the poet wishes no more than to conjure up a certain atmosphere—Oriental or medieval or fairy tale—to suit the occasion.

In the works of his younger contemporary Novalis, however, the carbuncle assumes a much more striking symbolic significance. This is not yet the case in the fragmentary narrative *The Disciples at Sais* (*Die Lehrlinge zu Sais*, 1798) where toward the conclusion the teacher and his disciples assemble before the temple and engage in a conversation regarding the primal language of mankind and other philosophical matters. As evening approaches the teacher sends for "one of those rare luminous stones that are called carbuncles, and a strong bright-red light poured over the figures and costumes."[84] Here the stone merely contributes to the atmosphere for lofty discourse. It is to be sure the last of many stones mentioned in the course of the story, and thus apparently the most treasured of them; but it illuminates the scene literally, not symbolically.

At the time he wrote this fragment Novalis was a student at the Royal Mining Academy at Freiberg, where his teacher was Abraham Gottlob Werner, the father of modern mineralogy. Werner treated the history and lore of precious stones in his lectures, and we also know from Novalis' notebooks that he read, during this period, a number of medieval and Renaissance lapidary-books that cite the carbuncle. However, the important citations of the carbuncle take place later in Novalis' novel, *Heinrich von Ofterdingen* (1802). In the legend of Atlantis, which is recounted in the third chapter, a carbuncle establishes the relationship between the youth and the princess. On the occasion of her first visit in the house of the wise old scholar the princess loses a stone, which is said to be a "talisman" with the power of assuring the freedom of her person. On the following day the youth sees in the forest a bright radiance, which turns out to be a dark-red stone engraved with mysterious ciphers. Recognizing the stone as a carbuncle, the youth spends the entire night ecstatically contemplating it and, toward morning, jots down a few lines in which he describes the powerful impression made upon his heart by the stone with the puzzling sigils engraved into its glowing blood. Indeed, he finds that the stone resembles a heart within which the image of the unknown beloved dwells:

> Es ist dem Stein ein rätselhaftes Zeichen
> Tief eingegraben in sein glühend Blut,
> Er ist mit einem Herzen zu vergleichen,
> In dem das Bild der Unbekannten ruht.
> Man sieht um jenen tausend Funken streichen,
> Um dieses woget eine lichte Flut.
> In jenem liegt des Glanzes Licht begraben,
> Wird dieses auch das Herz des Herzens haben?[85]

The reference to the engraving upon the carbuncle suggests that Novalis, the trained mineralogist familiar with the history of his subject, was acquainted with the classical sources that emphasize the suitability of the stone for engraving, as well as the magical sources that point out the carbuncle's apotropaic powers. Above all, the carbuncle in this chapter is not simply decorative or allusive: it has the important plot-function of bringing girl and boy together; and Novalis develops the ancient association of *lux et vita* into a symbol that exemplifies the mystery of love.

From Ludwig Tieck's report concerning Novalis' plans for the continuation of the novel we know that this episode represents only the first occurrence of a motif that was supposed to become much more prominent as the work progressed.[86] At the end the emperor was supposed to show Heinrich an ancient document stating that Heinrich was to find "an old talismanic gem, a carbuncle for the crown for which a place had been left empty"—an allusion to the medieval connection between the carbuncle and the imperial crown. In the course of his search Heinrich arrives in a mystical realm, "the Golden Age at the end of time," where "the wedding of the seasons" takes place. In this timeless realm all the principal symbols and motifs of the novel come together when Heinrich discovers the Blue Flower, which turns out to be his beloved Mathilde, who is sleeping and holding the sought-after carbuncle. The emergence of the carbuncle as the image of magical transformation culminating in the *unio mystica* with the beloved alerts us to the readings in alchemy that paralleled Novalis' study of mining engineering. As a poet he recognized in the mystic stone a splendid and apt symbol for his romantic ideal of metamorphosis through *Bildung* and of the unification of all being. In *Heinrich von Ofterdingen* he created a romantic showcase—indeed, the Bible of German romanticism—in which the mystic carbuncle could be displayed for the edification of a new, post-Enlightenment generation.

Novalis was by no means the only romantic writer to make use of the carbuncle, which for several years showed up in literature with a frequency unmatched since the late Middle Ages. In Zacharias Werner's *Martin Luther, or the Consecration of Power (Martin Luther, oder: Die*

Weihe der Kraft, 1807) the stone is cited with the frequency that is perhaps inevitable in a drama about a miner's son that takes place in part among miners and in mines. The image is introduced in the prologue, which speaks of the three ideals: faith, art, and purity. In a manner consistent with late medieval usage the carbuncle is equated with faith, "the most radiant of all the Cherubim" surrounding the Lord:

> So sprach der Herr!—und es durchdrang ein Leben
> Die Thronen, Cherubim und Seraphinen,
> Die freudig um den Bronn des Lichtes schweben!—
> Der strahlendste von allen Cherubinen,
> Der Glaube, der—ein leuchtender Karfunkel!—
> Oft dem zertretnen Volk zum Heil erschienen,
> (Er leuchtet nur im mitternächt'gen Dunkel,
> Er zeigte sich den Sehern und den Kindern,
> Er glüht in Bildern, flammt in Sterngefunkel).[87]

With similar symbolic intent the stone supplies the central image for the "Carbuncle Song" (*Liedel vom Karfunkel*) that resounds in Luther's camp outside Worms. The song is supposed to represent a duet sung by the carbuncle and the hyacinth, the one resplendent in the night and the other filling it with its fragrance:

> D'rum ich, der Karfunkel, muß nach Dir zieh'n;
> Was oben ich strahle, mußt unten Du blühn,
> Du Duft, —ich Mondenschein.[88]

While Werner employs the carbuncle rather ponderously in its traditional Christian meaning of faith, other romantic writers introduce it as an image for glittering light. In his poetic drama *Kaiser Octavianus* (1804), which amounts to a catalogue of medieval lore familiar to German romantics, Tieck describes a lioness lying in her lair with "glittering carbuncle-eyes / As red as blood, as fiery as a flame."[89] Otto Heinrich von Loeben, who wrote under the pseudonym of Isidorus Orientalis, speaks in one of his poems of the darkness that lures him with its carbuncle:

Dir strahlt es hell, ich aber muß in's Dunkel.
Da schimmert mir der sehnende Karfunkel.[90]

Ludwig Uhland reaches back to the medieval legends for his poem "Roland Schildträger," which relates how Roland wins a carbuncle from a giant in the Ardenne Forest and then inserts it into his father's shield, where it glitters like the sun.[91] In sum, the German romantic poets were acquainted with all the old associations that linked the carbuncle to religious faith, imperial emblems, and alchemistic transmutations.

At the same time, the writers of the romantic generation were also aware of the ambivalence surrounding the mystic stone since ancient times. E.T.A. Hoffmann alludes slyly to the association of carbuncles and dragons when, in *The Golden Pot* (*Der goldne Topf*, 1814), Archivarius Lindhorst recalls that his brother left his family to go among the dragons. "Now he dwells in a cypress wood near Tunis, where he watches over a famous mystic carbuncle," which he tries to protect against the machinations of an evil necromancer.[92] In Hoffmann's account of *The Mines at Falun* (*Die Bergwerke zu Falun*, 1819) the stone that lures the crazed miner Elis to his death is a sparkling almandine, "more beautiful than the most splendid blood-red carbuncle."[93] In Johann Peter Hebel's popular dialect poem "Der Carfunkel" (from his *Alemannische Gedichte* of 1803), which describes the fulfilment of a fateful prophecy, the carbuncle exercises an evil function.[94] While having her fortune told, a woman draws four times: the first card is the ace of diamonds, which signifies a red carbuncle—not a good fate: " 'es bidütet e rote Charfunkel; / 's isch ke guete Schick." Meanwhile her husband is playing cards in the inn with a sinister fellow who turns out to be the devil himself. When Michel wins the hand, he accepts in payment a magical ring set with a sparkling carbuncle that possesses the magical power of filling empty pockets with money. The possession of the carbuncle turns out, as prophesied in the cards, to be the beginning of Michel's terrible end, which the poem depicts in all its horror. Among romantic poets and their readers, therefore, the lore of the carbuncle, which had been lost during the decades of the Enlightenment, was recovered.

Small wonder, in the light of its renewed popularity as an ambiguous image of good and evil, that the carbuncle provoked satirical comment. In his novel *Premonition and Present* (*Ahnung und Gegenwart*, 1815) Eichendorff portrays an ecstatic young poet who declaims a lengthy dithyramb "about God, Heaven, Hell, Earth, and the Carbuncle-stone."[95] Later (Bk. III, Chaps. 21-22) he depicts a madman to whom has been assigned, as an image of his insanity, the sobriquet "carbuncle-seer" (*Karfunkelspäher*). In both cases the carbuncle is cited as an image of ecstasy bordering on madness. In one of his anti-romantic polemics the ageing classicist Johann Heinrich Voss ridiculed August Wilhelm Schlegel's "noble Secret Society for the reestablishment of the canonical age of Hildebrand," which spends most of its time practicing songs for the envisioned revelations of the "carbuncling Orient" and the southern sunlight.[96] The two principal documents, however, involve two of the most amusing parodies of German romanticism, which take the carbuncle as the comprehensive symbol of the entire movement. The "handbook for fulfilled romantics and for prospective mystics" that Jens Baggesen edited in 1810 satirizes not only the obsession with carbuncles but also the sonnetophilia of later romanticism. The work is allegedly the report of a certain Danwaller, who claims to possess the carbuncle, "the Philosopher's Stone, the *arcanum* of sonnets, in a word, the whole secret of the only possible and only genuinely poetic poetry."[97] By means of this mystical stone Danwaller succeeds in incorporating a company with a sonnet factory capable of turning out an average of seven hundred sonnets per week in three working hours per day. The method amounts to a simple production line: the rhyme words are selected at random and written down in the proper sequence; then the fourteen lines are filled in as rapidly as possible by various workers. The almanac contains examples from the three main periods of carbuncle history (the genial, the romantic, and the mystic periods). Two other sonnets display precisely the same rhyme-scheme as the following more-or-less nonsense poem entited "To Romantica":

Es flossen Blitz' aus jedem Edelsteine;
Mondstrahlen träufelten aus allem Golde;
Es weinte Liebesfunken jede Holde;
Rings dampften alle Berge Glut vom Weine;

Die Fluten alle loderten—nicht eine
Der Flammen, die da stehn in Lichtes Solde,
Vom Glanz der Sterne bis zum Schein der Dolde,
Blieb übrig—jede Blüthe ward die deine.

Geathmet all' in einem einz'gen Kusse,
Sich selbst in neuer Strahlung zu gebähren,
Verschlang sie dein jungfräulich keusches Dunkel.

So that dein Schoos, durchbohrt vom Himmel, Buße;
Und die Empfängniß selig zu bewähren,
Gebahrst du den schwarzleuchtenden Karfunkel.

(p. 68)

In a cascade of neologisms based on the common root we hear about the "carbuncle-smoothness" ("Karfunkelglätte," p. 72) and "carbuncle-hardness" ("Karfunkelhärte," p. 73) of the sonnets, which are produced in a "total breakthrough of carbuncling grace" ("das vollkommene Durchbrechen der karfunkelirenden Gnade," p. 109) by the members of the "carbuncling society" ("der karfunkelnden Gesellschaft," p. 110) as a result of their "quiet longing for the carbuncle stone" (p. 124) with "carbuncling skill and agility" ("karfunkelirender Geschicklichkeit und Fertigkeit," p. 114). The sequence of sonnets ends with a "General Hymn to the Carbuncle, or Klingklingel-Kyrie-Eleison" (p. 145), and the appendix contains two further romantic-mystic narratives in sonnet form: "Icicle and Frostflower, or the Carbuncle

Transformed into a Phoenix" and "Frog and Toad, or the Phoenix Transmuted into a Primal Carbuncle" ("Der in einen Phönix verwandelte Urkarfunkel").

Although the second example does not teem so resplendently with carbuncles, *Die Karfunkelweihe* by Till Ballistarius (pseudonym for J. L. Caspar) attests to the popularity of the carbuncle among romantic writers by quoting literally from contemporary works that employ the image. This "romantic tragedy" describes a battle that the romantic poets, stirred up by the whore-goddess Licentia Poetica, wage against classicism. Before the battle Little Hans, the young poet, is led into the oracle's cave, where he is offered a drink from the barrel of Inspiration: "Scoop seven times with this hollowed carbuncle," he is told.[98] Soon Little Hans, dreaming of blossoms and carbuncles, recites a poem inspired by Licentia Poetica which expresses the hope that he too will find a carbuncle blooming in the dark:

> So erblüht noch mir aus dem Dunkel
> Einst ein leuchtender Karfunkel!
>
> (p. 78)

It is scarcely necessary to quote further from these two delightful parodies, for it should be obvious that the opponents of romanticism seized eagerly upon the carbuncle as a conspicuous and generally acknowledged symbol of the romantic movement in Germany—an image that exemplified in its unreality what the rationalists regarded as the hollow fantasies of Novalis and his followers.

The poets of German romanticism stumbled upon the carbuncle in the course of their studies in alchemy and medieval-renaissance culture and, sometimes, in their practical training in mineralogy and mining. The mystic stone that glows in the dark appealed to them in part as an image of their reaction against the Enlightenment, which had sought—especially in the trivialized form of the late German *Aufklärung*—to banish all wonder from the universe. Their appropriation was informed by the romantic conviction that the world, like its microcosmic analogy the human psyche, is a place of darkness and mystery that requires magical illumination. The mystic stone in all its ambivalence—as an image of faith as well as evil, the image of the *unio mystica*—was the suitable icon. The revival was limited principally to Germany, and when the brief vogue was dispelled by parody the carbuncle again disappeared for decades from a literature that became increasingly realistic all over Europe. (It is worth noting that the delayed romanticism that occurred in the United States brought forth at least one work conspicuously employing the mystic stone: Hawthorne's tale "The Great Carbuncle: A Mystery of the White Mountains.")

We are now in a position to appreciate more fully the revival of the legend that took place during the *fin de siècle*. In part the Decadent delight in the mystic stone was a reaction against that realism which, at the beginning of the century, had ridiculed the carbuncle as an image of romantic excesses. The *fin de siècle* witnessed a revival of interest in several romantic writers, most notably Novalis, in whose works the carbuncle was singularly important. In part it was an expression, as we noted, of the Decadent fondness for the exotic in material objects. But we are now able to be more precise about the implications. We now recognize, for instance, the sources that Wilde cites in *The Picture of Dorian Gray*—notably the treatise of Camillus Leonardus, which recapitulated the entire classical and medieval lore concerning the stone and which had been translated into English as recently as 1750. However, the references to the legends surrounding Alexander the Great and to the recently edited letters of Prester John make it clear that Wilde was attracted primarily by the exotic lore surrounding the wondrous stone that glows in the dark. Huysmans, in contrast, had different motivations. It is likely that Huysmans was acquainted with the work of Fernand de Mély, whose publications on Hellenistic and medieval stone-lore were paralleled by extensive studies of the cathedral at Chartres. Yet in *La Cathédrale* Huysmans refers explicitly enough to his sources—Marbodus, Middle High German Mariological lapidaries, and interpretations of the high priest's pectoral—to make clear the nature of his interest in the carbuncle. Unlike Wilde, Huysmans makes no reference to the exotic contexts in which the stone often appears; instead, as a devout Catholic with mystic proclivities he revives the carbuncle explicitly as a religious image in the traditional medieval sense. If Wilde extends the medieval literary traditions for which the carbuncle represents an image of adventure and mystery and if Huysmans draws on the medieval Christian lapidary hermeneutics, there is nothing in George's poem to suggest that he went beyond the German romantic poets—notably Novalis—whose works were being revived in Germany and France during the nineties.

In general, the writers of the *fin de siècle* incorporated existing lore into their works for purposes of atmosphere. More recent writers, in contrast, have explored and enhanced the symbolic implications of the stone. Paul Claudel begins his essay on "La Mystique des pierres precieuses" with some general comments on the attractions of stones.[99] Alluding in passing to the carbuncle that regularly shows up in the *contes* concerning Melusine, he speculates on the inevitability with which gems assume occult or even astrological virtues, both medical and mystical. He gives evidence of his familiarity with Marbodus' *Liber de Gemmis* as well as the lapidaries of Albertus Magnus and others. For the greater part of his essay, however, Claudel simply recapitulates the commentary of Cornelius a Lapide on the stones in the foundation of the Heavenly Jerusalem, in which each stone is equated first with one of the twelve apostles and then with one of the twelve articles of faith in the Catholic credo. The third stone—the ruby, which Claudel identifies with the carbuncle—represents the Lord, who has been conceived by the Holy Spirit and has come to bring fire into the world to illuminate and glorify it.

Whereas Claudel, as one might expect in the case of

a pronounced Catholic writer, clings to the conventional religious associations of the mystic carbuncle, Hermann Hesse bestows upon the ancient stone conspicuously modern associations. In the fantasy *Pictor's Metamorphoses* (*Pictors Verwandlungen*, 1922) the theme of transformation, which obsessed Hesse in many of his fictional works and concerned him often in his essays, is metaphorically portrayed through the transmutation of the person in a manner possible in the realm of the fairy tale.[100] When Pictor enters the garden of paradise, he recognizes that paradise consists of the potentiality that all beings possess to transform themselves freely and unceasingly into ever new forms of existence. He sees a bird that changes itself successively into a flower, a butterfly, and finally into a glittering crystal. By means of this (here still unspecified) stone Pictor is enabled to transform himself into a tree. The condition lasts for years, but Pictor takes no pleasure from his arboreal state, for he senses that something important is missing. One day a girl comes into the garden, and Pictor feels an urgent desire to be united with her. Only complete union, he realizes, can fulfill his happiness. At this moment a bird comes flying along and drops from its beak something that glows with flamelike brilliance against the green of the foliage. The girl, stooping to pick it up, sees that "It was a crystal, was a carbuncle, and where it is, it cannot be dark." As soon as the girl holds this magic stone in her hand, Pictor's wish is fulfilled. She joins him in the tree, and they spend the rest of eternity in the bliss of constant transformation and renewal—a magical process that Hesse delighted in rendering in the water-colors he drew to illustrate the various holograph editions of the fantasy he prepared for friends and collectors.

Hesse is making use here of many vaguely recognizable elements. The garden is an adaptation of the biblical paradise with its tree of life and tree of knowledge, which are here somehow combined. The carbuncle as the means of magical transformation is appropriated from Novalis, whose works Hesse knew in intimate detail. (During this very period he was preparing a one-volume popular edition of Novalis' works.) And Hesse was quite familiar with the Latin Middle Ages, from which he had edited or translated many works: accordingly, he knew the legends of the carbuncle from older sources as well. Yet the mystic carbuncle assumes in this delightful fantasy a function that, going beyond traditional associations, suggests a modern understanding of symbolism.

We have already had occasion to note that C. G. Jung contributed significantly to the serious study of alchemy in the twentieth century and to the interpretation of alchemistic symbols in the light of modern depth psychology. It is essential to remember that this research was for Jung anything but an academic exercise. The chiseled reliefs (e.g., the face of the Trickster) and the free-standing sculptures ("Atmavictu" and the "Serpent Stone") with which he adorned his retreat at Bollingen—the famous tower—make it amply clear that Jung had a mystical appreciation of stones. As he noted in his autobiography, "At any time in my later life when I came up against a blank wall, I painted a picture or hewed a stone. Each such experience proved to be a *rite d'entrée* for the ideas and words that followed hard upon it."[101] Of all these stones, none was more important than the one Jung called simply "The Stone" and inscribed with various alchemistic formulae in Greek and Latin. "The Stone stands outside the Tower, and is like an explanation of it. It is a manifestation of the occupant, but one which remains incomprehensible to others."[102]

The stone assumed this central role in Jung's thought because it came to represent in his eyes the *coniunctio oppositorum* of *anima* and *animus*, the integration of self that he saw as the goal of all psychological development. "The unity of the stone is the equivalent of individuation, by which man is made one; we would say that the stone is a projection of the unified self."[103] In his alchemical studies Jung discovered the most suitable images for this thought. "The dual being born of the alchemical union of opposites, the Rebis or Lapis Philosophorum, is so distinctively marked in the literature that we have no difficulty in recognizing it as a symbol of the self."[104] One of the most common synonyms for the *lapis philosophorum*, as Jung pointed out, was *carbunculus*, cited with conspicuous frequency in Jung's essays (see the indices to his works). In its capacity as *Lapis*, in turn, Jung's carbuncle symbolizes the ancient association of *lux* and *vita* (analogous in Jung's system to *anima* and *animus*) as well as the alchemistic notion of transmutation. In one of his essays he approvingly quotes the exhortation of the alchemist Gerhard Dorn: "Transmute yourselves from dead stones into living philosophical stones."[105]

Jung's alchemistic studies could have had no direct influence on Hesse's fantasy. Although the two men were acquainted and occasionally saw each other during the period immediately preceding the composition of *Pictor's Metamorphoses*, Jung did not undertake his serious study of alchemy for several more years. It is more likely that Hesse received the carbuncle as a symbol of transformation from a literary source—Novalis' *Heinrich von Ofterdingen*—and, given the similarity of concern, used it for similar symbolic purposes. Regardless of the precise stages of transmission, however, it is evident that Claudel, Hesse, and Jung had a more profound appreciation of the mystic carbuncle than did the three representative writers of the *fin de siècle*, for whom it was largely an exotic and decorative image. Drawing on sources in religion, literature, and alchemy, the modern thinkers restored symbolically to the carbuncle the powers of mystical illumination and spiritual transformation it had possessed for hundreds of years until its radiance was extinguished in the cool light of the *Aufklärung*.

This reluminescence is consistent with the larger pattern evident in the history of the mystical stone, which extends over more than two thousand years. What characterizes the carbuncle preeminently is its marvelous power of adaptation and accommodation. It is par excellence the luminescent stone, but it has otherwise no stories about itself. Rather, it is easily attracted to other legends that need for their own purposes a stone with precisely this power: to symbolize Christ or the Virgin, to illuminate a temple or a dangerous cavern, to adorn the person of the king of Pegu or the emperor's crown, to irradiate the ignorance of paganism or the dark night of the soul, to transmute gross matter into spirituality or to unite the lovers in fantasies by Novalis or Hesse. The mystic carbuncle is ultimately a signal—a red light that flashes from time to time in the history of human culture to alert us to spiritual energies coursing beneath the surface at depths of religion or psychology that have always remained inaccessible to the clear light of reason.

Chapter Three

TALKING DOGS:
THE CANINIZATION OF
LITERATURE

I

THE WOOLLY, longhaired narrator of Kafka's late story "Investigations of a Dog" (1922) is a profoundly troubled animal. No longer a dog among dogs, he has withdrawn from the social harmony of the canine community. The tendency to rumination that alienated him from dogdom he traces back to an unsettling experience in his youth. One night while out for a run he encountered a troupe of seven small dogs illuminated by a strange radiance and dancing to the rhythms of a powerful music. When the pup asked the dogs what force compelled them to dance, they violated the laws of caninity by refusing to answer. Indeed, they offended all accepted standards of canine decency by strutting on their hind legs and displaying their nakedness. Then they vanished as suddenly as they had appeared. It was his failure to get a satisfactory explanation for this mysterious event that incited the dog to devote his life to metaphysical investigations.

The dog begins his enquiries with the most basic speculations: what does the canine race nourish itself upon? This question leads quickly to the more general one: whence does the earth procure this food? The dog has noticed that most food comes from the ground, a fact underlying the fundamental law governing the canine community: go forth and water the earth. But he has also observed that some food comes not from the ground but from above, produced not by watering but by incantations, dance, and song. The other dogs regard him as foolish for troubling his head with such questions. If he needs food, they say, they will share with him according to the practice of the canine community. Why worry about its source? In his effort to discover the truth about nourishment the dog decides to fast in a secluded spot. But after a few days he is driven away by a great hound, who is accompanied by a penetrating melody that almost bursts his eardrums. Just at this point, when the canine narrator has decided that it would be more productive to shift his investigations from food to music, the lengthy fragment breaks off.

Many of the riddles of Kafka's perplexing narrative can be readily explained by the fact that the dog does not acknowledge the existence of people: "all that I cared for was the race of dogs, that and nothing else. For what is there actually except our own species?" (p. 218).[1] Once the reader puts the dog's experiences into a human context, much becomes clear. The music-dogs that provoke the pup's investigations are trained dancing dogs at a circus or fair. Confusing cause and effect, the pup assumes that the music to which they respond is produced by them. Similarly, the ear-piercing sound that heralds the magnificent hound is the huntsman's whistle. The mystery of the food that appears from above in response to incantations is resolved as soon as we see the dog in a human environment, being fed by his master.

Kafka is using an animal story to present an essentially human situation. In metaphysical matters, he implies, man is as blind as the dog that pursues its investigations without realizing what it owes to mankind. His canine narrator, in fact, displays all the characteristics of the typical Kafkaesque hero: pedantic and a compulsive talker, this pathological worrier is dissatisfied with purely material explanations for existence and longs for an irrational faith in some sort of supernatural being, as attested by his belief in the strange *Lufthunde*, which no one has ever seen even though everyone talks about them. Despite all its complexities, then, the basic meaning of the fragment is reasonably clear. But interpretation alone, since it takes the facts of the narrative for granted, does not come to grips with the really startling question posed by Kafka's story. What is a philosophizing dog doing in twentieth-century literature?

Kafka frequently resorts to animal images as drastic analogues for human relationships. "Investigations of a Dog" belongs to a group of four major stories narrated by animals: "A Report to an Academy" (1917) is delivered by a monkey, who portrays his gradual *embourgeoisement*; in "The Burrow" (1923-24) a badger describes his extensive underground realm and the sinister forces that threaten it; and in Kafka's last story a rodent chronicles the destiny of "Josephine the Singer, or the Mouse Folk" (1924). It is clear where the "Investigations of a Dog" belongs within the context of Kafka's works and their images. But have we exhausted all the implications of the motif of the talking dog if we simply point to analogies in other works by Kafka? Or can we establish a literary tradition to which this garrulous canine belongs?

The decades around the turn of the twentieth century produced so many canine scribblers that they would be entitled to a separate listing by the Westminster Kennel Club. In the United States alone we find *Vic: The Autobiography of a Fox Terrier* (1892), *The Autobiography of an Irish Terrier* (1904), *Pup: The Autobiography of a Greyhound* (1905), *Fairy: The Autobiography of a Real Dog* (1907), and *The Autobiography of Jeremy L., The Actor Dog* (1910).[2] During the same period, dogs all over the world were churning out their "diaries," their "mémoires," their "observations," and their "letters." One especially poetic pup penned *The Rubaiyat of a Scotch Terrier* (1926). Anatole France disclosed twenty philosophical "Meditations of Riquet" (1900), Monsieur Bergeret's dog. In Italo Svevo's story, "Argo and His Master" ("Argo e il suo padrone," posthumously published in 1934), a convalescent in the mountains learns his dog's language in order to record his dog's ruminations. An internationally popular tear-jerker entitled *Where's Master* (1910) was attributed to Edward VII's dog, Caesar, who recounts to his friend, the terrier Daisy, the events surrounding the king's illness, death, and funeral. In a sense, therefore, Kafka was appropriating for his own purposes a familiar minor genre of his age.[3] But to note this caninization in the literature of the early twentieth century raises another question. Did these literary dogs simply come out of nowhere, strange mutants produced by a genetic quirk? Or can they claim a respectable literary pedigree?

II

MEN HAVE long regarded the dog with an affection that often borders on reverence.[4] This attitude is due in large measure to the fact that *canis familiaris* was the first animal that Mesolithic man succeeded in weaning away from the wilderness and domesticating. As the animal that overcame its bestial impulses to rise above the wolves and the jackals from which it emerged, the dog gained a reputation for sagacity and even for a certain spirituality. According to Isidore's *Etymologiae* (XII, ii, 25): *Nihil autem sagacius canibus; plus enim sensus ceteris animalibus habent.* The esteem the dog enjoyed has produced a variety of cultural practices through the centuries. In ancient Italy, hunting dogs were crowned at the annual festival of Diana of Nemi—a practice that anticipated today's awards to the Dog Hero of the Year or election to the Animal Actors Hall of Fame. During World War II the mongrel Chips, a member of the K-9 Corps, was awarded a Silver Star (subsequently revoked) for heroism in battle. The City of Vienna has a special institution—its Kynologisches Museum (Karl-Schweig-hofergasse 3, 1070 Vienna)—dedicated to the history, genetic development, and domestication of the dog family, with exhibits containing over one thousand skulls of house dogs, wild dogs, foxes, wolves, and jackals.

Dogs have long played a major role in the folklore of power. Warren Harding's airedale Laddie Boy had a special chair in which he attended Cabinet meetings.[5] In American folk art, dogs have often provided a favorite motif for paintings, sculpture, pottery, textiles, weathervanes, and jewelry.[6] Chekhov addressed many letters to his wife Olga with variations on the heading "Dear Dog"; the poet Mayakovsky customarily signed his letters to his mistress "Puppy"; and when Richard Wagner's dog Pohl died in 1866, the composer was so distraught that he ordered a special coffin, shrouded the body in a coverlet, and performed a bizarre burial ritual.

In his *Theory of the Leisure Class* (1899) Thorstein Veblen argued (Ch. 6) that the dog "commends himself to our favour" because of his conspicuous uselessness, his fawning subservience, and his predatory impulse. A less cynical point of view has emerged from the motivational-research surveys commissioned by dog-food manufacturers to determine the "psychographic" profile of dog owners.[7] These "dog-owner typologies" agree that owners tend to "humanize" dogs far more than other pets. In a period of declining birth rates, dogs become "surrogate children." Through "ego projection" the owner attributes to the dog tastes that reflect his own. This humanization of dogs justifies chic dog boutiques, such as Le Chien in Manhattan, where the owner can purchase for his or her pet items ranging from jewelry, boots, and sweaters to fashion T-shirts labeled "Pierre Cardog," "Christian Dog," of "Goochie Poochie." In 1977, Saks Fifth Avenue's Dog Toggery advertised Christmas cards for dogs to send to their veterinarians: "I am such a lucky pet—Cause I have you for my Vet." After the dog's demise the grieving owner can announce the event on dog note paper (sealed with dog sticker stamps), commission a monument at "Petstones," and bury the deceased at an institution like Pleasant Plains Pet Cemetery—a New York counterpart to the Happier

Hunting Grounds portrayed by Evelyn Waugh in his California satire *The Loved One* (1948).[8]

But this anthropomorphic reverence, however gratifying its intent, has not been an unmixed blessing for the dog. Because of the spirituality attributed to them, dogs were prized as sacrificial offerings all over the ancient world—from Luzon and Assam to Argos and Sparta, where they were consecrated to the deities of fertility and war. In other places—from Egypt to Hawaii and Ireland—it was acceptable to substitute dogs for human beings in sacrificial rites. (An analogous practice sent dogs in place of men on the early space flights and still exposes dogs to a variety of unpleasant medical tests for which the National Anti-Vivisection Society invites our indignation.) The Greeks had an elaborate vocabulary to designate festivals where dogs were slaughtered (κυνοφόντις) or deities worshipped with sacrifices of dogs (κυνοσφαγής). Indonesians as well as American Indians ate dogs in the hope of assimilating their bravery, and the Romans and the ancient Peruvians practiced cynophagy at their major festivals.

The close identification of dogs with men also produced the widespread practice of cynotherapy. In Siberia, New Guinea, and Burma, dogs were sacrificed to ward off plagues. Elsewhere such diseases as measles and whooping cough were transferred to the dog by laying the dog on the sufferer or by feeding the dog a few of the patient's hairs. Hippocrates recommended dog flesh for consumption; Pliny prescribed dog's urine for warts, dog's blood for poison, and dog's tooth for toothache; dog's tongue, dried and suspended around the neck, was long considered a cure for scrofula. As recently as the eighteenth century, medical treatises prescribed liniments distilled from dog fat for bruises and rheumatism. A preparation known as "dog oil" is still used in sections of England and the United States as a remedy for arthritis. And "a hair of the dog that bit you"—now reduced to a proverb recommending a drink

to cure a hangover—is a linguistic reminiscence of ancient prescriptions for dogbite and rabies.

It seems inevitable that a beast endowed with such
associations would play an important role in myth and
legend, and classical antiquity teems with examples. The
goddess Artemis is always surrounded by her pack of
hounds; Apollo as god of the hunt is known by the
epithet Cynegete ("leader of the dogs"); the physician
Asclepius numbers the dog along with the more familiar
serpent among his attributes; Pan is the dog-breeder of
the gods; and the two-headed New Year's dog Orthrus,
subsequently slain by Hercules, fathered a quartet of
beasts even more remarkable than himself: the Chi-
maera, the Sphinx, the Hydra, and the Nemean lion. In
ancient Egypt the reverence of dogs was especially fer-
vent. Anubis, the cynocephalic god of the dead, was the
patron saint of embalmers because he invented the art
of mummification to preserve his beloved companion,
Osiris. At Assiut in central Egypt, where the canine god
Wepwawet was honored, dogs were the object of popular devotion: at their deaths they were mummified and
interred in a special canine burial ground.

In the Middle Ages the ancient beliefs were simply
translated into Christian terms. Dogs were attached as
a symbol of loyalty to various saints, notably St. Dominic
and St. Bernard. According to the *Legenda Aurea* St.
Bernard's mother dreamed of a whelp barking in her
womb. When she recounted this dream to a priest he
prophesied: "Thou wilt be the mother of a very good
little dog, which will be the guardian of the house of
God, and will pursue its enemies with loud barking; for
he will be a peerless preacher, and will cure many with
the healing grace of his tongue."[9] Popular etymology
regards the Dominican friars as the hounds of God (*do-
mini canes*). In medieval art the dog provided a familiar
iconographic image: at a woman's feet it represented
affection and fidelity; at a man's feet, courage and mag-
nanimity. The reputation for loyalty perseveres in the
once popular name for dogs, Fido. And the claim of
unusual sagacity can be seen in the "Wise Dogs" or

"Dogs of Knowledge" that were featured as stage prod-
igies by seventeenth-century traveling players, at eight-
eenth- and nineteenth-century fairs, and in twentieth-
century vaudeville.

The love of dogs, especially strong among Indo-Eu-
ropean peoples, was by no means universal in the ancient
world.[10] In the Old Testament all the references to dogs
express contempt: "As a dog returneth to his vomit, so
a fool returneth to his folly" (Proverbs xxvi:11). Still
today devout Muslims feel that they must bathe if they
have been defiled by touching a dog. Even among cynophilic peoples the reverence was qualified by a certain
ambivalence. Men feared that the dog might revert to
the bestial state from which it had emerged, becoming
once again an evil force, all the more menacing because
of its position of trust within the human community.
Thus in many medieval folktales the devil assumes the
shape of a dog in order to insinuate himself into human
society[11]—a motif that Goethe appropriated for his *Faust*,
in which Mephistopheles first enters the scholar's study
in the form of a poodle.

The ambivalence toward dogs is reflected semantically
in shifts in the metaphoric use of the word: in the sixteenth century a dog was simply a "cur" whereas by the
eighteenth century the term had come to designate a
"noble animal."[12] This same ambivalence shows up in
literature as well. Cynophilia is evident in the many
popular dog stories featuring the faithful dog—from
Ouida's *A Dog of Flanders* (1909) through such sequels
as Walter A. Dyer's *Pierrot: Dog of Belgium* (1915)
down to films and television series about Rin-Tin-Tin
and Lassie. The cynophobic attitude is embodied in the
hound of hell, the great black dog with flaming eyes,
which appears in archetypal form in *The Hound of the
Baskervilles* as well as many folk-tales and horror stories. This negative image dominates Günter Grass's *Dog
Years* (1963), in which the succession of black, wolf-like
dogs—Perkun, Senta, Harras, and Prinz—exemplifies the
cur-like qualities Grass detects in the German character.

III

THE MODERN literary sensibility has frequently felt challenged to define its attitude toward the animal reputed to be at once so spiritual and so wild—that displays, in other words, precisely those schizophrenic characteristics that have fascinated writers in their human subjects. Few poets have been more preoccupied with dogs than Rainer Maria Rilke. In one of his letters to Benvenuta (17 February 1914) Rilke speculated how sublime it would be to "look into" a dog—"to let oneself into the dog precisely in his center, at the point where he is most dog, the place within him where God might have seated himself for a moment when the dog was created . . . to see . . . that he could not have been made better." At least two literary forms have emerged to fill this cynoscopic urge. The first type is represented by John Galsworthy's *Memories* (1912), Thomas Mann's *A Man and His Dog* (*Herr und Hund*, 1918), and Colette Audry's *Behind the Bathtub* (*Derrière la Baignoire*, 1962). For all the differences between the stories of Mann's short-haired pointer Bauschan, Audry's Alsatian Douchka, and Galsworthy's nameless spaniel, certain characteristics tie them together. All three writers analyze the dog's personality by projecting onto the dog human characteristics. Douchka, in fact, means "little soul." Galsworthy remarks that his spaniel was "certainly no Christian; but, allowing for essential dog, he was very much a gentleman" (p. 63).[13] And Mann, in his "Notes on Bauschan's Character and Manner of Life," describes his dog in terms that would be absolutely appropriate for the bourgeois figures in his early stories and novels.

To the extent that they are concerned principally with man's attitude toward the dog, these three classics are "relativised" or "anthropocentric" animal narratives. At the other end of the scale we find works that might more appropriately be called "absolute" or "cynocentric."[14] It would be difficult to imagine two writers more dissimilar than Jack London and Virginia Woolf or two dogs more utterly unlike than the gentle spaniel of *Flush* (1933) and the huge mastiff of *The Call of the Wild* (1905). Yet for all the differences between the authors, the dogs, and the setting—Elizabeth Barrett Browning's ultra-civilized London and Florence and the savage Klondike of the gold rush—a striking similarity links these two famous dog novels because both are cynomorphic: that is, they are narrated from the dog's point of view. A second common factor ties these works to the tradition of ambivalence mentioned earlier: the authors are fascinated by the atavistic longings that rule their canine protagonists. London's novel is a paean to "the call of the wild," which gradually shatters the veneer of domestication encasing Buck. Precisely the same kind of urge is conspicuous in Woolf's gentle spaniel. "It is universally admitted," the story begins, "that the family from which the subject of this memoir claims descent is one of the greatest antiquity."

There have also been recent examples of cynomorphic narrative, complete with atavistic impulses. In Richard Adams' novel *The Plague Dogs* (1977) two dogs—Snitter and Rowf—escape from a brutal animal experimentation laboratory and, suspected of bearing the bubonic plague, are pursued about the English Lake District for six weeks until they are reunited with Snitter's kindly master. One of the most stirring indictments of Stalinism emerges from Georgi Vladimov's *Faithful Ruslan* (1975), which portrays the dehumanizing effect of the Soviet gulag system from the viewpoint of a guard dog.

This exercise in literary cynology can help us to discriminate among the various forms in which literary dogs appear. But none of these forms—the popular dog tale, the intellectual meditation on the man-dog relationship, nor the cynomorphic narrative—explains Kafka's "Investigations of a Dog." To uncover the sources of this first-person account by the species that might be called *canis familiaris loquax* we must go back to classical antiquity.

IV

IN BOOK II of *The Republic* (374e-376b) Socrates discusses the qualities required by the ideal guardian of the state. The physical attributes are obvious: the guardian must be keen of perception, quick, and strong. But he must also possess certain spiritual qualities, for spirit alone "makes every soul in the face of everything fearless and unconquerable."[15] Yet these very attributes might well cause the guardian to be harsh to friends as well as enemies. "Where," ponders Socrates, "shall we discover a disposition that is at once gentle and great-spirited?" After arriving at the conclusion that a good guardian is an impossibility because no single individual can unite such seemingly opposed traits, Socrates brings forth his paradox. "You surely have observed in well-bred hounds that their natural disposition is to be most gentle to their familiars and those whom they recognize, but the contrary to those whom they do not know." If up to this point Socrates has drawn on the canine attributes generally familiar from folklore, he glorifies the quality of sagacity when he goes on to prove that dogs also display wisdom, being able to distinguish friend from foe by recognition of the one and failure to recognize the other. "How, I ask you, can the love of learning be denied to a creature whose criterion of the friendly and the alien is intelligence and ignorance?"

Platonists have long been embarrassed in their attempts to justify the reasoning in this remarkable passage. But regardless of its merits or deficiencies as logic, the literary image governing the passage caught the cultural imagination, and Plato's authority established the dog as the "philosophical" animal par excellence, a notion that remained lively to the end of classical antiquity.[16] Indeed, as late as 1534, in the Author's Prologue to the First Book of *Gargantua and Pantagruel*, Rabelais cited Plato's characterization of the dog as "the most philosophic beast" and urged his reader to crack the

bone of his symbols in order to suck out the marrow of
his meaning.

The derivation of the name Cynics for the influential
school of ancient philosophers is unclear: it has been
traced back variously to the earliest home of the school,
a gymnasium outside Athens called Cynosarges, and to
the Greek word for dog, in contemptuous allusion to
the uncouth mode of life flaunted by its adherents. In
any case, the Cynics gladly accepted the dog as their
symbol. When the Cynic Crates got married he coined
the term *cynogamia* ("dog-wedding") to designate the
occasion. And when Diogenes died the Corinthians erected
to his memory a pillar on which reposed a dog of Parian
marble.

It was the curious union of Plato and his philosophical
dog with the cynophilic philosophers that produced what
seems to be the first example in Western literature of a
philosophical dialogue involving a talking dog. The satirist Lucian did not assimilate Platonism and Cynicism
uncritically; but he learned the technique of the literary-
philosophical dialogue from Plato, and he was indebted
to the satires of the Cynic Menippus for many of his
ideas. These elements come together in the twenty-first
of his *Dialogues of the Dead*, to which Browning alludes
in the lines from *Pippa Passes* concerning "some Greek
dog-sage, dead and merry, / Hellward bound in Cha-
ron's wherry." When Menippus arrives at the gates of
Hades, he strikes up a conversation with Cerberus by
claiming kinship: "for Cerberus and Cynic are surely
related through the dog."[17] Menippus is eager to learn
how Socrates behaved on the occasion of his descent to
the underworld, and Cerberus obliges him with a detailed account. Though Socrates appeared calm while he
was still some distance away, he began to bawl like a
baby as soon as he saw the gloom inside. "All that sort
are the same, I tell you—bold resolute fellows as far as
the entrance; it is inside that the real test comes." Although Socrates turned out to be a mere theorist, unable
to live up to his own brave precepts, Cerberus certifies

that Menippus is a credit to the breed, like Diogenes before him. "You two came in without any compulsion or pushing, of your own free will, with a laugh for yourselves and a curse for the rest."

Lucian's dialogue, though only a few dozen lines long, displays several basic characteristics. First, our interest is solicited for the dog's comments on human affairs as witnessed from his unique and literally "cynical" point of view. Second, this philosophical comment is sustained by a strong narrative element. Third, the dog's ability to speak is not taken for granted: it is possible only because it occurs under unusual circumstances (that is, in the underworld) and because of the unique kinship between the dog and the human Cynic.

V

LUCIAN'S DIALOGUES were lost to the Latin Middle Ages. But when Lucian was rediscovered during the Renaissance his dialogues, seen to provide an ideal vehicle for the critical revaluation of religion and society undertaken by the humanists, were translated or imitated by virtually every major writer of the age.[18] Few works more clearly preserve the tradition of the Lucian dialogue than the enigmatic *Cymbalum Mundi* (1537) of Bonaventure des Périers—classics scholar, Bible translator, religious reformer, and *valet de chambre* of Marguerite de Navarre. The last of the four dialogues takes place in ancient Greece between two dogs, Hylactor ("barker") and Pamphagus ("eat-all").[19] In the opening monologue Hylactor bemoans his paradoxical fate: able and eager to talk, he has sworn never to utter a word in the presence of men until he finds another dog who can talk. To satisfy the compelling urge that he calls his logorrhea ("mon flux de langue") Hylactor mystifies his fellow canines by addressing them in human speech, he disturbs the peace by shouting "Murder!" or "Fire!" in the streets, and he plays pranks on man and beast alike. One day he meets Pamphagus, another talking dog. It emerges in the course of their conversation that they were both hounds in the pack of Actaeon. They obtained the power of speech when they ate his tongue after Diana had turned their master into a stag and set his own hounds upon him. When Hylactor expresses a desire to communicate with human beings so that he might be venerated in Greece as Anubis is worshipped in Egypt, Pamphagus declares emphatically that he would prefer to remain silent because people would want such a prodigy to live in a manner contrary to the nature of a dog: "I would be secluded in a room; I would be rubbed down, combed, clothed, worshipped, adorned, fondled." To Hylactor's query whether he wouldn't like to live like men, Pamphagus swears by Cerberus' three heads that "I prefer remaining what I am rather than living as wretchedly as they do and if only for one reason: that I'd have to talk too much as they do." Agreeing that it is wiser to remain silent than to divulge their marvelous ability, the two dogs decide to join the other hounds in the hunt. As the dialogue ends, Pamphagus is sure that the foolish Hylactor will be unable much longer to control his tongue in the presence of men.

The *Cymbalum Mundi* has perplexed its readers for four centuries.[20] Beyond the fact that it is a religious allegory, nothing about the work is clear—even such a fundamental question as whether Bonaventure was a believer or an atheist. It has been suggested that Actaeon is Christ, who was betrayed and then turned into a God by his Church; Actaeon's tongue symbolizes the Gospels; and the two dogs represent reformers (Luther and Calvin) who, having learned the message of Christ, are unable to make themselves understood by their fellows. Other critics have proposed that the dogs represent Bonaventure himself and his friend Estienne Dolet, both advocates of "hesuchism," a form of sixteenth-century quietism that advocated faith and piety in contrast to the more vocal Christian reform movements of the period.

Leaving aside the probably unresolvable problem of

meaning, what we find in this mysterious work is, formally, a philosophical dialogue involving two talking dogs and displaying a strong narrative element. The dogs' ability to speak is justified magically, and the discussion revolves around the question whether or not the dogs should disclose this ability to human beings. The canine point of view is exploited as an alienating device that enables us to look at human affairs with critical detachment. Although it is somewhat longer, this dialogue clearly shares the principal characteristics of the dialogue between Cerberus and the Cynic in Lucian's *Dialogues of the Dead.*

There is good reason to believe that Cervantes was familiar with Lucian's dialogues,[21] and it is likely that he knew Des Périers' *Cymbalum Mundi.* Either source, or both, could have provided the model for the "Colloquy of the Dogs" in his *Exemplary Tales* (1613). Here we find again a philosophically oriented dialogue between two dogs who are astonished to discover that they can talk. But Cervantes has augmented the narrative at least tenfold by developing two motifs that are present only rudimentarily in Des Périer's dialogue. The rationalization of the dogs' ability to speak is expanded into an elaborate framework narrative; and the inherent narrative tendency—evident in Cerberus' account of Socrates' descent to Hades and in Hylactor's report of his various pranks—has been intensified to incorporate a series of picaresque adventures.

The "Colloquy of the Dogs" is presented as a manuscript written by the Ensign Campuzano, who has spent several weeks in the Hospital of the Resurrection in Valladolid sweating off the syphilis inflicted upon him by his deceitful wife (the subject of the framework tale, "The Deceitful Marriage").[22] One night the ensign hears voices behind his bed. Listening attentively, he concludes that the speakers are none other than Scipio and Berganza, dogs belonging to the almoner Mahudes. For two consecutive nights Campuzano eavesdrops on the dogs and then writes down from memory the first night's colloquy. He submits the manuscript to his friend, the Licentiate Peralta, who encourages Campuzano to set down the second part as well.

Cervantes never suggests that Campuzano actually sees the two dogs talking. Instead, he *hears* someone chatting behind his bed and infers from their conversation that it is the two dogs. He overhears this colloquy, moreover, while he is feverish, weakened by illness, and undergoing sweat baths. Despite the ensign's protests that he could not have invented the dogs' conversation out of his own head, it is plain that Cervantes is providing us with a perfectly rational explanation for the colloquy of the dogs.

Basically the dialogue displays the same characteristics as the much shorter works by Lucian and Des Périers. It begins with an expression of astonishment by the dogs at their new-found ability to speak: "the unparalleled favor that Heaven has granted to both of us at the same time" (p. 247). Before settling down for their talk they look around to make sure that no one can overhear them—a gesture that recalls the motif of silence in the *Cymbalum Mundi*. Both dogs exhibit a pronounced tendency to philosophize—so much so that they almost become caricatures of the motif of the philosophical dog. In a passage that sounds like a parody of Plato, Scipio explains the etymology of the word "philosophy" after Berganza has conceded that "although I use the word, I do not know what it is; only I guess that it is something good" (p. 268). Berganza repeatedly interrupts his narrative for philosophical digressions: "Brother Scipio, may Heaven grant all your desires if you will allow me at present to do a little philosophizing without boring you" (p. 265). Scipio, who himself displays a tendency to moralize, accedes, but he warns Berganza against *murmuración* or "backbiting." "Take heed, Berganza, that your inclination to philosophize be not a temptation of the devil, because slander has no better cloak to hide its malice than the pretense that all it says are maxims of philosophers, and that the disclosure of the shortcomings of others is honest zeal" (p. 265). Finally, the canine viewpoint functions as an alienating device that exposes human affairs in a cynical light.[23]

This basic form is enlarged and modified by the inclusion of the picaresque narrative of Berganza's life. His adventures display a remarkably sophisticated structure:[24] five episodes on either side embrace the central episode in which a witch named Cañizares tells Berganza that he is in reality Montiel, the son of the witch Montiela. He was transformed at birth into a dog by the enchantment of the witch Camacha. It was this transformation, allegedly, that endowed Berganza with the power of speech.

This picaresque expansion has had a pronounced effect upon the dialoque. Above all, it significantly enhances the possibilities for cynical comment on the hypocrisy of human society, which Berganza witnesses unsuspected by the perpetrators: butchers who cheat their customers, shepherds whose life contrasts rudely with fashionable pastoral idylls, bailiffs who blackmail travelers and connive with thieves and prostitutes, the practices of soldiers, gypsies, moors, Jesuits, actors— scarcely an aspect of early seventeenth-century Spanish society fails to come under the cynical eye of the dog Berganza. This narrative element was already present in the dialogues of Lucian and Des Périers. But the expansion that it undergoes in Cervantes' tale affects the form of the dialogue itself: for "The Colloquy of the Dogs" is no longer a true dialogue; it is a monologue punctuated by comments of the second interlocutor. As a result, the dialogue is not primarily dialectical and philosophical; it is a picaresque tale in monologue form, interrupted from time to time for comments of a generalizing and generally critical nature.

VI

IN ONE BRILLIANT EFFORT Cervantes perfected the dogs' colloquy as a fictional form. When his works began to be discovered outside Spain in the middle of the eighteenth century, the story was widely imitated.²⁵ In England it was the picaresque narrative that appealed to readers. Cervantes' tale was one of the principal inspirations for the *History of Pompey the Little; or, The Life and Adventures of a Lap-Dog* (1751), by Francis Coventry.²⁶ This novel, dedicated by its youthful author to Henry Fielding, aspires to be a canine *Tom Jones*. Beginning with "A Panegyric upon Dogs," it traces the education and travels of Pompey from Bologna, where he was born in 1735 in the apartments of a "celebrated Courtesan," to London, where he died on June 2, 1749. Along the way Pompey passes from owner to owner and from place to place, providing a perfect vehicle for the author's comments on the ills of British society and for much gossip in this lightly disguised *roman à clef*.

The turn of the century produced several dog stories that are indebted to *Pompey the Little*: the children's classic, *Keeper's Travels in Search of His Master* (1798), by Edward Augustus Kendall; the anonymous *Dog of Knowledge; or Memoirs of Bob, the spotted terrier: supposed to be written by himself* (1801); and the hugely popular *Biography of a Spaniel* (1797), allegedly a translation from the German but most likely the product of a minor British writer. We can trace a clear line of continuity from Cervantes' "Colloquy of the Dogs" down to these late eighteenth-century canine picaresques, but several changes have taken place. First, the dialogue form has been eliminated altogether so that we are left with a straightforward picaresque narrative, either in the third person or in the first person. Second, the canine hero is no longer a philosophical dog since his opinions do not matter; he merely provides the occasion for stringing together various episodes. Finally, all subtlety of characterization is lost. There is a clear dialectical tension between the garrulous Hylactor and the more cautious and cynical Pamphagus; Berganza reveals himself indirectly to be as guilty of "backbiting" and hypocrisy as the human masters that he attacks in his digressions.

But these dogs who search for their masters or die for them have been reduced from complex characters to walking exemplars of canine loyalty.

No European writer enjoyed a greater reputatation among German romantic writers and critics than Cervantes.[27] Among the many translations and adaptations of his works we also find several new versions of "The Colloquy of the Dogs." The *Gespräch zwischen zwey Hunden. Nach Cervantes und Florian* (1804), by Janus Eremita (=Joh. Chr. Gretschel), for instance, is a free adaptation that retains the dialogue form and the basic topics of Cervantes' "Colloquy" while streamlining the dialogue and inserting into it episodes from other stories by Cervantes.

All this activity around the turn of the century—the adaptations, D. W. Soltau's three-volume translation of Cervantes' *Lehrreiche Erzaehlungen* (1801), and the general enthusiasm for Cervantes among such romantic critics as Friedrich Schlegel, August Wilhelm Schlegel, Ludwig Tieck, and Schelling—persuaded E.T.A. Hoffmann that public familiarity with the Spaniard's work was so widespread that he could take for granted among his readers an acquaintance with "The Colloquy of the Dogs." His "Account of the Most Recent Fortunes of the Dog Berganza" ("Nachricht von den neuesten Schicksalen des Hundes Berganza," 1813), which purports to be a continuation of Cervantes' tale, merely cites Soltau's translation in the note to the title page and otherwise assumes that his audience is able to supply any necessary background details from the Spanish original.[28]

Passing through a deserted park on his way home from a nocturnal revelry, Hoffmann's narrator—a self-styled "Traveling Enthusiast"—hears sighs and then a muted voice lamenting its terrible destiny: "Cursed Cannizares, is your rage still potent even after your death? Did you not find your infamous Montiela and her satanic bastard in hell?" (p. 148). Looking more closely, the narrator makes out a black bulldog on the point of dying from a seizure. After he has revived the dog with water from the nearby river, the narrator addresses him politely. Consoled by the narrator's words, the dog tells his story. It turns out that he is none other than that same Berganza about whom Cervantes had written some two hundred years earlier. Frightened one night by the witch Cannizares, Berganza ran away from his master Mahudes and his companion Scipio. His panicky flight brought him to a crossroad where seven witches were celebrating their rites. Seizing Berganza, in whom they maintained that they recognized the son of the witch Montiela, they smeared him with magical ointments in an effort to transform him back into human shape. When the cock crowed the witches departed and Berganza made his escape, but the ceremony left its mark on him. Although the transformation failed, the ointment rendered Berganza immortal so that now, like the Wandering Jew, he is cursed to roam the earth forever. His wanderings— here we come to the second part of the story—eventually bring him to Germany, where he lives for a time with the conductor Johannes Kreisler (the archetypal romantic artist who figures in many of Hoffmann's works). When the townspeople attempt to do away with the two of them on the grounds that Kreisler is mad and Berganza rabid, the dog makes his escape and ends up in a nearby house where he becomes the pet of the lovely Cäcilie and witnesses the salons arranged by her mother. Following an ill-fated attempt to rescue Cäcilie from the brutal lecher to whom she has been married off (another archetypal situation in Hoffmann's works) Berganza runs away again. Arriving in the narrator's town, he finds employment in the local theater as a dancing dog. This third section of his account contains a variety of observations on actors, producers, directors, writers, and the theatrical life in nineteenth-century Germany. When morning comes, Berganza loses his ability to talk and goes bounding off into the distance, leaving the narrator to ponder his words.

Hoffmann wrote a number of stories and fairy tales involving talking animals, and at least two other works are narrated by animals: "Account of a Sophisticated Young Man" ("Nachricht von einem gebildeten jungen Mann," 1814), the letter written by a conceited musical monkey named Milo to his girl friend, is the model for Kafka's "Report to an Academy"; and half of the novel *Tomcat Murr* (*Kater Murr*, 1820-22) consists of the autobiography of the vain and cocky eponymous hero. Since the "Account of the Most Recent Fortunes of the Dog Berganza" is the first of the tales in which Hoffmann used the motif of a talking animal, it is particularly revealing that it was demonstrably inspired by another literary work.[29]

Through his basic fiction—that he is presenting a sequel to the adventures of Cervantes' Berganza—Hoffmann alerts us to the conventions of the genre that he is exploiting. Once again we have a dialogue involving a talking dog, who uses his experiences as the basis for observations on human society. Hoffmann's Berganza shares that love of philosophical digressions that characterized him in Cervantes' account. "Your reflections on yourself and your race, dear Berganza, bear witness to your philosophical spirit, and so I am quite content if, from time to time, you interrupt your story" (p. 155). Although the dog's philosophy is satirized in some of his reflections—e.g., his digressions on the superiority of canine language over human language as a mode for expressing emotions, or on the rhetoric of tail-wagging—most of his comments amount to astute criticisms of human society as witnessed by an outsider—not just a dog but, as he points out, a seventeenth-century Spanish dog in nineteenth-century Germany. As such, he offers observations on the role of women in intellectual society, the cultural pretentiousness of the German bourgeoisie, the vanity of actors, the avarice of producers, the differences between true and false art, and a variety of other topics. In short, the talking dog appears here again in the role that has been conventional ever since Lucian. In keeping with the motif as it occurs in Des Périers and Cervantes, the role of criticism is balanced by the theme of silence: all the advantages of mankind, Berganza tells his interlocuter, "are not worth as much as the ability to preserve true meaning in a long silence" (p. 166). Finally, the colloquy is framed in such a way as to make it clear that it amounts to no more than the drunken vision of the narrator. We learn at the start that he is drunk; even Berganza, during his short time in the town, has heard that the narrator has a reputation for drunkenness. And everything that Berganza allegedly tells him can easily be attributed to the narrator's own experiences—from the literary allusions based on Cervantes' novella through the social gossip involving Kreisler and Cäcilie down to the cynical comments on the local theater society.

At the same time, Hoffmann would not be a German romantic if he did not parody the very conventions that he exploits. A high degree of irony is involved, first of all, in the literary playfulness that borrows its principal character from a famous work of world literature. We are dealing, after all, not with simply another talking dog but with Cervantes' Berganza. Hoffmann creates a delightfully ironic interplay between fiction and reality by causing his (fictional) characters to assume that Cervantes' (fictional) characters have a real existence. "Since the excellent Don Miguel de Cervantes Saavedra disclosed Campuzano's account to the world, I can assume that my adventures, which I related to my dear, unforgettable Scipio, are quite familiar to you" (p. 153). And he adds a further twist by making Berganza's interlocutor a person rather than another dog, as in the original. The narrator expresses the conventional astonishment at the wonder of a talking dog, but his astonishment is qualified: he finds the fact only "a bit strange" because he has never before heard a dog talk "so audibly" (p.

148). Much of our amusement stems from our recognition of the literary pattern that is being parodied here.

VII

It was Hoffmann's ironic play with literary conventions that impressed his Russian admirer, Gogol, whose "The Diary of a Madman" (written 1833-34) shows clear traces of Hoffmann's "Berganza."[30] "The Diary of a Madman" is the first-person account of the three or four months leading to the nervous breakdown and confinement of a forty-two-year-old petty government clerk.[31] In love with Sophie, the daughter of his director, he goes mad when he learns that she is about to be married to a handsome young officer. The last incoherent entries in his journal depict his commitment to an asylum while he is under the illusion that he is the king of Spain being escorted in honor to his own country.

One of the devices whereby Gogol reveals the incipient madness of his narrator is the motif of talking dogs. His journal begins with the observation that "an extraordinary thing happened today." As he is going to his office, he sees Sophie get out of a carriage on Nevsky Avenue and enter a shop. Waiting outside in the rain to catch another glimpse of his beloved, he notices that her lap-dog, Madgie, has also had to wait in the street. Then he hears a voice greeting Madgie. Two ladies pass by under umbrellas, but it is not they who are talking. Then he realizes that the dog following the two ladies is sniffing at Madgie, who explains that she has been ill. Although initially surprised to hear two dogs talking, the narrator overcomes his astonishment, recalling other occurrences of talking animals that he has read about. (In his qualified astonishment he resembles Hoffmann's narrator.) But he is completely dumbfounded when Madgie assures Fidele that she wrote to her during her illness. "Now, I'd be willing to forfeit a month's pay if I've ever heard of a dog that could write" (p. 9). When the dogs take their leave, he follows the second dog and notes where it lives.

For the next month the narrator lurks around the director's house, hoping to catch a glimpse of Sophie. Recalling the conversation between the two dogs, he makes up his mind to obtain the letters exchanged by them, reasoning that "a dog is an extraordinary politician and notices everything, every step a human takes" (p. 14). Returning to the house to which he had followed the dog, he rushes in and seizes a small bundle of papers that he finds beneath the straw in the dog's basket. The narrator is convinced that he will learn everything he wishes to know from these letters. "Dogs are a clever race. They know all about intrigue and so it's all bound to be in their letters" (p. 15). But instead of comments on human nature, he finds gossip about Madgie's own love affairs. "What rubbish! How much of her letters is she going to fill with such stupid stuff? I'm after *people*, not dogs! I need spiritual food and I am served these inanities" (p. 18). When Madgie does finally comment on the goings-on in her house, the narrator is chagrined to find himself portrayed and exposed in all his pitiable wretchedness. Learning about Sophie's wedding plans, he tears the ostensible canine epistle to shreds and, soon after, goes mad.

In Gogol's hands the dogs' colloquy and its expectations have been brilliantly transformed. The narrator approaches the dogs precisely because he shares the conventional belief in the philosophical dog, and he is disappointed to discover that they do not live up to his expectations. But the relationship between the parts—between framework and core—has been inverted. As we noted in the cases of Cervantes and Hoffmann, the framework was originally added in order to justify the wonder of the taking dog: through feverish imaginings and through drunkenness. Here too the framework justifies the motif—through madness. But the talking dog is no longer the center of the story; it has been reduced to nothing more than a symptom of madness whereas the framework has been expanded into the principal narrative—of a man so seriously disturbed that he imagines that he overhears dogs talking and reads canine comments into a miserable scrap of paper that he snatches from a dog's basket.

The philosophical dog is an essentially literary motif which passes from work to work because talking dogs do not occur in "reality." As a result, it is obvious in almost every case which source each writer used. Whereas Gogol, like so many of the Russian Hoffmannists, drew his inspiration from the German romantic writer, the Nobel-Prize-winning Spanish dramatist, Jacinto Benavente y Martínez, went back directly to his countryman, Cervantes, as the title of his dialogue reveals: "Nuevo Coloquio de los Perros" (1908).[32]

The story begins in a spirit of Cervantean playfulness that parodies the framework embracing Cervantes' "Colloquy," notably the specific detail regarding time, place, and circumstances under which Ensign Campuzano overhears the conversation between Scipio and Berganza. Here the witness remains nameless: he is characterized simply as an incorrigible night-owl. Benavente goes to great lengths to stress how inexplicable it is that the report contains no record of *where* his witness experienced this new prodigy. Even the occasion is described in playfully vague terms: it is a summer night of celestial magnificence, propitious for enchantments, like the time of Shakespeare's midsummer night. The site, described in considerable realistic detail, is totally unlike the hospital of Valladolid: the ramshackle establishment for selling stolen dogs is rumored to be a cover for enterprises of an even more illegal nature. One night, during his nocturnal wanderings, the witness arrives at this wretched dog pound and, for reasons unspecified, decides to spend the night there. Suddenly he hears two voices talking quietly and, edging closer, perceives to his astonishment that the voices belong to two dogs, who are sleeping outside to escape the heat. Tempted at first to waken people to witness this wonder, he thinks better of it, realizing that he would be thought mad if the dogs should fall silent. So he listens surreptitiously to the ensuing dialogue between the elegant Pomeranian Darling and the mongrel Ninchi.

Darling is explaining that his name, a distinguished English appellative, is pronounced with a silent "r." Ninchi has answered to many names during his lifetime, depending on the political persuasions of his various owners. The sophisticated Darling understands many languages, including Spanish, French, and English; Ninchi knows only the vernacular of dogs, which is the same wherever in the world one goes. But on this enchanted night, when the dogs acquire the unexpected power of speech, he is able to talk the kind of Spanish gutter dialect that he has heard for most of his life. Following these preliminaries they agree that each shall tell the story of his life, beginning on the first night with Darling.

Born in an elegant pet shop on the Champs Elysées, Darling is sold to a Parisian actress. Most of the story is taken up by Darling's account of the actress's life with her manager-husband, her Rumanian lover, and her homosexual fashion designer. Following an argument with her husband, the actress goes off to South America with her lover. When she returns to Paris, she is reconciled with her husband and takes a role in a new play that promises to be a brilliant success. Suddenly she dies, and Darling is given as a memento to the fashion designer, who turns out to be a great hypocrite: fawning to his wealthy patrons, he tyrannizes less affluent customers and works out his considerable aggressions on his servants and, from time to time, on Darling. The dog is therefore pleased when he is passed along to a trio of rich American women, who take him with them to Spain. Here they are so greatly swept along by their Iberomania that they neglect Darling. Mistreated by the servants, Darling runs away one day in pursuit of a cute little bitch and is captured by the servant of two wealthy, aristocratic old spinsters, who are delighted with him. But since their consciences are troubled by the possession of stolen goods, they determine to consult their priest, who will surely show them a way to keep the dog and, at the same time, to assuage their feelings of guilt. At this point, before we learn how Darling was reduced to his present deplorable state, signs of dawn appear. In accordance with their agreement never to speak in the presence of men the dogs fall silent, planning to continue their colloquy that same night.

This conventional picaresque narrative offers Darling occasion to comment on a variety of social phenomena in France, South America, and Spain. He satirizes the theatrical profession, the *beau monde* of Paris, the pretensions of wealthy American expatriates in Europe, the religious hypocrisy of the Spanish aristocracy, the thievishness of the Spanish lower classes—little escapes his eye. The colloquy, in other words, exploits the genre's tendency toward social criticism and cynical comment. Benavente's dogs, moreover, are real "philosophers," as individually characterized as Scipio and Berganza. The dogs have made the conventional vow not to betray their gift of speech to human beings lest they be exploited and placed in even greater bondage. Better dead than slaves, exclaims the fiercely independent Ninchi, who can sing the Marseillaise and who has associated with anarchists. Both dogs are greatly concerned with social injustice. Darling, who believes that conditions affect character, defends the servants against Ninchi's criticism, pointing out that need and servitude produce evil in men. As a result, the dogs agree to avoid moral comment on the behavior of the characters in their tales— a rule that both of them repeatedly break as they become incensed at the behavior of the human beings they have known and observed.

The conversation between Darling and Ninchi includes several direct allusions to Cervantes' text. Thus the dogs agree to avoid "backbiting" (*murmuración*) for the simple reason that they would never get to the end of their tales if they paused to comment on everything that deserved criticism (p. 874). They discuss narrative style, criticizing the human tendency to include irrelevancies in accounts. Their inability to adhere to their resolutions shows, just as clearly as in Cervantes' stories, that the dogs are as culpable as are human beings of the various ills they lampoon. Benavente's "Nuevo Coloquio" is a witty and sophisticated up-dating of the "Colloquy of the Dogs." But more than that: it is an intensely "literary" work that is conscious at every moment of the tradition within which it is operating. As a result, a great deal of our pleasure in reading this dialogue comes from having a very specific set of expectations and seeing how cleverly a modern writer manages to play with them for his own purposes.

VIII

WE ARE NOW in a position to locate Kafka's "Investigations of a Dog" within a larger context. Kafka's fragment plainly differs in three important respects from the works that we have considered up to this point. It is a monologue rather than a dialogue; the dog is not gregarious but cut off from the canine community; and the human witness is absent. At the same time, we are clearly dealing with a talking dog who displays a pronounced proclivity for philosophical disquisition. We know that Hoffmann's animal narratives had a profound influence on Kafka, who was thus aware of the tradition.[33] We have noted a growing tendency toward the narrative monologue even when the form is still technically a dialogue. In Kafka's story this tendency is carried to its logical extreme. Similarly, the alienation of Kafka's dog— the circumstance that incapacitates him for dialogue— is meaningful only if we take into account the conventional eagerness of dogs in literature to talk to one another—an expectation that is alluded to in the text. Finally, although this dog lives entirely within a canine world and makes no explicit comment on mankind, he is an outsider who is implicitly talking about human society and the limits of human understanding. If we seek to locate Kafka's tale within an existing literary tradition, it makes more sense to link it by inversion to the motif of the philosophical dog and the genre of the dogs' colloquy than, say, to the beast allegory, where animal talks only to animal. If we accept this connection, the tale takes on a final ironic implication fully worthy of Kafka: to the extent that we are privy to the dog's "investigations," we are thrust unwittingly into the role of the crazed witness who understands—or thinks that he understands—the language of the dog.

No motif that has survived almost two thousand years simply disappears. Contemporary popular culture displays a variety of non-literary examples in which it has quite literally gone to the dogs. The figure of the philosophical dog can be recognized quite clearly in a popular 1910 Schlitz beer advertisement, which shows two bespectacled dogs sitting at a table, smoking cigars, and quaffing beer while they chat. And in the seventies Leigh Grant designed a widely familiar series of greeting cards featuring a thoughtful-looking dog who is always shown reading a book. The figure is also evident in Snoopy of Charles Schulz's comic strip *Peanuts*: it is no accident that Schulz chose a dog, rather than a cat, for the outside observer who lies on top of his doghouse making cynical observations on the foibles of human nature; that has been the dog's role since Plato. Similarly, TV viewers sit and listen seriously while talking dogs—singly and in choruses, howling or chortling—extol the succulence of their favorite dog-food.

However, it is not only in the form of cultural trivializations that the motif has persisted. It has also continued to show up in works by representative writers. But for the past fifty years the motif has undergone deformations of the sort that we encounter in Mikhail Bulgakov's novella *Heart of a Dog* (written in 1925),[34] which is set in Moscow in the winter of 1924-25. It begins with what appears to be the first-person narrative of a filthy mongrel who has just been scalded by boiling water. As he shivers in a doorway licking his wounded flank, the dog makes cynical comments of the sort we have come to associate with the genre: on the miserable existence of kept women, on butchers who cheat their customers, on the differences between gentlemen and proletarians, and so forth. These comments show Sharik to be a true descendant of Berganza. Then, when a strange gentleman appears and offers the dog a sausage, the narrative unexpectedly shifts to the third person, and it becomes clear that the dog's thoughts amount to an interior monologue within a larger framework.

The kindly stranger turns out to be Professor Philip Philipovich Preobrazhensky, a brain specialist who maintains on the side a flourishing practice in sexual rejuvenation through hormone injections and organ transplants.[35] The professor takes the dog home and nurses him back to health. Several weeks later the professor and his assistant obtain the corpse of a twenty-five-year-old thief and perform an experimental operation, transplanting into the dog the human testes and pituitary gland. Within a few days the first startling changes take place: a sudden moulting of hair on the forehead and torso is accompanied by a distinct alteration of timbre and lowering in pitch of the bark. A few days later the dog utters its first word: "delicatessen." From that point on his progress is rapid: he loses hair everywhere except on his head, chin, and chest. "Elsewhere he is bald, with flabby skin. His genital region now has the appearance of an immature human male" (p. 62). A month after the operation the dog has been transformed into "a short man of unpleasant appearance. His hair grew in clumps of bristles like a stubble field and on his face was a meadow of unshaven fluff. His brow was strikingly low. A thick brush of hair began almost immediately above his spreading eyebrows" (p. 71). The dog, who now goes under the name Comrade Sharikov, has a personality to match his unsavory appearance: he not only smokes, drinks, and curses, using the gutter language he has picked up and stored in his brain; he molests women, chases cats, and mouths Party jargon. Finally the monster gets a job with the municipal Sanitation Department, where he is put in charge of eliminating stray cats by strangulation. When he turns informer, denouncing the professor as a counter-revolutionary, the professor decides to take action: performing a second operation, he transforms Comrade Sharikov back into the dog Sharik. When the police appear to investigate the murder of Comrade Sharikov, the professor confounds them by producing the dog. Sharik, in his concluding interior monologue, congratulates himself on the warm and peaceful existence he can enjoy in the doctor's apartment, now that the nightmare of operations is past.

Bulgakov presents us with an exuberant inversion of the genre. His novella gives every appearance, for the first three or four pages, of belonging to the conventional genre of picaresque narratives recounted by a dog; our expectations lead us to believe that another dog will appear to pick up the conversation. No other dog shows up, however. Instead, the doctor performs an operation that enables the dog literally to talk, thus providing an ironic modern twist to the conventional justification of speech. We are no longer dealing with a feverish patient or a madman who thinks that he hears dogs talking: Comrade Sharikov actually does talk. A second inversion is evident in the fact that the dog, who begins as a cynical critic of human society, following his operation degenerates into the worst specimen of human being. His behavior causes the professor and his assistant to make cynical observations on the nature of dogs—a total reversal of the normal convention of the genre.

It is known that Bulgakov saw himself in the succession of Gogol, that he was influenced by Hoffmann, and that he was an admirer of Cervantes, whose *Don Quixote* he adapted for the stage.[36] From a variety of sources, then, Bulgakov was aware of the convention of the dogs' colloquy, which he wittingly parodied. Our pleasure in Bulgakov's novella is considerably enhanced by our awareness of the literary play with conventional genres and expectations: the philosophical dog turns out to be a degenerate; the "picaresque" dog, locked up in an apartment, is unable to wander; the enframing "justification" turns out, as in Gogol's tale, to be the main story; the colloquy (with a human being) deteriorates into gutter language and denunciations.

It seems inevitable that such a popular and offbeat motif should appeal to writers of modern fantasy, and we find an amusing variation in Clifford Simak's novel, *City* (1952). In eight loosely related chapters Simak traces the history of a family named Webster from the year 1990, when human civilization begins to disintegrate and men leave Earth for Jupiter, down through the next 20,000 years. At this point the few remaining men have withdrawn into a city called Geneva, where they live sealed off from the rest of the world, which is run by talking dogs who are cared for by robots. In our context the stories are less relevant than is the framework fiction. The stories have allegedly been edited and annotated by a trio of scholarly dogs named Tige, Rover, and Bounce (author of *The Myth of Man*). These dogs live at a date in history so remote that they regard mankind simply as a legend produced by the primitive canine consciousness. "Man may have risen in the early days of Doggish culture as an imaginary being, a sort of racial god, on which the dogs might call for help, to which they might retire for comfort" (p. 8).[37] In these academic disputes among the dogs (which parody twentieth-century anthropological works) we hear a reminiscence of Kafka's perplexed canine, attempting to explain reality to himself with no reference to man. "Rover believes that in the first tale we are dealing with almost pure myth and that as a result no situation or statement can be accepted at face value . . ." (p. 12). The cynical comment is quite evident in the canine notes on the story of human civilization. Speaking of the city, for instance, the dogs regard it as an impossible institution. "No creature of the highly nervous structure necessary to develop a culture, they point out, would be able to survive within such restricted limits. The result, if it were tried, these authorities say, would lead to mass neuroticism which in a short period of time would destroy the very culture which had built the city." Other notions that they know from the legend of mankind are equally disturbing. "Rover, in his study of the legend, is convinced that the tales are much more primitive than is generally supposed, since it is his contention that such concepts as war and killing could never come out of our present culture, that they must stem from some era of savagery of which there exists no record" (p. 12).

Simak uses the convention of the philosophical dog to make a comment on human civilization as a whole; a recent novella takes up the motif to spoof many shibboleths of contemporary American society. The heroine of Rosalyn Drexler's *The Cosmopolitan Girl* (1974)[38] is Helen Jones, a Swinging Single who dashes around Manhattan searching for glamorous jobs, her life dictated by the prescriptions of her favorite magazine. When a young man unexpectedly comes to see her, Helen rushes into a flurry of activity. "How could I believe I was beautiful unless I saw myself through his eyes? Unless I made *sure* he'd go ape over me. I turned to my longtime friend and adviser *Cosmopolitan* magazine. 'Oh, *Cosmo*,' I pleaded, 'how can I look superstunning on short notice? Help me!' " (pp. 58-59). For a time a boy friend named Pablo moves into her apartment, where he spends most of his time writing dirty letters to pornographic magazines. Resenting Helen's jealous protectiveness, Pablo eventually leaves her to become a model for an artist in SoHo, who creates life-size replicas of him in various poses. Helen finally manages to get in touch with Pablo again through a radio talk show and rescues him from a rundown hotel in the Bowery. They get married, and the moderator of the talk-show moves in with them to form a *ménage à trois* so chic and trendy that it is documented by a camera crew for educational television.

This story of social absurdity is precisely the kind of tale that the philosophical dogs have traditionally loved to relate cynically. What gives Drexler's novella its unique twist is the fact that the story is not told by a dog; the dog is introduced into it as a main character. Pablo is not a man but a talking dog Helen claims from the police dog pound after he breaks into twenty-one homes in Scarsdale. "I am a woman and Pablo is a consenting adult male . . . dog" (p. 80). There is no attempt in this fantasy to justify the dog's power of speech. Pablo is at the same time a typical dog and an ironic commentator. By the end of the book the whole world has been turned topsy-turvy. Pablo no longer tries to act like a human being, hiding his ears under a hat or straining for an upright position. As a result of the television documentary "Saks has introduced the Pablo Look: men want to look like dogs. Hair shirts are 'in,' padded palms and soles de rigueur, wet noses chic, and fetch-and-carry is swiftly taking the place of golf and tennis" (p. 189).

True to their picaresque peregrinations, talking dogs have also made their way into two recent Italian novels. Elsa Morante's *History: A Novel* (1974) does not belong strictly speaking to the category that we have been defining. To be sure, Bella's barks, growls, and wags become intelligible speech in the mind of Useppe, her epileptic young master. But since Bella emerges as a character only toward the end of the lengthy novel, she does not constitute the focusing consciousness of the work. Moreover, she exemplifies canine loyalty and therefore does not function as a cynical commentator on human reality. In Morante's novel the dog is closer to the talking dogs of fairy tales and children's stories than to the canines of our tradition.

But Carlo della Corte's novel *Cuor di Padrone* (1977)[39] recapitulates almost all the characteristic motifs we have encountered. Della Corte's awareness of the literary tradition within which he is operating is indicated by the fact that his book is dedicated to Thomas Mann and Mikhail Bulgakov; the title, in fact, is an inversion combining Bulgakov's *Heart of a Dog* and Mann's *Herr und Hund*. At the same time, the book seems to owe something to the social satire of such writers as Benavente and Svevo. A sort of *dolce vita* involving the prosperous architect Giulio Arcangelo, his mistress Gilda, and their friends, the action takes place in Arcangelo's villa in the lake district near Milan. The various infidelities culminate in a scene in which Arcangelo catches Gilda and the journalist Morandoni making love on the living-room sofa. This gives Giulio the opportunity he has been waiting for to get rid of his mistress.

What rescues the novel from tawdry triviality is the point of view: the entire story is told—actually, typed on an Olivetti—by the dog Box, a mongrel who has read Montesquieu on liberty and Foucault on semiotics; who is inspired by his knowledge of Saussure to speculate on canine semantics, who has studied Havelock Ellis on sexuality, and who disagrees with Pavlov for reducing memory to mere reflex. Box has contemplated the sculpture of Rodin and Giacometti and talks knowingly about literature, architecture, and art—of Brecht, Kokoschka, and Signac. The writing is possible because, according to the fiction, Box succeeds in forcing his own spirit into Arcangelo's body, which he uses for a time as his own.

The act of spiritual violation that occurs toward the end of the novel, when Giulio has just thrown Gilda out of the house, is made plausible by the subplot of the work: people are shown in increasingly dehumanizing situations and Box emerges as more human than the people surrounding him. Box, for instance, dislikes hunting, but he is forced to participate by the gardener Remigio, who delights in being cruel to animals. (The motif of human insensitivity shows up in several places: e.g., people select their dinner trout from an aquarium while listening to recordings of Debussy's *La Mer* or of Jean-Louis Barrault reciting *Le Cimetière marin*.)

The action begins when the drunken Remigio threatens the maid-servant Irpinia with a knife. Box bites him, thereby incurring her affection and Remigio's wrath. After Remigio torments him, Box manages to murder the gardener by sabotaging the stone beside the lake where he sits to fish. When Box gets sick, Giulio wants to abandon him, but he is rescued by Irpinia. Irpinia is finally fired—she has witnessed too many indiscretions of her employers. As the relations between man and dog deteriorate, Giulio becomes increasingly bestial: his eyes are said to be "vulpine" (p. 160), and he takes a sadistic pleasure in extinguishing his cigarettes on Box's fur. Box, in turn, is rendered almost preternaturally insightful by his hatred: "Hatred doesn't divide; hatred is a bridge, a magnetic charge that enables you to live within someone else" (p. 100). He begins to have visions of entering Giulio's body. As he becomes more "human," he practices speaking—the vowels go quite nicely, and he skips the more difficult consonants. By the end of the book the way is paved for the mystical interpenetration, in the erotically animated house, that produces "a single hybrid creature" (p. 185). As the novel ends, Box wanders around the empty villa, listening to music on the stereo and typing his memoirs. On the last page, however, his animal nature begins to reassert itself and his hand-paws can no longer manipulate the Olivetti. His final words deteriorate into nonsense syllables: "Ma eco la stanchezza che pre ne tuto, no vorei ma, ste zampe che confusionano la mente; ò çççgaggax amrei ecatw" (p. 191).

Despite all characteristic differences these treatments of the philosophical dog since Kafka display several basic similarities. First, they all represent inversions of the conventional form: it is easier to understand the works within the tradition than completely independent of it. Indeed, the authors often count on our recognition of their sources as the necessary background for their humor. Second, the inversions of form reflect an inversion in the nature of the philosophical dog. These canines are no longer detached witnesses, standing apart and passing judgment on mankind; they have become troubled participants who suffer from all the afflictions of mankind. Yet despite all deformations the philosophical dog is still being used for the purpose of cynical social comment that has been conventional since Lucian. For these dogs—Kafka's disturbed metaphysician, Bulgakov's seedy degenerate, Simak's uncomprehending scholars, Drexler's jaded swinger, and Della Corte's sophisticated voyeur—exemplify modern society and its discontents, an image that is all the more shattering when we see it manifested in animals whose natural innocence has been corrupted by the pernicious influence of mankind. It is a final irony that so many of these dogs have given up speech and the natural community it implies for the solitary act of writing—even Bulgakov's Sharik, who indites denunciations to the secret police, and Drexler's Pablo, who scrawls dirty letters to sex magazines.

We have seen how the motif of the philosophical dog emerged from ancient cultural beliefs in the dog's sagacity and accommodated itself initially to the form of the philosophical dialogue. Following its rudimentary beginnings in classical antiquity the dialogue of the dogs reached a sudden and brilliant culmination in Renaissance France and Spain, producing a host of imitations, both plodding and genial, during the Enlightenment and romanticism, before its inversion into parody in the twentieth century. Any set of works that pass through such pronounced stages—beginnings, fulfillment, imitation, parody—can be said to constitute a coherent genre rather than a series of discrete texts. Indeed, the figure of the talking dog has been accompanied since its beginnings by a consistent configuration of motifs. If we locate a specific text—e.g., Cervantes' "Colloquy"—in this generic context, we are enabled to understand certain elements that might otherwise remain problematic. At the same time, while the structural motifs have remained constant enough to enable us to identify the genre, the *content* of the genre shifts from century to century to reflect each author's perception of his society and its problems. Perhaps you can't teach an old dog new tricks; but writers from Lucian to the present have surely taught their new dogs the tried and tested old ones.

Chapter Four

FIGURES ON LOAN:
THE BOUNDARIES OF
LITERATURE
AND LIFE

I

In 1808 a remarkable document of German romanticism was published anonymously under the title *Karl's Trials and Tribulations*.[1] This "double novel" (*Doppelroman*) actually amounts to a "quadruple novel" inasmuch as it was written jointly by four members of the Berlin writers' club known as the North Star League (*Nordsternbund*): Karl August Varnhagen, Wilhelm Neumann, August Ferdinand Bernhardi, and Friedrich de la Motte Fouqué. But the term, which was used routinely by the writers and their friends to designate their collective effort, is symptomatic because it calls attention to one of the two main sources of the work: Jean Paul, who coined the word in his novel *The Years of Indiscretion* (*Die Flegeljahre*, 1804) to designate the cooperative novel written by the brothers Walt and Vult. A second paradigm, evident at every stage of the exuberant plot, was Goethe's exemplary *Bildingsroman, Wilhelm Meister's Apprenticeship* (1795-96). Of course, to specify Jean Paul and Goethe as influences upon a novel of German romanticism places that novel into a rather large category. Yet the four young authors of *Karl's Trials and Tribulations* found a unique way to pay their ambivalent homage to the two masters they venerated.

The hero of the novel rapidly emerges as one of the most thoroughly unpleasant heroes in the history of the German novel. The first chapter is barely underway when Karl kills his mistress's husband, who is awakened by the commotion as Karl attempts to rape her. Forced to flee, Karl ends up at a country estate, where within a few hours he manages to pick a fight with one of the other guests. When the latter—Friedrich—is prevented from meeting him in a duel, Karl kills his substitute and once again takes flight. As he walks along the following morning, he overtakes an open carriage.

> . . . he had scarcely glanced into the chaise, when a joyous "*Bon jour*, my dear fellow!" resounded, and at the same time a young man leaned over the door and extended his hand. The travel clothes, particularly the nightcap drawn deep down over his face with a leather hood over it, prevented Karl from recognizing the speaker immediately. But he hesitantly extended his hand, and the other continued: "Gracious! I hope, dear friend, that you are not returning from some unpleasant affair. Your appearance alarms me as greatly as it pleases me!" "Don't worry," replied Karl, who at this moment recognized Wilhelm Meister. . . . (pp. 168-69)

Awakened by the conversation, Wilhelm's traveling companion, who is described as a graceful Lombard, peers out. "Without difficulty Karl recognized the marchese, whom we already know from Wilhelm Meister's Years of Apprenticeship, as Goethe had written them" (p. 169). The two travelers invite their new acquaintance to share their carriage and to accompany them to the nearby estate of a widowed countess.

In the course of their conversation Karl satisfies his curiosity concerning details of Wilhelm's life that Goethe left unclear—e.g., the age of Wilhelm's son Felix. Wilhelm takes the opportunity to point out that Goethe is inconsistent and inexact about his life on a number of occasions. It soon becomes evident, however, that Wilhelm has no thoughts of his own. Indeed, he quotes his own words from the *Apprenticeship* so often that at one point the marchese reproves him. "Is that really supposed to be your own opinion, your inner feeling? I fear that these words belong more to a writer than to you" (p. 175). Elsewhere Karl is astonished that Wilhelm has changed his attitudes so radically that he now utters as well-tested truths thoughts that he formerly had rejected indignantly. Finally, Wilhelm and the marchese carry on such lengthy discussions on topics familiar from the *Apprenticeship* that Karl falls asleep from sheer boredom.

Meanwhile Karl's enemies are also making their way, as it happens, to the same estate. When they reach the surrounding park, they notice a stout man gathering strawberries in the bushes although his corpulence makes stooping clearly difficult and perspiration streams from his broad forehead.

> Approaching the man Friedrich said teasingly: "The strawberries must truly be very sweet since you are giving yourself such a sour time to pick them." "No more than any others," said the stranger, straightening up. "But they become so thereby. And has not our wise Mother done well to let the rasp-, black- and strawberries of life grow so low that they become sweeter for us through the effort?" "You seem very familiar to me," said Friedrich, "and yet I cannot recall having seen you anywhere before." "Oh, friend," said the stranger, "precisely that is the lofty privilege, the *jus imaginum* of noble men, that they can reciprocally possess each other's image without ever having seen each other, and that one fraternal soul can extend the warm hand of love to another across the wide green earth. And must not the goose itself supply the connecting piece that makes our hands long enough to touch? Do we not pluck from her wing the wing upon which we soar up to the pinnacles and down into the caverns in order to fish pearls of tears from the sad

eye of our loved ones and those who are to become such?" "Now I know you," said Friedrich, "unless I am quite mistaken." (p. 186)

This remarkable person—of whom it is later said that "anyone who has read only a single page of yours must recognize you from the first four words you utter" (p. 196)—is none other than Jean Paul himself, who is also present as a guest at the countess's estate.

We have no need to detail the complications of plot that occupy the characters during the following chapters. Suffice it to say that both Wilhelm Meister and Jean Paul enter fully into the conversations and activities of their new friends. Jean Paul turns out to be utterly charming, talking amiably and being as helpful as possible to everyone. Wilhem Meister, in contrast, reveals himself to be a complete ass. Karl finds him "disgusting" (*widrig*) and Friedrich—using a word that expresses utter contempt in the age of Goethe—regards him as wholly "insignificant" (*unbedeutend*). Despite the "sensation" that his arrival initially produces, it is soon rumored that he is "the coldest among all the people present" (p. 221). He shocks the company by his bitterness and ingratitude toward Goethe, asserting that he would not even bother to accompany the marchese to Weimar if "the divine Schiller" were not also there. When Karl and Friedrich resume their quarrel, Meister tries to soothe Friedrich with some sententious words, but Friedrich ignores him. When Meister will not desist, Friedrich slaps the "troublesome peacemaker." Meister is dumbfounded. "Because of the celebrity that Goethe had given him, he was accustomed to be regarded everywhere in Germany with a kind of holy awe; and through the misfortune that now afflicted him so unexpectedly he saw himself suddenly plunged so profoundly from his heights that all his experience, all the culture that such an interesting life had vouchsafed him, did not suffice to restore the composure that he had lost at a single blow" (p. 350). The marchese has their carriage hitched up and departs with his famous friend in all haste from the estate and at the same time from the novel, which after a few more chapters dissolves in the turmoil of the Napoleonic wars.

Through this witty personification of their esteem, the four young romantic writers paid their respect to their two great models. Jean Paul expressed his delight at the witty caricature of his personality and, above all, at the brilliant parody of his distinctive literary style.[2] E.T.A. Hoffmann called the novel "one of the wittiest, most ingenious, and liveliest books I have ever seen" (p. 168), citing in particular the appearance of Jean Paul as a figure. In a retrospective review of 1825 Willibald Alexis singled out the parodies of Jean Paul as especially original. But though the contemporaries were generally amused by the introduction of Jean Paul, they were dismayed and even indignant at the treatment of Wilhelm Meister. Rahel Levin chided her future husband, Varnhagen: "How could you possibly let Wilhelm Meister depart with those slaps! Infamous!" (p. 135). And when Varnhagen paid his respects to Jean Paul in Bayreuth, even he thought that they had gone too far with their outrageous (*frevelhaft*) treatment of Meister. " 'Children, what have you done!' he said pensively. 'You should have left that out! Goethe is sacred; he is different from all the others" (p. 130).

The mixed reaction of the contemporaries is revealing. At first glance it might look as though they were merely reacting to the seeming slight, by means of literary parody, to the most venerable cultural hero of the age. But Rahel and Jean Paul were not aggrieved simply by the implicit disrespect directed at the living writer. They were perturbed explicitly by the insult to Wilhelm Meister—that is, to a fictional figure! The question calls for our closer scrutiny.

II

THE SHATTERING of poetic illusion through the introduction of alien elements belongs to the familiar tech-

niques of romantic irony. But various possibilities need
to be differentiated. Most frequently we are dealing with
the intrusion of a figure from everyday historical reality
into a fictional world. From Clemens Brentano, who
introduced his own friends and other contemporaries
into his novel *Godwi* (1801), down to the present, many
writers have exploited this device. Hermann Hesse includes several of his acquaintances as well as his wife in
the fictional world of *The Journey to the East* (*Die Mor-
genlandfahrt*, 1931). Freud and Jung show up among
the characters in E. L. Doctorow's *Ragtime* (1975), where
they take a boatride through the Tunnel of Love on
Coney Island. George Seferis and Lawrence Durrell make
guest appearances in C. L. Sulzberger's *The Tooth Merchant* (1973); Richard Nixon plays a role in Robert
Coover's *The Public Burning* (1977) as well as Kurt
Vonnegut's *Jailbird* (1979). And Henry Kissinger has a
brief walk-on part in Joseph Heller's *Good as Gold*
(1979). Usually these appearances amount to minor roles
not inconsistent with historical probability. But occasionally writers go further and reshape historical fact.
In Alan Lelchuk's novel *American Mischief* (1973), for
instance, Norman Mailer is killed by a student revolutionary who shoots him in the anus with a .38 automatic
in an *acte gratuit* inspired by Nietzsche. It needs to be
stressed that this ironic device differs from the technique
of the historical novel—from Walter Scott, James Fen-
imore Cooper, and Alessandro Manzoni down to the
most recent popular historical romances—which characteristically introduces a historical figure, or group of
figures, into a recognizable historical situation.[3] Here,
in contrast, we are dealing with works in which the
context is wholly fictional, so that the actual figures—
usually contemporary—are felt to be so intrusive that
they shatter any fictional illusion.

Other writers have varied the same basic device by
introducing themselves into their own fictions—a device
popular in German romanticism, where it was used by
Brentano, Ludwig Tieck, E.T.A. Hoffmann, Adalbert

von Chamisso, and others. Indeed, Jean Paul's predilection for this device must have made him doubly amused to see his own figure show up in the fiction of the North Star Leaguers. Passed along by writers like Karl Immermann, who introduces himself into Book VI of his eccentric novel *Münchhausen* (1838-1839), the technique shows up frequently in twentieth-century fiction. In *Anniversaries* (*Jahrestage*, 1970-73), Uwe Johnson describes himself objectively—with his bald head, glasses, black leather jacket, and cleaning his pipe—as he addresses a meeting of the Jewish-American Congress of New York (entry for November 3, 1967). John Barth gives freer rein to his imagination in his novella *Dunyazadiad*. Again the description is accurate: "a light-skinned fellow of forty or so, smooth-shaven and bald as a roc's egg. His clothes were simple but outlandish; he was tall and healthy and pleasant enough in appearance, except for queer lenses that he wore in a frame over his eyes."[4] But his function is anything but realistic: Barth turns out to be the genie conjured up by Scheherazade, who tells her the 1001 stories that she recounts to the king each night to stave off her execution. It emerges that Barth knows the story because he has already read it in the *Arabian Nights*.

In all these cases we are dealing with the same basic phenomenon: the intrusion of reality into fiction, whether the figure introduced is a historical figure like Freud, a contemporary person like Hesse's wife, or the author himself. Although the degree of probability may vary, the aesthetic problem remains the same as when Jean Paul appears in *Karl's Trials and Tribulations*. But with the appearance of Wilhelm Meister in that novel altogether different assumptions begin to be in force. For here we are no longer dealing with the relationship of fiction to reality but, instead, with the relationship of one fictional world to another—a situation that involves wholly different aesthetic rules and implications.

In general we can regard a figure on loan—and at this point let us define the term specified in the title as a fictional character that a writer takes out of its original context and inserts into another one—as a kind of quotation. Accordingly, many of the comments that Herman Meyer makes about literary quotations in fiction apply equally well to our figures on loan. In a very precise sense, for instance, Wilhelm Meister is "a bit of preformed linguistic property shaped by another author."[5] The act of incorporating Wilhelm Meister into another literary work is an act of narrative integration that maintains the same "unique tension between assimilation and dissimilation" as does the quotation. For if the figure should be so fully integrated as to become unrecognizable, the intended effect would be lost. Like the quotation, therefore, the figure on loan must step into a new context and at the same time remain detached enough to remind us constantly of its source. Like the quotation, moreover, the figure on loan depends for its effect upon a shared cultural tradition that enables the reader immediately to recognize the alien body that has entered the fiction.

Keeping these guidelines in mind, we can distinguish our category from two other types to which it bears a superficial resemblance. In the first place, the criterion of "preformed linguistic property" distinguishes the figure on loan from those mythic or mythological figures whose lives are retold in one literary form or another or reshaped typologically. Such figures, though they may sometimes be identified closely with a particular writer, have an existence that is independent even of their classic formulations. Faust simply does not belong to Goethe to the same extent or in the same manner that, say, Wilhelm Meister or Werther do, or Julien Sorel to Stendhal, or Raskolnikov to Dostoevsky. For this reason the various literary metamorphoses of Faust or Don Juan or Prometheus or Odysseus never produce the same sensation of astonishment that we feel when a figure on loan appears.[6]

In the second place, the criterion of narrative integration distinguishes our category from what might be called

the Extended Lives of literary figures. To this genre belong such works as Pustkuchen's spurious accounts of
Wilhelm Meister's later years,[7] Jules Janin's extension
of E.T.A. Hoffmann's Kreisler tales,[8] or the many extensions of such popular figures as Frankenstein's monster and Sherlock Holmes. Even such parodies as Friedrich Nicolai's *Joys of Young Werther* (*Die Freuden des
jungen Werthers*, 1775) or Julius Gross's poem "A Vision,"[9] in which Faust and Gretchen get married and
live happily ever after, remain within the limits of the
genre because the authors make no attempt to extricate
the figures from their original fictional context. Instead,
they reshape the context created initially by the author.
For reasons that would be worth exploring, this genre
has become increasingly popular in recent years, attract-
ing such a variety of writers as Mikhail Bulgakov, who
updated Gogol's *Dead Souls* in his story "The Adventures of Chichikov" (in *Diaboliad*); Jorge Luis Borges,
who completed José Hernández' classic Argentine folk
poem *Martin Fierro* in his story "The End" (in *Fic-
ciones*); and Heinrich Böll, who appended a humorous
"Epilogue" to Adalbert Stifter's classic of poetic realism
Indian Summer ("Epilog zu Stifters *Nachsommer*"). In
a recent anthology a group of German writers extend
the stories of famous figures from world literature in
manners ranging from the gently ironic to the scurril-
ous.[10] In Horst Krüger's extension of Hölderlin's romantic classic *Hyperion*, for instance, Hypi, now married to Didi (Diotima), has become a male prostitute in
Berlin and his friend Bellarmin has been called to Tübingen as a professor of poetics.

III

In *Karl's Trials and Tribulations*, in contrast, we are
faced with different assumptions altogether. The four
authors establish the fictional reality of their narrative,
which for the first two hundred pages we accept according to the usual conventions of literary reading. When

Wilhelm Meister suddenly appears—without transition, motivation, or forewarning—we are shocked: not just because the immediate fictional world has been shattered by this intrusion but also because we realize subsequently that another reality has also been fragmented— the reality of Goethe's novel, whose integrity is violated so that Wilhelm Meister can step out of it to enter the new fictional context and whose authenticity is crudely undermined by Wilhelm Meister's constant criticism of Goethe's version of his life. Precisely the same effect is apparent if we now turn to a totally different example of the same phenomenon.

In 1740 Samuel Richardson published the first two volumes of *Pamela, or Virtue Rewarded*, an epistolary novel that immediately won a broad audience in England and soon, in translation, exercised a profound influence on the development of fiction on the continent. The novel promptly elicited a number of parodies, among which Henry Fielding's first novel, *Joseph Andrews* (1742), is conspicuous for its virtuosity. Fielding's "comic romance" is based on the fiction that the virtuous maidservant Pamela Andrews has an equally virtuous brother named Joseph. Joseph is in service as a footman to Lady Booby, the lecherous aunt of that same Mr. B. whom Pamela married at the end of Richardson's novel. The first ten chapters of Fielding's tale are motivated almost wholly by the parodic impulse, as Joseph is exposed to seductive dangers that parallel those undergone by his sister in Richardson's moralizing work. Soon, however, Fielding's own creation, the quixotic Parson Adams, moves into the center and dominates the bulk of the narrative. It is only toward the end that the plot shifts back to Joseph Andrews, who is on the point of marrying his beloved Fanny. Lady Booby is still enraged at this news when a servant notifies her of the arrival of her nephew and his wife. Lady Booby has not yet heard that her nephew is married, but in the next moment he enters and presents his new wife with the words: " 'Madam, this is that charming Pamela, of whom I am convinced you have heard so much' " (Bk. IV, Chap. 4)—an ironic allusion within the fiction to the other fiction that was currently enjoying such a vogue. In the following chapters Pamela, a character from Richardson's edifying tearjerker, steps into the utterly different fictional world of Fielding's ironic romance. It soon turns out that the former maid-servant has become so pretentious since her marriage that she tries to dissuade her brother from marrying a girl she considers beneath her station.

> "Brother," said Pamela, "Mr. Booby advises you as a friend; and no doubt my papa and mamma will be of his opinion, and will have great reason to be angry with you for destroying what his goodness hath done, and throwing down our family again, after he hath raised it. It would become you better, brother, to pray for the assistance of grace against such a passion than to indulge in it."—"Sure, sister, you are not in earnest; I am sure she is your equal, at least."—"She was my equal," answered Pamela; "but I am no longer Pamela Andrews; I am now this gentleman's lady, and, as such, am above her.— I hope I shall never behave with an unbecoming pride; but, at the same time, I shall always endeavor to know myself, and question not the assistance of grace to that purpose." (Bk. IV, Chap. 7)

The problem is resolved when it is revealed, a short time later, that both Joseph and Fanny are the children of persons enjoying considerable social standing; they marry and live happily ever after. But the entrance of Pamela betrays a conspicuous similarity to the appearance of Wilhelm Meister in *Karl's Trials and Tribulations*. In both cases the figure is introduced with an ironic allusion to his literary fame. In both cases we are amused because the figure on loan deviates so greatly from our expectations: Wilhelm Meister has become a tedious and conceited do-gooder, and Pamela has degenerated into a calculating social climber. In both cases, finally, the ideological premises of the source are implicitly criticized by the appropriation of the title-figure.

The figure on loan can serve other purposes, as we see if we consider the example of E.T.A. Hoffmann's *New Year's Eve Adventure* ("Die Abenteuer der Silvester-Nacht," 1815).[11] To recover from one of those social humiliations commonly experienced by Hoffmann's heroes, the narrator makes his way into Thiermann's Inn in Berlin, where he dulls his misery with beer and tobacco. In this condition of "sublime philistinism" he watches as the innkeeper escorts a new guest into the room. The newcomer, who incongruously has fitted a pair of elegant slippers over his boots, edges along the wall and takes a seat facing the narrator, whereupon he also orders beer and a pipe. For a time the narrator looks on as the stranger occupies himself with all sorts of exotic plants, which he takes out of a case. The narrator reacts just as Friedrich had reacted to Jean Paul's mannerisms: "Increasingly a premonition stirred within me, and it seemed to me as though I had not so much *seen* the stranger as, rather, often *imagined* him." For the moment, however, his attention is distracted as another guest enters the room and demands that all the mirrors be covered up. The three men engage in a desultory conversation until, following a seemingly trivial comment, the more recent arrival storms out of the room in a fury, taunting the other about his shadow. The latter, deathly pale, sinks back into his chair and heaves a deep sigh. " 'That evil man has reminded me of my deepest misery. Oh—lost, irretrievably lost is my—Farewell!' Getting up, he strode across the room and out the door. Everything remained light around him—he cast no shadow. Filled with delight I ran after him—'Peter Schlemihl—Peter Schlemihl!' I cried joyfully, but he had cast off his slippers." The narrator sees how the stranger—now identified as the hero of Adalbert von Chamisso's popular tale, which had appeared the year before—strides away in his Seven League Boots and disappears into the night. Following this incident Hoffmann turns to his own story, and Peter Schlemihl does not appear again. But the brief scene makes it sufficiently clear that Hoffmann is not employing the figure on loan for parodistic purposes, as was the case in the *Doppelroman* and in Fielding's "comic romance." On the contrary: he treats the episode in full seriousness as an analogy to his own "Tale of the Lost Reflection." That story, familiar to many as one of the three tales incorporated in Offenbach's *Tales of Hoffmann*, is appropriately introduced by the encounter in the beer cellar, in which Chamisso's hero, who has lost his shadow, meets Hoffmann's creation, who loses his mirror image. Both figures suffer from the characteristic fragmentation and schizophrenic anxiety of the romantic hero: the lost shadow and the purloined reflection exemplify the souls they have forsaken in their pursuit of forbidden earthly possessions.

In later romanticism the figure on loan belongs to the standard equipment of fantastic narrative in Germany as well as France. In his "Account of the Most Recent Fortunes of the Dog Berganza" (1813) Hoffmann exploits as a figure on loan one of the canine heroes of "Colloquy of a Dog" in Cervantes' *Exemplary Novels* (1613).[12] In 1818 Chamisso wrote an extension of the fragmentary *Karl's Trials and Tribulations* in which he brought Karl together with his own Peter Schlemihl, who now—exploited and impoverished by his publishers—ekes out his existence as a "Wunderdoctor" practicing the fashionable science of mesmerism.[13] In Eichendorff's story *Much Ado about Nothing* (*Viel Lärm um nichts*, 1832) the author includes, along with various figures appropriated from his own works "a strange man with a long white beard and a wide pleated cloak" who turns out to be the mad harpist from *Wilhelm Meister's Apprenticeship*.[14] In explicit imitation of the parodic recognition scenes he introduces Count Leontin from his earlier novel *Premonition and Present* (*Ahnung und Gegenwart*, 1815), whom the others recognize because he cannot make even the most trivial remark without striking a chord on his guitar. Théophile Gautier borrowed a whole coterie of figures in *Onophrius, ou les Vexations fantastiques d'un admirateur d'Hoffmann*, to embody the emotional disturbance of a young painter so totally obsessed with Hoffmann's works that he sees himself constantly surrounded by figures from that strange fictional world.[15] Terrified by the tales of Peter Schlemihl and the "New Year's Eve Adventure," he refuses to look into mirrors lest he see no reflection or to look down at the floor lest he miss his shadow. Sinking into a cataleptic state, Onophrius finally starves himself to death in direct response to the "Witches' Sabbath" of figures on loan.

If the allusion to Goethe's harpist in Eichendorff's story is fleeting and if the figures from Hoffmann in Gautier's tale are imagined rather than "real," in Balzac's early nouvelle *Melmoth réconcilié* (1835) we find once again the full-fledged appropriation of a figure on loan from Charles Maturin's Gothic classic *Melmoth the Wanderer* (1820). Maturin's powerful novel consists of a succession of episodes, in each of which the chief character is offered relief from his suffering by Melmoth in return for assuming the pact with the devil through which Melmoth lost his soul and was condemned to eternal wandering. In Maturin's story all the protagonists reject the pact, and Melmoth is condemned to continue his wandering. Balzac's story begins when Castanier, a former dragoon and now, at forty, a cashier in a large Paris bank, absconds with a huge sum in order to run away with his mistress. Finding himself betrayed, he sells his soul to Melmoth and acquires power to repay the stolen money, destroy the evidence of his crime, and indulge all his passions. But when he discovers that Melmoth has died repentant, he regrets his loss of soul. Buying the soul of another man, he dies in peace. The power and pact of the devil are passed along from hand to hand until finally they are extinguished when a young cleric, who sold his soul out of love for a courtesan, dies of a poison used in an effort to cure his venereal disease.

In all these cases we can single out a few common

features that characterize the figures on loan. First, the writers from Fielding to Balzac always create a fictional world of their own, into which the borrowed figure enters as an alien; they count on the amusing or frightening shock-effect that Todorov and other theoreticians of the fantastic have identified as a characteristic of that mode.[16] Second, these writers always make use of figures from works so familiar that their literary pedigree is instantly recognizable. Third, the figure does not serve as an end in itself; rather, it has a significative function that points beyond the work. In the parodistic novels it serves above all for ideological criticism (e.g., of Richardson's notion of virtue or Goethe's conception of *Bildung*). In other works it alerts us to psychological problems whose analysis interests the writer, or it contributes to the atmosphere of the fantastic surrounding the work.

IV

It would be misleading if, on the basis of these examples, the impression were given that the motif of the figure on loan was widespread. Apart from Fielding, we are dealing with a coterie of writers in Berlin and their French imitators. What matters, however, is not the frequency but the representative quality of the examples. Because so many gifted writers from Fielding to Balzac employed the motif, it lends itself to comparative analysis.

If we now ask under what circumstances the motif was passed along to the twentieth century, it becomes evident that the relationships have changed radically. The motif which formerly the writer controlled with sovereign skill by means of his irony has suddenly become problematic. The figures on loan no longer point significatively at extraliterary conditions of society, education, or psychology; they now frequently serve the criticism of literature itself. Symptomatic of this change is the fact that the modern figures on loan on the whole do not come from easily identifiable contemporary bestsellers but from the increasingly inaccessible cultural tradition of the past.

Hermann Hesse's *Journey to the East* (1931) initially arouses the impression that it is nothing but a traditional, massive borrowing of figures according to the familiar romantic pattern. We have already noted that Hesse introduces into his fantasy various people from his immediate circle of friends. He also brings in a succession of figures on loan. "My company consisted of the favorite figures of my books," the narrator confides (Ch. 1). "Almansor and Parzival rode beside me, Witiko or Goldmund, or Sancho Pansa."[17] But if we compare Hesse's tale with *Karl's Trials and Tribulations*, we see how much the circumstances have changed. In Hesse's work the literary figures appear along with their authors. But whereas in the romantic *Doppelroman* Jean Paul and Wilhelm Meister allegedly exist on the same level of reality, in the modern narrative the fictional figures on loan have gained reality at the expense of their creators. The narrator is struck by the fact that "the figures imagined by them were without exception much livelier, lovelier, happier and in a certain sense more right and real than the poets and creators themselves." In one place, for instance, E.T.A. Hoffmann shows up with figures from his tale, *The Golden Pot* (*Der goldne Topf*, 1814). "Flickering and rather drunk, Hoffmann darted back and forth among the guests, talking a lot, small, gnome-like, and he too, like all of them, was only half real in shape, only half present, not completely solid, not completely genuine, while Archivar Lindhorst, for his amusement playing the part of a dragon, breathed fire with each breath and like an automobile." It adds to the irony of the tale that, for the purposes of this comparison, Hesse used none other than Hoffmann, who after all made use of figures on loan in his own stories. But whereas Hoffmann referred to contemporary works that every reader would instantly recognize, Hesse alludes to many books that can be appreciated only by the reader with a literary education. In addition, although Hesse borrowed the motif from Hoffmann, whom he admired almost without reservation, he adapted it to underscore his own characteristic theme: the rendition of poetic reality, which for Hesse had greater authenticity and integrity than mere everyday "reality."

We encounter a similar example in Walter de la Mare's fantasy, *Henry Brocken* (1924). Here the growing dominance of literary figures is rendered visible through the fact that they can no longer be extricated from their own contexts. Instead, the fictional hero of the romance must on each occasion enter the figures' reality. The landscape through which he wanders on his mare, Rosinante, is not our everyday "reality" but a world of fantasy already shaped by other writers. Early in his journey, for instance, Henry ambles languidly across a green moor. After a while "I espied betwixt me and the deep woods that lay in the distance a little child walking. She, at any rate, was not a stranger to this moorland."[18] The child turns out to be Wordsworth's "Lucy," who is wholly at one with the surroundings in which Henry Brocken is an outsider. Traveling a bit further, he comes to a sequestered garden. "When I had advanced a few paces, I met face to face a lady whose dark eyes seemed strangely familiar to me. She was evidently a little disquieted at meeeting a stranger so unceremoniously, but stood her ground like a small, black, fearless note of interrogation" (p. 28). The lady turns out to be Jane Eyre, and Henry is invited to spend the night with her and Mr. Rochester in the house described by Charlotte Brontë. In the course of his further wanderings he journeys through the land of the Yahoos and Houyhnynms from *Gulliver's Travels*; he meets figures from poems by Herrick and Chaucer, from plays by Shakespeare, from *Pilgrim's Progress*, and from the whole history of English literature.

From the romantic writers to De la Mare and Hesse we have come almost one hundred eighty degrees: from works into which a fictional figure is imported for purposes of ironically undermining a different fictional reality to works in which the fictional reality is so powerful

that figures from the realm of ordinary "reality" prove
to be ineffectual foreign bodies. To put it another way:
we have moved from the fantastic, which is characterized
by an eruption of the seemingly inexplicable into the
rational world, to the fantasy, which takes place in another world governed by laws different from our own.[19]
Although we seem to be dealing superficially with the
same literary motif we saw in Fielding, Hoffmann, and
Balzac, the shift in the relationship between fiction and
reality alerts us to the fact that we have arrived, in the
cases of Hesse and De la Mare, at writers in whose works
the claim of art as against mundane life has become more
or less absolute. In view of this new superiority vouchsafed the literary figures it is hardly surprising that the
authors of twentieth-century fiction find from time to
time that they must set their figures straight.

This topos is evident in Miguel de Unamuno's novel
Mist (*Niebla*, 1914), when the hero, Augusto, reaches
such a nadir of spiritual despair that he makes up his
mind to commit suicide. Before taking the final step, he
decides to discuss the matter with the author of his story.
In a conversation that in essence anticipates the theory
of contemporary *Rezeptionsästhetik*, Unamuno reminds
Augusto that he cannot kill himself because he has no
life of his own. "No, you don't exist any more than any
other creature of fiction exists. You are not, my poor
Augusto, anything more than a figment of my imagination and of my readers' imagination, when they eventually read this story of your fictitious adventures and
mishaps that I have invented for you. You are a mere
protagonist in a novel, or *nivola*, whatever you'd like to
call it."[20] Similarly, in Kurt Vonnegut's story *Breakfast
of Champions* (1975) the author is sitting with his character, Kilgore Trout, in the cocktail lounge of a Holiday
Inn. Vonnegut tells Trout that he is a novelist and that
he invented Trout for use in his books. " 'I'm your Creator,' I said. 'You're in the middle of a book right now—
close to the end of it, actually.' "[21] As the novel ends,
the author decides to "set at liberty all the literary char-

acters who have served me so loyally during my writing career"—just as Tolstoy freed his serfs and Jefferson his slaves.

To follow this development to its logical conclusion, we will examine two recent examples that feature figures on loan who want to assert their independence in different ways. In the first case we encounter a figure who would like to flee out of the fiction to which she belongs in order to escape various circumstances that she finds intolerable. *A Dangerous Liaison* (*Een gevaarlijke Verhouding*, 1976) by the Dutch writer Hella S. Haasse consists of the alleged correspondence of the author with the Marquise de Merteuil, who at the end of Choderlos de Laclos' *Les Liaisons dangereuses*, ravaged by small-pox and blind in one eye, is said to have escaped "in the direction of Holland." In her remarkable work, which combines fiction and essay, Haasse imagines that the marquise settled for a time in Daal-en-Bergse Laan (Hill and Dale Lane) on the outskirts of Den Haag because its name reminded her of her lover and fellow conspirator, Valmont. Inspired by the *genius loci*, Haasse addresses a series of letters to the fascinating *femme fatale*, which elicit epistolary responses from the marquise, who thrives on—indeed, exists exclusively in!—letters. The correspondence fills in a number of fictional details that supplement Laclos' account—notably concerning the marquise's youth and the motivation of her hatred of Madame de Tourvel—and then updates her life following the conclusion of Laclos' report: her initial life of retirement in Holland, the ennui that drives her into a new plot to dupe a Dutch advocate of his fortune, and her eventual escape—this time back to revolutionary France and possibly to London. These narrative passages are interspersed with sections of social and literary criticism in which the marquise and her modern correspondent debate from their respective points of view the merits and significance of various heroines of history and literature. (The book constitutes, among other things, the record of the author's struggle against the allure of the arrogant marquise and her cynical interpretation of life.)

In the most precise sense the Marquise de Merteuil never actually enters the author's contemporary world: the fiction implies that the correspondence takes place by means of some sort of time warp. Yet she is very much a figure on loan, and this fact produces interesting speculations on the nature of fictionality. The marquise, for example, bitterly resents the fact that she is condemned by Laclos to spend the rest of her life in the windy country she detests. She is further indignant that, merely because she exists in a novel, she is forever exposed to the fantasies of her readers and the interpretations of critics. Having learned from her reading that people escape reality by means of literature, she decides by a process of inversion to escape from literature into everyday life. But her correspondent must ultimately remind her of a hard fact. "Personages from novels never escape through breaches in its reality *out of* the fictional world. They have no other existence than what is bestowed upon them by an author. You are in Holland, madame, every time a reader completes his perusal of *Les Liaisons dangereuses.*"[22]

The insight that literary figures who owe their whole existence to books can communicate only through letters is carried to its extreme in a novel that consists exclusively of letters the author exchanges with figures from his own earlier novels: John Barth's *Letters* (1979). At one point the author writes to Todd Andrews (the hero of *The Floating Opera*), "soliciting the latter's cooperation as a character in a new work of fiction."[23] Andrews obliges Barth with a résumé of his activities since 1954 (the date of *The Floating Opera*). Another character, Jerome Bray (from *Giles Goat-Boy*), writes to Todd Andrews requesting his counsel in a legal action against Barth for plagiarizing and misrepresenting his story. (The complaint of the literary figure against its creator is a topos that reminds us of Wilhelm Meister's lack of gratitude to Goethe in *Karl's Trials and Tribulations*.) A new figure that Barth had used in no previous work of fiction, Lady Amherst, introduces herself to the author in a series of autobiographical letters in which she gives a detailed account of her love affairs with various well-known *hommes de lettres*—notably James Joyce, Thomas Mann, and Hermann Hesse.

Barth displays an accurate if ironic sense of literary history when he writes to Todd Andrews: "Given your obvious literary sophistication, you will agree with me that a Pirandelloish or Gide-like debate between Author and Characters were as regressive, at least quaint, at this hour of the world, as naive literary realism: a Middle-Modernist affectation, as dated now as Bauhaus design" (p. 191). We have already observed how frequently the motif occurs in the early twentieth century. But it is symptomatic of Barth's artistic consciousness that in the subtitle he designates his book as "An Old-Time Epistolary Novel" explicitly patterned after the model of Richardson's fiction. If the era of figures on loan began with Fielding's borrowing from Richardson, it reached its high point, if not its absolute end point, two hundred fifty years later with John Barth. We are dealing, in short, with a more or less closed genre, whose history displays a clear development. At this point it would be worthwhile to look more closely at the significance of our figures on loan from the standpoint of literary history.

V

ANY LITERARY MOTIF, regardless of its inherent charm, demonstrates a certain symptomatic significance as the expression of deep-lying tendencies of the age that exploits it. To explain the popularity of figures on loan in romantic narrative it would be appropriate to point to two tendencies that no doubt contributed to its use: romantic irony with its inclination to shatter aesthetic illusion through the intermingling of fiction and reality,[24] and the arabesque, which Friedrich Schlegel posited as the basic model for the romantic novel because it seeks to organize a chaos of heterogeneous elements into an aesthetic unity.[25] The figure on loan, as an interpolated foreign element, has something in common with both tendencies: it undermines the fictional illusion of aesthetic unity, and it contributes to the arabesque-like nature of the literary work. But irony and arabesque, though relevant in a general way, cannot fully account for the specific phenomenon. Let us pose the question in a different form: Why did it occur to the romantic writers in Berlin to choose, as a means through which to express their irony and from which to construct their arabesques, an element so exotic as literary figures borrowed from another writer's work? At this point literary history provides us with some assistance, for the romantic writers belonged to the first literary generation that grew up with the conviction that character is the most important element in any work of literature. To put it most bluntly: you cannot have a figure on loan until literature has provided you with a figure to borrow.

It is symptomatic that Fielding singled out *Pamela* as the object of his parody, for Richardson's novel is generally regarded as the first "novel of character" in English (and more generally European) literature. Earlier fiction and drama had "characters," of course: but in accordance with neo-classical doctrine they tend to be so universal and typical that they display few individualizing features.[26] In his *Poetics* Aristotle insisted that "the plot is the first principle, and, as it were, the soul of a tragedy. Character holds the second place." This order of priorities was observed until the middle of the eighteenth century. Gottsched, in the more than eight hundred pages of his *Essay on Critical Poetics* (*Versuch einer kritischen Dichtkunst*, 1730) devoted only two pages (II, 1, x) to the question of character, essentially recapitulating Aristotle's dictum that characters must be consistent with history and consistent within themselves. However, as critics in England and Germany began to challenge the neoclassical unities in drama, their interest shifted away from plot toward character—a shift that led, among other things, to the appreciation of Shakespeare. There is no more passionate evidence for this new attitude than the statement that the young Goethe proclaimed in 1771 in honor of Shakespeare's name day. "I didn't hesitate for a moment to renounce the regular theater. The unity of place gave me such a sense of dungeon-like anxiety, the unities of plot and of time seemed no more troublesome fetters of the imagination." The French and Germans who have been infected by neoclassical doctrine are incapable of appreciating Shakespeare's achievement. "Most of these gentlemen are offended particularly by his characters. And I exclaim: Nature! Nature! nothing is so much Nature as Shakespeare's human beings."[27] This shift in point of view led to a radical reorientation of criticism. The many works that now began to come to grips with Shakespeare's plays discussed the characters almost as though they were human beings who possessed an existence outside the plays in which they appear. Maurice Morgann's *Essay on the Dramatic Character of John Falstaff* (1777) was influential upon all such investigations.[28] Coleridge's Shakespeare criticism belongs almost wholly to the tradition of eighteenth-century character studies,[29] and the same type of criticism is best represented in Germany by Goethe's discussions of Hamlet in *Wilhelm Meister's Apprenticeship*.

This shift of interest, which can be regarded as the literary reflection of the new individualism that resulted from the late eighteenth-century liberal revolution, began in the criticism of drama, but soon moved to fiction. Indeed, Blanckenburg in his *Essay on the Novel* (*Versuch über den Roman*, 1774) suggested that this genre emerged in specific response to the new interest in human character. "The tragic poets could not attain their goal with these more complete characters; the result to be achieved would not have been appropriate to the cause: this is the real reason why we find no such characters in the works of Aeschylus, Sophocles, Euripides. The drama, in my opinion, cannot in general tolerate such complete characters as the novel requires. This difference arises from the difference between the two genres, and it is therefore as essential as any other."[30] In the novel, according to Blanckenburg, "what matters are not the incidents befalling the persons but their sensations" (p. 60)—not the plot, in other words, but the characters. It is entirely appropriate that the first work of literary theory in which an entire section was devoted to character should be the *Elements of Aesthetics* (*Vorschule der Ästhetik*, 1804) by none other than that model of the Berlin romantic writers, Jean Paul. In his "X. Programm" Jean Paul discusses the nature of character in general, the origin of poetic characters, their representation and expression. The new romantic view of character, which accords to literary creations virtually a reality of their own, emerges vividly in the following passage. "The character itself must firmly preside before you, alive, in the hour of inspiration; you must hear him and not simply see him; he must tell you what to say, as happens in dreams, and not you him, and that must happen so intensely that in the cool period preceding you might be able to predict more or less What, but not How. A writer who must consider whether he must let a character in a given situation say Yes or No—discard him! He's a stupid cadaver."[31] Not until we reach this stage has the literary figure become so vivid and autonomous that it is capable of being appropriated into other works. Irony and arabesque provide the technique and point of view; but the new fictional figure provides the substance.

The persistence of the romantic conception of autonomous literary figures throughout the nineteenth century is attested by the opposition and irony it engendered. Edgar Allan Poe, for instance, is generally enthusiastic in his 1845 review of Hazlitt's *The Characters of Shakespeare*. Yet he is moved to conclude that "in all commentating upon Shakspeare, there has been a radical error, never yet mentioned. It is the error of attempting to expound his characters—to account for their actions—to reconcile his inconsistencies—not as if they were the coinage of a human brain, but as if they had been actual existences upon earth."[32] When the poet Rattengift ("Rat Poison") in Christian Grabbe's play *Jesting, Satire, Irony, and Profound Significance (Scherz, Satire, Ironie und Tiefere Bedeutung,* 1827) meets the devil (II, 2) he takes the opportunity to ask what many of his contemporaries have wanted to know: "Since you know what's going on in Heaven, I implore you to tell me what those immortal heroes of virtue are doing, whom I have chosen to be the guiding stars of my life and my poetry. Above all, what has happened to that sublime model of friendship, the divine Marquis Posa?" Rattengift is chagrined to learn that the hero of Schiller's drama is not in heaven but in hell, where he has become a pimp and opened a beer-hall "At the Sign of Queen Elizabeth." But that disappointment cannot undermine his fundamental belief in the reality of fictional figures. Consistently enough, he inquires about Wallenstein and other literary heroes before it occurs to him to ask about the writers themselves. Exemplary for this belief is the legend according to which Balzac, on his death-bed, called out for Dr. Bianchon, the physician he created to play a role in several of his novels.

It is by no means only writers themselves who believe in the reality of fictional characters. According to Q. D. Leavis's study of *Fiction and the Reading Public* "fiction for very many people is a means of easing a desolating sense of isolation and compensates for the poverty of their emotional lives."[33] The quotations from authors and readers she offers bear this out. One writer, for instance, remarks that her readers "constantly write about [my characters] to me as if they're alive and ask for more news of them!" The urgent curiosity that prompted readers to wait eagerly to learn the fates of characters in Dickens' serial novels has been transferred, a century later, to the destinies of characters in television serials. The point of absurdity in this identification of life and fiction is reached when Congressional committees invite as authorities to their hearings on medical problems ac-

tors who are qualified solely by their television perform-
ances as doctors! Adorno uses the tendency of the reader
to identify with fictional characters as the essential mark
of the "pre-aesthetic" cultural philistine.[34]

The modern equivalent of this romantic attitude shows
up in the works of Hesse, De la Mare, and other writers
who attribute greater reality to the fictional creations
than to their creators. In his reflections in *Our Lord Don
Quixote* Unamuno claims: ". . . though we oftentimes
consider a writer to be a real, true, and historic person
because we see him in the flesh, and regard the characters
he invents in his fictions as purely imaginary, the truth
is exactly the reverse. The characters are real, it is they
who are the authentic beings, and they make use of the
person who seems to be of flesh and blood in order to
assume form and being in the eyes of men."[35] Consistent
with this view is his serious claim that "Don Quixote
and Sancho have more historical reality than Miguel de
Cervantes Saavedra, and more than the author of these
lines, and that far from Cervantes being their creator, it
is they who created Cervantes" (p. 430). A similar view
is evident in Pirandello's preface of 1925 to *Six Characters in Search of an Author*, a play about characters
who, having been conceived in their author's imagination, now demand an aesthetic realm in which they may
live. "I can only say that, without having made any effort
to seek them out, I found before me, alive—you could
touch them and even hear them breathe—the six characters now seen on the stage."[36] This view was supported
by the Freudian interpretation of literature, of which
Ernest Jones's book *Hamlet and Oedipus* (1949) is representative. "In so far and in the same sense as a character in a play is taken as being a real person, to that
extent must he have had a life before the action in the
play began, since no one starts life as an adult."[37]

By the twenties the neo-romantic view of fictional
figures as autonomous reached such extremes that it
summoned forth the inevitable critical reaction. T. S.
Eliot began his essay on *Hamlet* (1919) with an assertion

that "Few critics have even admitted that *Hamlet* the play is the primary problem, and Hamlet the character only secondary."[38] Minds like Goethe, who made of Hamlet a Werther, and Coleridge, who made of Hamlet a Coleridge, created a critical vogue of the most misleading kind. E. M. Forster felt himself constrained in his Clark lectures to point out to his audience the seemingly obvious fact: "Amelia or Emma, we shall then say, cannot be at this lecture because they exist only in the books called after them, only in worlds of Fielding or Jane Austen. The barrier of art divides them from us."[39] Moll Flanders cannot be here "because she belongs to a world where the secret life is visible, to a world that is not and cannot be ours, to a world where the narrator and the creator are one." A few years later, in an amusing essay on the theory and practice of Shakespeare criticism, L. C. Knights attacked the current trend, which he traced back to the late eighteenth century, of regarding Shakespeare preeminently as a great creator of characters. He complains that most critics are concerned with Shakespeare's characters, his love of Nature, or his philosophy—with everything, in short, except the words on the page. "The habit of regarding Shakespeare's persons as 'friends for life' or, maybe, 'deceased acquaintances,' is responsible for most of the vagaries that serve as Shakespeare criticism."[40] And certain contemporary theorists have carried their antipathy toward character even further. Thus Hélène Cixous attacks it as one of the "machines of repression" invoked by a dehumanizing society. "So long as we do not put aside 'character' and everything it implies in terms of illusion and complicity with classical reasoning and the appropriating economy that such reasoning supports, we will remain locked up in the treadmill of reproduction."[41]

The growing critical relegation of fictional characters back into the fictional world of words from which they emerged found its analogy, as we have seen, in the tendency of contemporary writers like Barth, Vonnegut, and Hella Haasse to remind their own disruptive and self-assertive characters of their essential textuality. This attitude is anticipated in one of Paul Ernst's *Imaginary Conversations*, where King Oedipus boasts proudly that "we, the creations of noble poets, are more than mere mortals, who after all are the creatures of the gods." But when his interlocutor, the heroine of Heinrich von Kleist's drama *Penthesilea*, asks him why he doesn't sit down, he must confess: "My author has made me to stand up. He did not give me the ability to sit."[42]

What, in the last analysis, does all this mean? Is the significance of the figures on loan exhausted when we determine that the motif has been used by various writers since the middle of the eighteenth century for purposes of ideological criticism, psychological analysis, and reflections on the nature of literature itself? That its development, moreover, is paralleled by the changing view of character in literary criticism since 1750? Explanations of this sort suffice if we understand literature exclusively as an object of study and interpretation. But anyone who believes in the existential meaning of literature will go a step further.

The figure on loan, as we have seen, is a vivid image for the frangibility of literary reality. One world must break apart in order that the figure may emerge; another must be opened up in order that it may enter. It is the aura of frangibility surrounding it that arouses the sense of anxiety we feel every time we encounter a figure on loan. Whether the context is humorous or horrendous, we are always driven to the question: what protects our own so-called reality from the fragmentation that these figures on loan inevitably signify? That mystery accounts for the fascination that figures on loan have exerted on readers for two hundred years. It also helps to explain why contemporary analytical philosophy is so urgently concerned with the ontology of fictional existence[43]—a question for which the phenomenon of figures on loan constitutes a perplexing case.

The subtle anxiety that troubles us as we deal with this seemingly playful object has been understood more clearly by Borges than by most theoreticians of fictional discourse. In his essay on *Don Quixote* the Argentine writer asks himself why the reader finds it so eerie when Don Quixote, at the beginning of the Second Book, appears in the role of reader of his own earlier adventures. "I believe I have found the reason: these inversions suggest that if the characters of a fictional work can be readers or spectators, we, its readers or spectators, can be fictitious."[44] It is ultimately because of this implicit reference to the uncertainty of our own world as well as the possible fictitiousness of our own existence that the appearance of figures on loan ever since *Karl's Trials and Tribulations* has always produced the ambiguous effect of weird amusement and existential anxiety. Who, after all, can assure us that we, as readers of the figures on loan, are ultimately more than—people on loan?

Chapter Five

THE RESURRECTION: A MOTIF FROM NINETEENTH-CENTURY THOUGHT IN TWENTIETH-CENTURY FICTION

I

IN THE PREFATORY LETTER to his dramatic sketch *The Apostle* (1911) George Moore outlined his experiences on reading the Bible for the first time. Moore was particularly fascinated by the figure of Paul, about whom—he says—"my pen could scratch on for ever" (p. 29).[1] At the same time, he continues, he was familiar with legends according to which Jesus had originally been an Essene monk and had not died on the cross. "Why, then, . . . should not Christ have returned to his monastery, having been cured of his wounds at the house of Joseph of Arimathea? Why should not Paul, after a day's preaching amid the Palestinian hills, have knocked at the door of that monastery? What a wonderful meeting that would have been!" (p. 33). And a wonderful meeting it is indeed as Moore depicts it in his scenario. On the one hand the fanatical Paul, whose entire faith—not to say the justification of his existence—is based on the conviction that "Jesus of Nazareth died on the cross on Calvary, and three days after was raised from the dead by the glory of his Father in heaven, and if this be not so the world still is thrall to sin, and we have preached falsely" (p. 74). On the other hand a very sober and human Jesus, who is prepared to go back to Jerusalem once more "to save the world from crimes that will be committed in the name of Jesus of Nazareth, if I deny not before the people the Godhead thou hast thrust upon me" (p. 99). What is the apostle to do in this moment of confrontation? Troubled by the prospect of the "strife and discord and dissension" (p. 97) that would follow Jesus' untimely appearance at such a late date, Paul strikes Jesus, who falls down and dies. As the play ends, the apostle hastens away to fulfill his mission. "If that man has spoken a lie he is worthy of death, and Christianity is saved by his dying; but if he spake the truth? . . . The truth is in the hands of God, and I go to Rome to meet my death, and through death to meet my Christ, my gain, the fruit of all my labour" (p. 100).

When the Anglo-Irish writer expanded this scenario into one of his finest novels, *The Brook Kerith* (1916), he softened this drastic ending. Paul is still dismayed by the "madman" who threatens to undo all his missionary work by returning to Jerusalem to reveal that he neither died nor was resurrected. But in the end the apostle persuades Jesus to return to his duties as shepherd of the Essene community and to "leave the world to him" (p. 476).[2] Paul is thus able to set out for Rome without burdening himself with guilt for the death of Jesus.

Moore was already in his fifties when he first came to the Bible, and he had no more than a hearsay acquaintance with the higher criticism as it was practiced in Germany and France. Yet in both the dramatic scenario and the later novel, his apostle strikingly embodies the crisis of conscience faced by many nineteenth-century Life-of-Jesus scholars who wrestled with the dilemma of the Jesus of history versus the Christ of faith. "Men need a miracle," argues Moore's apostle in the play, "and faith in Christ and his resurrection have filled our hearts with love for each other, and gathered men and women together in peace, humility, and obedience as the law has never done" (p. 98). Moore's Paul literally kills Jesus in order to preserve the miracle. But on another level dozens of scholars had to come to grips with the same problem. For it was possible to rationalize away virtually every other miracle in the gospels without undermining the central tenet of Christian faith. But what happens to Christianity when even the miracle of the resurrection is questioned? Should the scholar, discovering that the evidence for Jesus' death and resurrection is insufficient, kill him off for the sake of Christianity like the apostle in Moore's play? Or should he let him live, like the apostle in Moore's novel, and search for other means to justify his faith?

The theological situation around 1835 was summed up quite succinctly by David Friedrich Strauss in his epoch-making *Life of Jesus*. For centuries, Christian faith had been content with a literal and supernatural reading of the gospels: Jesus died on the cross, and then was resurrected from the dead. But this supernatural belief had been increasingly undermined by the rationalism of the seventeenth and eighteenth centuries. As Strauss puts it in his chapter on the resurrection: "The proposition: a dead man has returned to life, is composed of two such contradictory elements, that whenever it is attempted to maintain the one, the other threatens to disappear. If he has really returned to life, it is natural to conclude that he was not wholly dead; if he was really dead, it is difficult to believe that he has really become living. . . . Hence the cultivated intellect of the present day has very decidedly stated the following dilemma: either Jesus was not really dead, or he did not really rise again."[3]

Theological rationalism of the period 1750 to 1815, largely accepting the former opinion, devoted its ingenuity to proposing subtle explanations of the means whereby Jesus might have survived his ordeal on the cross—explanations that usually involved a group of secret helpers. Yet Strauss, in accordance with the dialectics of his method, is just as unhappy with the improbabilities of a super-subtle rationalism as with the implausibilities of supernaturalism. He tends, to be sure, "to doubt the reality of the resurrection rather than that of the death." Yet in effect he leaves the whole question suspended by advancing a so-called "mythical" explanation of the miracle. Strauss asks us to "transport ourselves yet more completely into the situation and frame of mind into which the disciples of Jesus were thrown by his death." It is important for our purposes to note his emphasis of the fact that it was ecstatic women who first claimed to have witnessed the resurrected Christ and who brought news of the miracle to the disciples. Faced with the psychological necessity of reconciling the death of Jesus with their idea of the Messiah, they entered into an exalted visionary state in which they convinced themselves that they had actually seen and heard a resurrected Jesus. "When once the idea of a resurrection of Jesus had been formed in this manner," Strauss concludes, "the great event could not be allowed to have happened so simply, but must be surrounded and embellished with all the pomp which the Jewish imagination furnished." According to Strauss's theory, then, the resurrection as recorded in the gospels is the product of over-excited imaginations, fleshed out typologically with motifs supplied by the Old Testament.

Strauss, though he rejected naive supernaturalism as well as thorough-going rationalism, was equally—indeed, principally—concerned with explaining the "miracles" as they are recounted in the gospels. Like Moore's apostle, he believed that "men need a miracle." For this reason he examined the emotional state of the various figures reported in the gospels to have witnessed the resurrection. It was Strauss's teacher, Ferdinand Christian Baur, who shifted the emphasis of New Testament scholarship away from the life of Jesus with all its miracles and wholly into the consciousness of the early Church. It is no accident that Baur wrote no Life of Jesus and that he came to grips with the question of resurrection in his magisterial volume *The Church History of the First Three Centuries* (1853). Rejecting the classic belief in absolute miracle as an interruption of the natural continuity of cause and effect, Baur argued that the question of resurrection properly stands outside the framework of any legitimate historical investigation. What history requires is "not so much the fact of the resurrection of Jesus as the belief that it was a fact. . . . The important 'historical fact' is the consciousness of the disciples that Jesus had risen from the dead. As a fact of their consciousness, it was as real to them as any historical event."[4] Baur criticizes Strauss for devoting so much attention to the stories of the Bible and for attempting to account for their origin: rationally, psychologically, mythically, or otherwise. It was more important, he insisted, to understand the rhetorical purposes for which they were written—a shift in emphasis that prepared the way for modern form criticism of the gospels.

By the middle of the nineteenth century, in other words, at least four principal strategies existed to account for the "miracle" of resurrection.[5] According to one view, resurrection was a supernatural event that occurred and that must simply be accepted as an item of faith. According to another position, the so-called "miracle" can be explained rationally: for one reason or another Jesus did not die on the cross; certain of his followers actually did see him subsequently and therefore had good reason to believe in his "resurrection." According to Strauss's theory, Jesus probably did die on the cross; but for various reasons his followers, ecstatic to the point of hysteria, came to believe that they had witnessed his resurrection and began to proclaim it as a miracle with all the embellishments that the ancient world expected in such cases. Finally, the historicism advocated by Baur and his school argued that the life and death of Jesus have very little to do with belief in the resurrection, which must be understood historically as a projection of the expectations and concerns of the early Christian community.

At this point it is worth pausing to stress the fact that these theological attitudes regarding resurrection reflect to a remarkable degree a more general tendency in the cultural history of the nineteenth century. To the extent that the resurrection is considered a "miracle," its theological explanation closely resembles the treatment of other supernatural phenomena in nineteenth-century literature: specifically as the explanation passes through the stages of magic, rationalism, psychology, and historicism.[6] Let us consider briefly as a parallel example the attitude toward a related phenomenon: the animation of inanimate matter. Gothic novels of the late eighteenth century and romantic literature of the early nineteenth century are filled with walking statues, portraits that climb down from their frames, and artificial creatures that are brought to life: think of the haunted ancestral portrait in Horace Walpole's *The Castle of Otranto* (1764), the *commendatore*'s statue in *Don Giovanni* (1787), or the monster in Mary Shelley's novel *Frankenstein* (1818). These frequent cases of animation of the inanimate are metaphors, of course; but they are most emphatically *not* simply wild poetic ravings. Rather, they are literary images embodying a belief supported by philosophical theories of the age, in particular German *Naturphilosophie*. According to this influential philosophy of science, the borderline between animate and inanimate, between life and death, is not absolute, but a matter of degree. Schelling concluded his *Ideas for a Philosophy of Nature* (1797) with the famous statement that "nature is visible spirit, while spirit is invisible nature." Galvani's experiments with electricity as well as Mesmer's experiments with hypnosis seemed to lend credence to the notion that mind has control over matter.[7] Novalis believed that spiritual energy could heal a withered limb; and Mary Shelley specifically cites German *Naturphilosophie* as the theoretical basis for her novel, in which Dr. Frankenstein succeeds in bringing to life an inanimate creature by means of galvanic processes. In other words, in the early nineteenth century—and especially in Germany—it was a widely held belief, based on contemporary scientific evidence and supported by philosophical theory, that the dead could in fact be brought to life—a belief wholly compatible with the supernatural view of the resurrection. This is not mere speculation. While he was still a student, Strauss himself wrote a prize essay entitled "De Resurrectione Carnis" (1828), in which he proved "exegetically and by the philosophy of nature" that the resurrection of the dead is possible.[8]

At the same time, a rival rationalistic theory reasoned that such apparent occurrences of the supernatural were purely illusory, brought about by sophisticated illusions or mechanical devices. To remain with the example of animated statues: in the late eighteenth and early nineteenth centuries the art of constructing mechanical automata had reached true heights of virtuosity. Mechanical geniuses like Jacques Vaucanson and Johann Nepomuk Maelzel produced automata that could sing, dance, play the trumpet or flute in an eerily lifelike manner. Edgar Allan Poe was fascinated by Von Kempelen's Turkish chessplayer when it came to the United States; and E.T.A. Hoffmann—like the hero as portrayed in Offenbach's *Tales of Hoffmann*—lived in mortal fear lest he fall in love with an automaton so brilliantly contrived that he would take it for real. In short, the contemporary cultural situation supported not only a supernatural view of animation of the inanimate, but also the most sophisticated rationalistic view.

As a result of this contest between supernaturalism and rationalism, many writers of the next generation chose to take a compromise position. Literature of the eighteen-thirties—in Germany, France, England, the United States, and Russia—is filled with works in which the author leaves open the question of whether or not a certain incident is natural or supernatural in its occurrence. Poe, Hawthorne, Gogol, and many others are true contemporaries of Strauss in this respect. Let me cite as a single brilliant example Prosper Mérimée's story "The Venus of Ille" (1837), a retelling in modern garb of the medieval legend of Venus and the Ring. According to this legend, on his wedding day, a young man accidentally plights his troth to Venus by putting his ring on the finger of her statue. Whenever the young man seeks to approach his bride, the figure of Venus interposes itself and prevents any conjugal affection. In the medieval version the difficulties are resolved by an exorcist, who at the expense of his own life contrives to recover the fatal ring from the goddess. But Mérimée proposes a different solution: his bridegroom is strangled to death in his wedding bed. As a rationalist, Mérimée is unable to accept the notion that statues come to life: he presents the reader with the plausible possibility that an enemy of the young husband crept into the bridal chamber and killed him. At the same time, as a late romantic writer he is unwilling to dispense wholly with the titillations of the supernatural. So he sets his tale in a community of superstitious peasants who do in fact believe in the supernatural and who persuade themselves that the statue actually came to life and avenged itself on the faithless young man. As author, Mérimée leaves the ending open so that the reader can decide according to his own preference whether he wants a supernatural or a rational explanation for the young man's death. But this strategy—allowing the supernatural and the rational explanation to cancel each other out, thereby leaving room for a psychological explanation underlying the growth of a legend—bears a remarkable generational resemblance to Strauss's mythic interpretation of miracles and the resurrection.

Up to this point writers and theologians alike have been concerned principally with miracle or, at least, the appearance of miracle. Among succeeding generations of writers, however, there were many who flatly rejected any appearance of the supernatural—just as Baur rejected the possibility of miracle. Yet they need to account somehow for the phenomenon of people who, for one reason or another, actually do believe in miracles. To remain with the example of animated statues, let us consider Henry James's early story, "The Last of the Valerii" (1874). Here, in contrast to Mérimée's ambiguous narrative, there is never the slightest suggestion that

the statue unearthed in a Roman garden is in fact magical; and there is not the least hint that it comes to life
at any time. Like Baur, however, James is interested in
the consciousness of a man who regards the animation
of the statue as a fact. He portrays his hero, Count
Valerio, as a handsome, good-natured, and rather slow-
witted young man who, in his spiritual naiveté and physical energy, is the model of natural man. Uncomfortable
with the doctrines of Christianity, he has spontaneous
sympathy for the gods of his ancestors. Appropriately
enough, he feels far more at home in the Pantheon than
in St. Peter's. As a result of these emotional characteristics, when a statue of Juno is unearthed in his garden,
Camillo is predisposed to be smitten by love. For a time,
in fact, he is so profoundly enchanted by the statue that
he neglects his young American wife until she astutely
has the statue buried again in the earth from which it
had been unwisely removed. The point is simply this:
like Baur and the historicists, James does not accept the
possibility of miracle. But he is fascinated by the spiritual
expectations and emotional circumstances that could make
a man susceptible to a belief in the supernatural—whether
it be the animation of a statue or the resurrection of a
deity. (He was after all the brother of William James,
who in 1902 published that classic of the psychology of
religion, *The Varieties of Religious Experience*.)

To sum up, then, nineteenth-century attitudes toward
the resurrection, far from being a phenomenon restricted
to theology, in fact reflect very precisely the more general
sentiments of the times toward magic and the miraculous
altogether. The process begins with acceptance of the
supernatural, which is initially qualified by rational explanations, then rendered ambivalent by a mythicizing
psychological interpretation, and finally disqualified altogether by a skeptical historicism. However, these stages,
once they have been superseded, do not simply disappear. Here we encounter a principle that might be called
the Conservation of Cultural Energy: *no* vivid cultural
image ever disappears, even after its original justification

has been forgotten or disqualified. Instead, these images are simply shifted to another cultural level. To remain with our previous example: few people today believe in the animation of the inanimate; yet children's literature—from Winnie the Pooh and Raggedy Ann to the little Gingerbread Boy and Pinocchio—is teeming with examples of precisely that phenomenon. By the same token, the various attitudes toward resurrection do not disappear once they have been superseded: they simply move into fiction. For if we turn now to twentieth-century fictionalizing representations of the resurrection of Jesus, we see that they tend to fall roughly into one of the four categories that, as we noted, originally emerged in a loosely historical sequence. In other words, diachronic succession is flattened out into cultural synchronism. Obviously, the strategy that is invoked in each case gives us some insight into the religious attitudes of the author, ranging from reverence to skepticism. But from a strictly literary point of view the choice of strategy has further important implications, for the manner in which the resurrection is handled in a fictionalizing life of Jesus can determine such matters as structure, characterization, and narrative standpoint.

II

ONE OF the international literary sensations of the nineteen-twenties was the *Life of Jesus* (1921) written by Giovanni Papini very frankly as a work of edification "to set Christ the Ever-Living with loving vividness before the eyes of living men . . ." (p. 10).[9] The work of a man who underwent a spectacular conversion late in life, Papini's book specifically opposes the growing rationalism and biblical scholarship that, in his opinion, has "been trying desperately to kill Jesus a second time—to kill Him in the hearts of men" (p. 3). (Papini's rhetoric suggests that he has come fresh from a reading of George Moore's play.) A book undertaken with such evangelical zeal would predictably accept the resurrection at face value, and this assumption turns out to be the case. Papini even chides the disciples for their reluctance to accept the miracle of the resurrection when Mary Magdalene reports that she has spoken to Jesus in the garden near the tomb. "They believed in the resurrection of the Master, but not before the day when all the dead would rise again, and He would come in glory to rule His kingdom. But not now: it was too soon, it could not be true: waking dreams of hysteric women!" (p. 383). But gradually, despite their reluctance to admit what Papini himself concedes to be "an extraordinary infraction of the laws of death" (p. 399), the disciples begin to share Papini's faith in the resurrection, which is presented as a straightforward factual occurrence.

Although Papini has nothing but contempt for those "enemies of Christ" (p. 395) who question the resurrection, he specifically concedes that Jesus always resisted the challenge to perform miracles indiscriminately, being unwilling to persuade men by the cheap means of wonders (p. 66). The only exceptions were the miracles of healing (p. 136 ff.), which Papini explains as psychosomatic cures. Much the same approach is evident in a hugely successful book of the nineteen-forties, Lloyd C. Douglas's *The Big Fisherman* (1948). Here again the miracles are reduced to wonders of healing—healings that bear a conspicuous resemblance to the wish-dreams of Douglas's own Christian Science. But when we get to the resurrection, once again all the stops are pulled. The first few appearances, to be sure, are represented as hearsay. "There were various versions of the story. Reduced to its simplest form: certain women, devoted followers of the Master, had gone out at dawn on Sunday to the beautiful Garden of Sepulchers to anoint the mangled body with myrrh. They had found the tomb open and empty. Then they had seen him, strolling among the flowers. After a tender moment of ecstatic recognition the women were told to notify 'my disciples—and Peter' " (p. 492).[10] And when Jesus appears to the disciples at supper and to Cleophas and his friend on the road to

Emmaus, there is a certain degree of doubt concerning his substantiality: did he actually pass through unopened doors? Did he actually partake of the food? All this leads us to believe that the author may be building up to the "hysterical women" theory. But on the next two occasions the narrator of the novel actually portrays Jesus as being physically present. When he appears to Peter on the Sea of Gennesaret, he is present in the text and not merely in Peter's imagination. "Beside the fire, warming his hands, stood the Master. He raised his arm, waved a hand, and called: Peter!" (p. 500). Similarly, when Jesus dispatches the disciples to Jerusalem he is portrayed as being literally present—although the author hedges a bit by adding: "when, at length, they lifted their eyes, he was gone" (p. 501). From a literary point of view, however, you cannot have it both ways: as long as a phenomenon is represented through a third person—for instance, Mary Magdalene or Peter—the miracle does not have to be accepted by the reader as having literally occurred. But when it is presented by the author himself, then we must accept it as true—at least within the framework of the story. Like Papini, then, Douglas suggests a rational explanation for the healing miracles; but his faith impels him to depict the resurrection as literally true.

These two examples might suggest that faith is not the best prerequisite for fiction. Even charitable critics would not argue that the books by Papini and Douglas have much value as literature, apart from any merits that they may have as edifying works. Papini's aggressive and somewhat ill-tempered fundamentalism often turns out to be almost boorish in its insistence on a literal reading of the gospels and in its attacks on modern biblical scholarship. Douglas garbles even the rudimentary historical facts underlying his novel, and the troublesome matter of faith necessitates, as we have seen, certain aesthetically intolerable shifts in narrative point of view. Yet these two fictionalizing lives are perhaps the two most popular and representative examples of a

genre whose general level of literary excellence is no-
toriously low.

The finest writers have tended to be challenged by a
more skeptical and rational approach to the gospels and
their miracles. Among the writers who have suggested
that Jesus did not die on the cross, almost from the start
the notion has been common that he must have been
aided by friends or by a secret society since otherwise
he could hardly have recovered from his ordeal on the
cross. Often this collaboration is attributed to the Order
of the Essenes. According to Karl Friedrich Bahrdt—first
in his *Popular Letters about the Bible* (*Briefe über die
Bibel im Volkston*, 1782) and then in his *Explanation
of the Plan and Aim of Jesus* (*Ausführung des Plans und
Zwecks Jesu*, 1784-1792)—Jesus is chosen almost at
birth to become a member of the Order. It is the Order
that furthers him in his career and whose members assist
him, without the knowledge of his somewhat slow-witted disciples, in his various miracles. The crucifixion and
resurrection constitute an elaborate hoax staged in an
effort to win public support for the Order's teachings.
According to a carefully planned time-table, Jesus pro-
vokes his own arrest and condemnation. Luke the physician has prepared his body with ointments and drugs;
Nicodemus makes sure that the Sanhedrin demands immediate crucifixion before the effects of the drugs wear
off; Joseph of Arimathea bribes the centurion not to
harm the body while it is on the cross and arranges with
his friend Pilate to remove it within a few hours; then
Luke revives Jesus once again so that he can retire and
live secretly in the Order, appearing in public from time
to time in order to maintain the legend of the resurrection.

Karl Heinrich Venturini's *Non-Supernatural History
of the Great Prophet of Nazareth* (*Natürliche Geschichte des grossen Propheten von Nazareth*, 1800-1802)
has much in common with Bahrdt's rationalization—
notably Jesus' association with the Essenes. In this case,
to be sure, there is no cynical political motivation: the

arrest and crucifixion are not planned and stage-managed by the Order. But after Jesus' alleged death on the cross, Joseph of Arimathea notices that there are still signs of life. Jesus is successfully revived and, again, sent off to live out his life secretly in the sanctuary of the brethren. In both cases, the miracle of the resurrection is based upon reports of witnesses who actually saw the real Jesus without knowing the secret facts of his crucifixion and resuscitation.

Venturini and Bahrdt provided the early models imitated by many authors in the past hundred and fifty years, right down to Hugh Schonfield in *The Passover Plot* (1966). No doubt the finest literary example of this category is afforded in *The Brook Kerith* by George Moore, who—wittingly or unwittingly—follows Venturini very closely. As we noted above, the novel moves in its second half toward the dramatic confrontation between Paul and Jesus, whom the apostle finds many years after the crucifixion still living as the shepherd of an Essene commmunity in the hills above Jericho. But the first half of the novel, narrated from the point of view of Joseph of Arimathea, culminates in the crucifixion. Here again Jesus is portrayed as a humble member of an Essene commune until his conversion to action by John the Baptist. But no Essene plot is involved in the crucifixion, which Jesus brings upon himself. When Joseph of Arimathea, an admirer of Jesus, learns of his crucifixion, he is eager simply for humane reasons to obtain the body and bury it: "far worse than the death he endured would be for the sacred body to be thrown into the common ditch with these malefactors." Bribing the centurion not to harm the body and persuading his friend Pilate to release it prematurely, Joseph transports the body to the tomb before he notices that Jesus is still barely alive. With the aid of his servant Esora, who concocts a healing balsam from a recipe that goes back to the Queen of Sheba, Joseph nurses Jesus slowly back to health until he is able to return to the mountains to life with the Essenes. Sobered and disabused of his messianic zeal, he remains hidden there until he is discovered accidentally by Paul many years later.

From all that has been said, it should be clear that D. H. Lawrence, consciously or unconsciously, was continuing an old tradition rather than creating a new one when he described the resurrection of Jesus in his story *The Man Who Died* (1931). His Jesus, to be sure, is not aided and abetted by Essenes. In fact, the lack of any rational justification for his survival might be counted as a weakness in the narrative. Jesus awakens alone in the tomb where he has been placed, bandaged and rubbed with ointments and wrapped in a linen sheet. Lawrence uses the resurrection for his own purposes—not for a grand confrontation between Jesus and his apostle in the manner of George Moore. Lawrence's Jesus realizes upon reawakening that his public career is over: he shares the disenchantment of Moore's savior. But like all Lawrentian heroes he rejoices in that fact. "Now I can wait on life, and say nothing, and have no one betray me. I wanted to be greater than the limits of my hands and feet, so I brought betrayal on myself. . . . For I have died, and now I know my own limits. Now I can live without striving to sway others any more" (p. 174).[11] It is this new affirmation of life that leads him, in the second half of the story, into the liberating embrace of the priestess of Isis.

Yet as a rationalization of the resurrection legend the story fits into the model established a century and a half earlier. As he leaves the tomb, Jesus meets Mary Magdalene, who is initially bitter because Jesus has risen for himself alone and refuses to come back to his former followers. "She went away, perturbed and shattered. Yet as she went, her mind discarded the bitterness of the reality, and she conjured up rapture and wonder, that the Master was risen and was not dead. He was risen, the Saviour, the exalter, and wonder-worker! He was risen, but not as man; as pure God, who should not be touched by flesh, and who should be rapt away into Heaven. It was the most glorious and most ghostly of the miracles" (p. 176). It is Lawrence's delicious irony, of course, that this "most ghostly" of the miracles, resulting in a deity who should not be touched by flesh, actually turns out to liberate Jesus to the pleasures of the senses in the arms of the priestess. Yet the rationalization—that Jesus did not die on the cross—is still followed almost immediately and automatically by the customary beginnings of the legend.

All the novels of rationalization are characterized structurally by the fact that the crucifixion scene comes long before the end because the authors are interested in depicting what happens to Jesus after he is removed, living, from the cross. With the notable exception of Lawrence's story, works of this category tend to develop the characters of the Essene associates, particularly Nicodemus and Joseph of Arimathea. Another group of novelists, in contrast, begins with the Straussian assumption that Jesus died on the cross and that there was no supernatural resurrection. This assumption also has certain obvious implications for the structure of the work, for it moves the crucifixion to the end. As Ernest Renan remarked in his *Life of Jesus* (1863), "for the historian, the life of Jesus finishes with his last sigh."[12] And some novelists have taken this advice quite literally. Nikos Kazantzakis' *The Last Temptation of Christ* (1953), for instance, ends abruptly with the last flicker of consciousness as Jesus expires on the cross. But other writers append a brief epilogue to account for the beginnings of the legend of the resurrection, and in this they generally follow in the footsteps of Strauss with his "hysterical women" hypothesis. Even Renan suggests possibilities of this sort. "But such was the impression he had left in the heart of his disciples and of a few devoted women, that during some weeks more it was as if he were living and consoling them. Had his body been taken away, or did enthusiasm, always credulous, create afterward the group of narratives by which it was sought to establish faith in the resurrection? In the absence of opposing documents this can never be ascertained. Let us say, however, that the strong imagination of Mary Magdalen played an important part in this circumstance. Divine power of love! Sacred moment in which the passion of one possessed gave to the world a resuscitated God!" (p. 302).

Emil Ludwig's *The Son of Man* (1927) takes a similarly hardheaded approach. In his Introduction the author stresses the fact that his book "deals with 'Jesus' and has not a word to say about 'Christ.' "[13] He assures us that "when any reference is made to the miracles, they are interpreted naturalistically, for I am writing history." As a result, the book ends with the unequivocal death of Jesus. Yet in the last paragraph Ludwig summarizes the various rationalizing explanations of the resurrection, and his final sentence attempts to account psychologically for the origin of the myth already growing up around Jesus—again, according to the hypothesis of the hysterical women.

> Next day, all Jerusalem has heard the news. A hundred rumors fly through the city. What to believe? Some say that Pilate has regretted giving Jesus' body to his friends, and has had it hidden. A second story is that the priests have stolen the corpse, lest the multitude should idolize it. A third notion is that the gardener must be at the bottom of what has happened, being afraid that a great multitude at the tomb would trample his flowers. According to a fourth version, some of the rascals who plunder tombs of anything they can get money for must have been at work. A fifth theory is that of those who say that no one has ever died after only three hours on the cross; that the Nazarene's disciples have revived Jesus from apparent death, and have got him away into safe hiding. The priests go to Pilate, berate him for being so pliable, and foretell endless troubles, now that the prophet's followers have been allowed to steal the body, in order to tell the people that their Master has risen from the dead.

But the women, who love him, believe that in waking dreams they have seen the risen Jesus in the flesh.

It takes little imagination to perceive that Ludwig is a disciple of the mythicizing tradition that goes back to Strauss.

The same visionary explanation has been used by several other authors of modern fictionalizing lives of Jesus. In his popular *Life of Jesus* (1936) Edzard Schaper accounts for the resurrection as a psychological-optical phenomenon, carefully making it stylistically clear that in every case the people in his book are experiencing a vision rather than actual reality. When Mary Magdalene encounters Jesus in the garden, she thinks at first that it is the gardener who has taken her by surprise. But when she hears the familiar voice of Jesus calling her, she "raised herself up and looked around with blinded eyes, without seeing anything but the flaming light of the sun that had just risen over the gardens" (p. 248).[14] It is on the basis of this vision, catalyzed by her own longing and the early-morning light, that Mary proclaims her irrevocable faith in the miracle of resurrection. At first the eleven disciples are unwilling to credit her account. But Cleophas and his friend, inspired by her words, have a similar vision on the road to Emmaus. From that moment on the vision hardens into gospel truth.

In Frank G. Slaughter's *The Crown and the Cross* (1959) it is again Mary Magdalene who precipitates the accounts of the resurrection. After Peter and John discover that the tomb is empty, they return to wake the others while Mary remains behind, weeping at the seeming desecration of the tomb. "Kneeling there, it suddenly seemed to Mary that the tomb was illuminated for a moment and she saw two men in white sitting inside" (p. 440).[15] But the sound of her own voice speaking to them in the empty sepulcher startles her. Then she feels a hand touch her shoulder. "A man stood beside her, only half visible in the dim light of early dawn. Kneeling,

Mary could not see his face, but she recognized by his dress that he was not a soldier." When Mary finally recognizes the figure beside her, who utters nothing but her name, her eyes swim with tears of joy. "Mary turned blindly toward her beloved Master but he was no longer there." Yet this eidetic vision suffices, once again, to catalyze the series of visionary experiences that are subsequently rationalized into a theory of the resurrection according to the procedure outlined by Strauss.

The fictional lives of Jesus belonging to the category we have called loosely Straussian are distinguished by several traits. First, they tend to use a shifting point of view that focuses principally upon the figure of Jesus; second, in contrast to works based on the theory of an Essene conspiracy they tend to place the crucifixion scene close to the end; and, finally, they tend to develop the characters not of Essenes like Nicodemus or Joseph of Arimathea but of the women and the disciples in order to provide plausible motivation for the ecstatic visions at the end. The fictional inventiveness is limited, however, to the extent that the narrative is restricted by certain expectations concerning the life of the central figure, which dominate the plot and the action. In other words, in a novel about Jesus the action cannot wander too far from the familiar incidents as recounted in the gospels.

There is a final category, however, which enjoys much more fictional license: namely, those novels that recount the life of Jesus not from a modern point of view that seeks to rationalize or to psychologize the events of the gospels, but rather from the standpoint of a historical contemporary of Jesus—a person whose account of the events is both restricted and enhanced by his historical limitations. This strategy, which has usually been adopted by the finest writers who have dealt with the story fictionally, provides a close literary counterpart to the historicism of Baur and his followers: disregarding the question of miracle, it attempts to comprehend attitudes toward the resurrection in its historical context. For purposes of illustration let us briefly consider three works that tell the story from a non-Christian point of view, thereby objectifying the entire account of the resurrection.

If we discount its framework fiction, Sholem Asch's brilliant and learned account in *The Nazarene* (1939) is told from three entirely different points of view. The events up to Jesus' arrival in Jerusalem are recounted first by a Roman officer, Ciliarch of the Antonia Fortress under the command of Pontius Pilate, and then in the form of an apocryphal gospel attributed to Judas; the events of the Passion week are narrated by a young disciple of Rabbi Nicodemon. These three interlocking accounts provide us with a rich panorama of life in Jerusalem at the time of Jesus and contribute to the intellectual fascination of the novel. Yet nothing in their point of view enables the narrators to apprehend a miracle like the crucifixion. When the Roman officer asks the young Pharisee what happened to Jesus after his death, the latter replies with absolute consistency: "That which happened afterwards with the Rabbi of Nazareth in Jerusalem has no relation to me" (p. 691).[16] When he is pressed, he finally admits that "in certain circles in Jerusalem secret rumors were current that the Rabbi had disappeared from his grave, that he showed himself in the life to his disciples, and that he told them what they still had to do" (p. 692). But the Pharisee himself takes no interest in the spread of these rumors, which he regards simply as a misguided but harmless ideological variation of the traditional Jewish messianic hopes. In this novel, in other words, Sholem Asch puts the question of resurrection into the context of contemporary Jewish faith and disqualifies the miracle by having it reported by an interested observer who is himself a non-believer. Like Renan and Baur, who argued that the topic of the resurrection belongs properly to the history of the early Church and not to the life of Jesus, Asch postpones his consideration of the subject to the sequel he wrote about

Paul, *The Apostle* (1943), in which the resurrection has already become an article of faith.

Whereas Asch puts his account of Jesus' life and death into the words of contemporary Romans and Jews, Robert Graves in *King Jesus* (1946) achieves a curious effect by having the story told around 90 A.D. by an Alexandrine scholar who, though no Christian himself, became an authority on the new religion when he harbored in his house a refugee bishop fleeing from the persecutions. The alleged date of the narrative means that the fictitious author has at his disposal information more or less equivalent to the synoptic gospels. Paradoxically, though he does not believe in the divinity of Jesus, the narrator is perfectly willing to accept the miracle of the resurrection, for in his eyes Jesus belongs to the familiar category of wonder-workers. "Not the least wonderful of Jesus' many feats was that, though certified dead by his executioners after a regular crucifixion, and laid in a tomb, he returned two days later to his Galilean friends at Jerusalem and satisfied them that he was no ghost; then said farewell and disappeared in equally mysterious fashion" (p. 3).[17] Because he belongs to an age that accepts miracles and magic as self-evident, the narrator can depict the resurrection in a matter-of-fact manner without making any concessions to Christian faith. There is no coyness whatsoever in the portrayal of the christophany before the three Marys and the disciples: Jesus simply appears. But unlike Douglas in *The Big Fisherman*, Graves is not asking us to accept the resurrection on his authority; rather, it is the narrator who accepts it for his own wholly non-Christian and historically circumscribed reasons.

Graves introduces a second historical justification for the narrator's acceptance of resurrection, for as a man of learning the narrator is familiar with the mythic origins and implications of crucifixion and resurrection. "Anciently, it seems, in every country around the Mediterranean Seas, crucifixion was a fate reserved for the annual Sacred King" (p. 402). Almost as though he had been perusing Sir James Frazer's *The Golden Bough*, the erudite old gentleman treats us to a disquisition on the attainment of immortality through death. In this novel, then, the motif of resurrection is treated almost precisely as Baur and the historicists recommended. Graves as author makes no comment on the miracle, which is taken for granted, and he makes no use of the psychological justification through hysterical women or exalted states. The resurrection is depicted simply as is the case in the gospels, and when Jesus appears before the women, they are calm and serene. But through the narrative method that he calls "analeptic" he makes plausible the willingness of men at the end of the first century to believe that such a phenomenon as resurrection might actually have taken place—in terms of contemporary magic and myth.

Pär Lagerkvist in *Barabbas* (1950) tells the story of the crucifixion and alleged resurrection from the point of view of the rather dull-witted man who was spared from the cross. (His Barabbas has none of the heroic dimensions of the Zealot leader as he is portrayed by Sholem Asch and others.) At the beginning of the novel Barabbas has wandered out to Golgotha largely out of idle curiosity about the man who took his place on the cross that morning. When Peter first tells him (p. 26)[18] that Jesus' followers expect their Master to rise from the dead on the morning of the third day, Barabbas calls this belief nonsense. All the same, he goes out before dawn the next morning and hides in the bushes opposite the sepulcher to see what happens. In fact, he sees nothing at all. When the sun rises, he realizes that the stone has already been rolled away and that the tomb must have been empty before his arrival. Yet Barabbas contributes to the growth of the myth. Years later, when he finds himself shackled in the mines to the Christian slave Sahak, out of a simple desire to please and console his friend he confides to him that he witnessed Jesus' resurrection. "No, not so that he had seen him rise from the dead, no one had done that. But he had seen an angel shoot down from the sky with his arm outstretched like the point of a spear and his mantle blazing behind him like a flame of fire. And the point of the spear had rolled away the stone from the tomb, pushing in between the stone and the rock and parting them. And then he had seen that the tomb was empty . . ." (p. 92). Again we are dealing with a phenomenon wholly different from the ecstatic hysterics of Strauss's women and disciples. It is made perfectly clear from the outset that no miraculous resurrection has taken place—or, more precisely, the witness from whose point of view the story is told does not see anything of the sort take place. Yet out of his simple human desire, years after the event, to lend support to the faith of his friend—which, incidentally, he too gradually begins to accept—Barabbas contributes to the myth of resurrection, which is created, as it were, within the early Christian community in response to its own messianic expectations.

In conclusion, we have seen that many of the most prominent fictionalizing lives of Jesus in the twentieth century fall into one of four rather clearly defined categories, depending upon the authors' views on "miracles" and the resurrection. Each of these four categories has certain implications for the form of the literary work— notably, the placement of the crucifixion scene, the development of secondary characters, and the determination of the narrative point of view. In other words, religious attitude determines literary technique. At the same time, the four categories correspond with fair precision to four stages in nineteenth-century Life-of-Jesus scholarship, and these four stages of religious attitude reflect in turn the general cultural climate of the age.

Chapter Six

THE ETHICS OF SCIENCE FROM ADAM TO EINSTEIN: VARIATIONS ON A THEME

I

THE HISTORY of postwar German drama might suggest to the casual observer that the contemporary theater is populated by a group of frustrated physicists. Writers of every generation, from Germany East and West as well as German-speaking Switzerland, and representing every theatrical vogue, have turned to nuclear physics for their subject matter. Carl Zuckmayer used the case of atomic spy Klaus Fuchs as the basis for a realistic drama entitled *Cold Light* (1955), which portrays the career of a young German émigré who is trained in England as a physicist, comes to the United States to work on the Manhattan project, and turns over classified information to the Russians. In *The Physicists* (1962) Friedrich Dürrenmatt takes us into a madhouse where two of the patients think that they are Newton and Einstein while the third, Möbius, imagines that he is visited by the spirit of King Solomon. It turns out that all three patients are sane: Möbius is a brilliant physicist who has made a discovery so potentially destructive that he has had himself committed to the asylum in order to avoid exploitation; "Newton" and "Einstein" are intelligence agents from opposing governments who feign madness in order to approach Möbius and win his services. The play ends when the three men, having agreed to preserve their secret in the interests of humanity, learn that they are in the hands of the sanatorium director, who is totally insane: having used her position to acquire Möbius' knowledge, she has set up a vast cartel with which she intends to take over the world. Heinar Kipphardt's *In the Matter of J. Robert Oppenheimer* (1964) is a documentary drama based on the proceedings initiated against the father of the atomic bomb in 1954 by the Personnel Security Board of the Atomic Energy Commission. Bertolt Brecht wrestled with the problem of the scientist and ideology for almost twenty years (from 1938 on) in the three versions of his *Galileo*. At the end of his life, moved by the death of Albert Einstein in 1955, he attempted to address the problem through a more contemporary material. Only a few fragments remain of his planned *Life of Einstein*—enough, however, to show that Brecht intended to focus on the dilemma of the theorist and pacifist who was compelled to put his knowledge at the disposal of war and who, having fled Nazi Germany, "found a new Potsdam in Washington."[1] Brecht's ideas were subsequently worked out by his followers in East Germany. In Karl Mickel's libretto for Paul Dessau's opera *Einstein*, the aging physicist, in his American exile, has come to the conclusion that both Germany and the United States were eager to use his discoveries to build weapons that threatened humanity; but Germany drove him into exile, and the United States now refuses to heed his political advice. So he burns up the manuscript containing a second great formula lest it too be used against mankind.[2]

It is immediately apparent that these dramatists are interested not in physics as such but in the ethical implications of a science that has suddenly come out of the laboratory into the public domain. As Zuckmayer explains in his afterword to *Cold Light*, "the theme of the play is not the splitting of the atom but the crisis of faith."[3] It is the particular appeal of ideological betrayal, according to Zuckmayer, that it produces a conflict of conscience that finds its closest analogy in times of religious wars. In Kipphardt's drama Oppenheimer puts the same thought another way: "It isn't the fault of the physicists that brilliant ideas always lead to bombs nowadays. As long as that is the case, one can have a scientific enthusiasm for a thing and, at the same time, as a human being, one can regard it with horror" (Part II, Scene 2).[4] Mickel's surrealist opera culminates in the hero's decision to destroy the results of his research rather than permit it to be used for inhuman purposes. And, in the most general statement of ethical principle, Dürrenmatt appends to his play twenty-one "theses" in which we read: "The content of physics is the concern of physicists, its effect the concern of all men."[5]

The popularity of this theme, found in several other German dramas of the sixties, is easy to understand. First, it is a subject with large and urgent implications. In the decades following Hiroshima and Nagasaki no theater-goer needed to be persuaded that the topic was worthy of his attention. Second, although the basic dilemma is by its nature an international one, many of its leading characters were German—a fact that engaged the interest of German audiences. Finally, as citizens of countries that were not themselves atomic powers yet vulnerable and exposed by their geographical location, German and Swiss dramatists keenly sensed the dangers of the Cold War and sought to analyze them according to their various ideologies. Though Zuckmayer was basically concerned with the crisis of belief experienced by any decent man, his play is written from an explicitly Western point of view. Zuckmayer, who spent the war years in the United States, views Russia and communism as the enemy, and his values are weighted accordingly. Karl Mickel, in contrast, writing from the German Democratic Republic, places the emphasis differently. His Einstein, like Brecht's, feels betrayed both by Germany and by the United States; the melody of the Internationale, introduced at the end of the opera, suggests that the only possible salvation lies in a communist society. Kipphardt, displaying the skepticism of a left-oriented West German, detects little innocence in the Oppenheimer affair: both the FBI and the military come off badly in his dramatization; he impugns the motives of many of the witnesses; and Oppenheimer's own integrity is questioned. Dürrenmatt, from his vantage-point in neutral Switzerland, leaves his audience with the distinct impression that all the nations involved in the struggle for nuclear power are either unscrupulous or insane or both.

Yet despite the shifts of political emphasis from one play to the next, a remarkably consistent pattern underlies all of them. In each case we encounter a scientist who initially pursues his science in a state of brash innocence, with no thought for the consequences. The discovery in each case is objectively value-free and a distinct contribution to human knowledge. But the political misuse of the discovery arouses the scientist from ethical innocence to a state of consciousness which necessitates a political act. Seen at this level of abstraction the plays are all based on an ambivalent conception of scientific knowledge, and this ambivalence enables us to grasp perhaps the most compelling reason for their success—a reason more subliminally insistent than the superficially urgent political factors. They all represent modern manifestations of a powerful archetypal structure familiar from myth and literature. We will come later to the religious implications of the structure, which are evident in the images that instinctively spring to the characters' minds when they reach the moment of insight in each play. But we must first deal with a more immediate source in which the archetypal situation assumed its exemplary shape for the modern imagination.

On October 29, 1949, following a meeting of the Atomic Energy Commission with Oppenheimer's advisory committee on the hydrogen bomb, David E. Lilienthal noted in his journal that James B. Conant flatly opposed the project on the grounds that "we built one Frankenstein."[6] Although the name Frankenstein does not occur in the German plays—the story of Dr. Frankenstein and his monster is an Anglo-Saxon invention—

it cropped up frequently in the discussions in this country surrounding the conflict between pure scientific research and its social implications. In the early sixties Dr. Philip Abelson, the director of the Geophysical Lab of the Carnegie Institution, warned that "government money has been the Frankenstein of big science, and in many instances, the monster has invaded the universities."[7] When Herbert J. Muller wrote "A Primer on Modern Technology and Human Values," in which he argued that man can control the technology that he has created, he entitled it *The Children of Frankenstein* (1970). In all of these representative cases the image is used loosely. It is never completely clear whether the speakers understand the difference between Dr. Frankenstein and his (nameless) monster. But that very ambiguity attests to the power of myth. Most people citing Frankenstein as exemplary for the scientist who in his search for knowledge creates a monster have never read Mary Shelley's novel. Instead, they have in mind the numerous "Frankenstein" movies that have been filmed since 1910 and that constitute an ineradicable aspect of American culture.[8] Although even the most trivialized film version or comic book preserves the structure of the archetype, it is to Mary Shelley's novel of 1818 that we must turn for the true analogue to the four German dramas that we have considered.

II

WHEREAS MOVIEGOERS today regard Frankenstein films as a venerable form of the fantastic, Mary Shelley based her novel on what she believed to be the most up-to-date scientific theories. To the extent that her narrative is consistent with, and a logical extension of, existing scientific cognition, it is an example of science fiction in the most rigorous sense of the word. When her husband wrote his preface to the work, he reminded his audience that "the event on which this fiction is founded has been supposed, by Dr. Darwin and some of the physiological

writers of Germany, as not of impossible occurrence"
(p. xiii).[9] It is unnecessary for our purposes to recapitulate the circumstances of composition: the competition
among the four young romantics spending the summer
of 1816 in Switzerland—Byron, Shelley, his wife Mary,
and their friend Polidori—to write a ghost story. What
matters is that Mary Shelley, as she tells us in her Author's Introduction of 1831, listened to conversations
between Byron and her husband, who was fascinated
by the latest scientific theories concerning the "principle
of life" and the possibility of creating life by electricity.
(As a student at Eton Shelley almost electrocuted himself
in the attempt to reproduce Franklin's experiment with
the kite.) "Perhaps a corpse would be reanimated; gal-
vanism had given token of such things: perhaps the com-
ponent parts of a creature might be manufactured, brought
together, and endued with vital warmth" (p. x). In her
novel Mary Shelley gave exemplary form to a romantic
dream embodied in the German *Naturphilosophie* and
shared by such writers as Novalis and Hoffmann—of
making animate the inanimate, of creating spirit from
inert matter.

The scientific rationalization of the novel must be
stressed, for if *Frankenstein* were purely fantastic—that
is, based on the intrusion of the irrational into the rational world—there would be no grounds for comparison with the later German plays. Like them, however,
it is based on what was considered the most exciting
science of the day. Like them, moreover, it appeared at
a critical moment in the history of science—at the moment, in fact, when decades of progress and achievement
had rendered science secure and unquestioning in its
accomplishments. Edward Teller, the father of the H-
bomb, once remarked: "I believed in the possibility of
developing a thermo-nuclear bomb. My scientific duty
demanded exploration of that possibility."[10] This absolute faith in the right and, indeed, the duty to pure
inquiry—what Erwin Chargaff has called the Devil's
Doctrine: "What can be done, must be done"—is an

attitude that emerged during European romanticism. Until the Renaissance, science, like the other intellectual disciplines, had served principally as a handmaiden of theology. The history of sixteenth- and seventeenth-century science is in no small measure an account of the struggle between religious authority and scientific discovery. By the end of the eighteenth century, however, as Carl Becker and other students of the period have pointed out, a naive faith in the authority of nature and reason had all but replaced the authority of the Church. It was one of the principal achievements of romanticism, and especially of the great reforms that established in early nineteenth-century Germany the first modern universities, to insist upon the right of scholarship in general and science in particular to pursue its free inquiry, uninhibited by any authority, spiritual or secular. Mary Shelley's *Frankenstein* expresses society's concern at what it perceived to be the mindless pursuit of knowledge with no thought for its social implications.

Mary Shelley tells the story of a brilliant young scientist, Victor Frankenstein, who succeeds in fulfilling the romantic dream of creating life from inert matter. But the monster he creates is so foul that he abandons it on the very night when he brings it to life. Lusting for vengeance, the creature kills all those who are dearest to Frankenstein and finally, after months of torment, destroys his creator himself. But the novel is much subtler than this stark outline suggests, and its subtlety is reflected in the complexity of its organization.

It consists not of a simple straightforward narrative but of a double framework. The outer framework comprises a group of letters written from Russia by a young British explorer, Robert Walton, to his sister in England. Half a year into a journey of discovery to the Arctic Walton encounters, drifting on an ice floe, an exhausted human being who turns out to be Frankenstein. During the days of his convalescence Frankenstein tells Walton the story of his life. The first five chapters recount Frankenstein's childhood and youth in Switzerland and his studies in Germany—notably his early obsession with the arcane researches of Albertus Magnus and Paracelsus, which leads to his pursuit at the university of the latest developments in "real" science. These studies culminate in the construction of a huge, sallow, yellow-eyed creature into which he manages to "infuse a spark of being" (p. 56). Chapters six through ten describe Frankenstein's illness produced by the shock of his creation, the news that his brother has been murdered, the trial and execution of an innocent servant-girl of the family, and Frankenstein's confrontation with the monster on a glacial field just beneath Mont Blanc.

At this point Frankenstein's narrative is interrupted for six chapters in which the creature recounts his own adventures during the intervening months: how he learned to talk by observing a family from his hideaway, how he educated himself by studying the literary classics, and how his attempts to enter human society by means of kind deeds were always repulsed by people horrified at his savage appearance. He ends his account by asking Frankenstein to create a female partner with whom he might share his loneliness in a self-imposed exile. The narrative now returns to Frankenstein, who tentatively agrees to the bargain and sets up a laboratory on "one of the remotest of the Orkneys." But at the last moment, overcome by the thought that he might be enabling the monster to propagate itself and destroy the human race, Frankenstein tears apart the still lifeless body he has assembled and flees. Now the monster's rampage of terror begins: in quick succession he kills Frankenstein's best friend and his bride; Frankenstein's father dies of grief. For months Frankenstein pursues his creature, but the monster manages to stay just ahead of him, from "the wilds of Tartar" to the Arctic wastes, always making sure that his creator catches sight of him often enough to continue his fanatical pursuit and that he finds enough food and shelter to keep himself barely alive. When the monster realizes that Walton is taking Frankenstein back to England to recover in safety, he boards the ship and murders his maker. In a final confrontation he assures Walton that, his vengeance now complete, he intends to destroy his own body on a funeral pyre so that "its remains may afford no light to any curious and unhallowed wretch who would create such another as I have been" (pp. 210-11). The novel ends as the monster springs from the cabin window and bounds away through the icy wastes, leaving behind a sobered Walton, who forsakes, for the benefit of his family and his crew, his bold dreams of scientific glory.

Mary Shelley was telling not just one story but three—not just the story of Victor Frankenstein but also that of his creature and of Robert Walton. Why does she spend six chapters—a quarter of the book—recapitulating the monster's adventures, which are unrelated to the rest of the plot? She wants us to understand that Frankenstein's creation is not evil in itself but has been made that way by society. Frankenstein's monster is not the plodding dull-witted creature as conceived by Boris Karloff. Though hideously ugly, it is awesomely strong and lithe, able to bound across mountain crags or Arctic wastes at superhuman speed. Its inherent intellectual abilities are so great that it learns, without assistance and within a matter of months, to speak a mellifluous Miltonic prose. Its sensibilities, nourished by the study of *Paradise Lost, The Sorrows of Young Werther*, and Plutarch's *Lives*, are noble; and its overtures to human society are all originally and instinctively beneficent. But every good act is rewarded with horror and violence by a society terrified at the creature's appearance. As he explains to Walton at the end of the novel, paraphrasing Milton's Satan: "Evil thenceforth became my good." "When I run over the frightful catalogue of my sins, I cannot believe that I am the same creature whose thoughts were once filled with sublime and transcendent visions of the beauty and the majesty of goodness. But it is even so; the fallen angel becomes a malignant devil" (pp. 209-210).

What we have here is more than the familiar topos of

natural man or the equally popular romantic notion that creatures created or born outside human history do not partake of original sin. We also find an emphatic statement that scientific creation is morally neutral, with a pronounced capacity—indeed, even a predisposition—for good, until it is corrupted by human society. This strong statement is necessary to balance Walton's narrative. For Frankenstein uses the account of his own experience to persuade Walton to renounce his dreams of discovery and scientific glory. "Seek happiness in tranquillity and avoid ambition, even if it be only the apparently innocent one of distinguishing yourself in science and discoveries" (p. 206).[11]

Situated between the inner narrative, which portrays the corruption of a good creation by society, and the outer framework, which depicts the enthusiasm and ambition of scientific discovery, Frankenstein's own story stands out in its full ambivalence. When we first hear Frankenstein's voice, shortly after he is rescued by Walton, it is the voice of a man utterly disenchanted with science. "You seek for knowledge and wisdom, as I once did; and I ardently hope that the gratification of your wishes may not be a serpent to sting you, as mine has been" (p. 28). Having seen the monster destroy his personal happiness, he has come to believe that it represents a threat to the entire human race. "My rage is unspeakable when I reflect that the murderer, whom I have turned loose upon society, still exists" (p. 190). But we must not forget that Frankenstein's entire narrative is colored by his ghastly experiences. The young Frankenstein, in contrast, was motivated by a passionate lust for knowledge. "The world was to me a secret which I desired to divine. Curiosity, earnest research to learn the hidden laws of nature, gladness akin to rapture, as they were unfolded to me, are among the earliest sensations I can remember" (p. 36). When we combine these remarks with the knowledge that the creature, though ugly, is by no means inherently evil, we begin to realize that scientific discovery, according to Mary Shelley, becomes

evil only when the scientist refuses to assume responsibility for his creation—that is, when he turns it loose
to be acted upon by an uncomprehending society. If
Victor Frankenstein had not been overcome by his initial
disgust, if he had responded to his creature with love
and understanding, it might have become an instrument
of good rather than of evil.

It would be inconsistent with everything we know
about European romanticism to think that Mary Shelley
meant her novel as a blanket indictment of the pursuit
of knowledge *per se*. Instead it is a cautionary tale against
a science divorced from ethical responsibility.[12] Whereas
the Enlightenment and early German romanticism had
often carried the obsession with science for science's sake
to extremes, and whereas religion, in reaction against
the Enlightenment, had sometimes revealed its hostility
to scientific discovery from astronomy to geology and
biology, later European romanticism was inspired by an
awareness of the ambivalence of scientific discovery and
the quest for truth. Victor Frankenstein is the linear
ancestor of the physicists in the modern German dramas.
Motivated at the outset by the quest for pure knowledge,
he makes a discovery that involves an enormous potential for good. But because he renounces the responsibility
for his discovery, it is subverted by society and becomes
a tool of evil. At that point the scientist rejects his earlier
attitude of pure investigation and makes the "political"
decision to destroy his findings and to dissuade others
from similar investigations.

Students of popular culture have observed that the
figure of the scientist as represented in works of pop-
science—notably comic books, monster movies, and TV
series—is overwhelmingly negative in our time.[13] And
the figure of Victor Frankenstein, as it emerges in most
of the popular versions of the story, has suffered from
this contamination. To the extent that Frankenstein himself is characterized as evil in the films, it is usually left
to an enraged populace to destroy the monster—a democratic uprising that has no parallel in Mary Shelley's

more elitist text. The figure of the romantic scientist is much more subtle and partakes of all the ambiguity attached to the questions of scientific ethics stirred up by the events surrounding the atomic bomb. But how did this ambivalence arise? I suggest that it emerges from the uncomfortable synthesis of two conflicting traditions regarding science and knowledge.

III

ONE OF THESE TRADITIONS is specified by the subtitle of the novel: *Frankenstein, or The Modern Prometheus*. As Raymond Trousson has shown in his magisterial study, Prometheus was one of the figures most appealing to the poets of European pre-romanticism, from Shaftesbury and Rousseau to Goethe and Herder.[14] Moreover, during the very years when Mary Shelley was writing *Frankenstein* her husband was composing his lyrical drama *Prometheus Unbound*. Yet after the title page the novel contains not a single reference to the mythological figure. It remains for the reader to deduce in what respects Victor Frankenstein can be said to be a modern Prometheus. The frequent references in the novel to electricity and lightning remind us that Prometheus incurred the wrath of the gods by stealing fire for mankind. A further analogy can be detected in the legend according to which Prometheus created the human race by fashioning men of clay. But that is as far as the analogy can be pursued. For his theft of fire Prometheus was punished by being chained to a mountain in the Caucasus, where each day an eagle appeared to eat away his liver, which renewed itself for the eagle's delectation every day for thirty thousand years. Unlike Frankenstein, however, Prometheus never succumbs to his punishment. He was beloved by the romantics precisely because of his titanic spirit of rebelliousness. Far from being beset by doubts, the romantic Prometheus is, in Shelley's words, "the type of the highest perfection of moral and intellectual nature, impelled by the purest and the truest motives to the best and noblest ends."[15] What distinguishes him from such rebels as Satan and makes him more poetical, Shelley continues in the preface to *Prometheus Unbound*, is the fact that "in addition to courage, and majesty, and firm and patient opposition to omnipotent force, he is susceptible of being described as exempt from the taints of ambition, envy, revenge, and a desire for personal aggrandisement. ...." These words could hardly be applied to Victor Frankenstein, who apart from his obsession with fire is a Prometheus *manqué*: he creates a man, to be sure, but it is a flawed man. Instead of serving society, Frankenstein becomes its nemesis, having created a monster that threatens its destruction. Indeed, his name itself has become anathema, the very definition of the evil scientist. The ambiguity of Mary Shelley's modern Prometheus is produced, I would argue, through its contamination by a parallel legend from a totally different source: the biblical Adam.

Here the text does help us, for although it lacks specific references to the myth of Prometheus, it is replete with images borrowed from the first few chapters of Genesis. Most frequently, to be sure, it is the monster himself, fresh from his study of *Paradise Lost*, who sees himself as a new Adam, gamboling in the fields of Paradise but abandoned by his creator. In this analogy, of course, Frankenstein is equivalent to God the Creator. But in several other passages Frankenstein uses biblical imagery to characterize his own situation. At one point, after the monster has warned him that he will seek him out on his wedding night, Frankenstein thinks of his beloved Elizabeth. "Some softened feelings stole into my heart and dared to whisper paradisical dreams of love and joy; but the apple was already eaten, and the angel's arm bared to drive me from all hope" (p. 180)—a clear allusion to the sin of knowledge, which Frankenstein took upon himself by his search for forbidden knowledge.

This cluster of images alerts us to another dimension of the novel. Adam, like Prometheus, is both functionally and by etymological designation a scientist. He performs the typically scientific functions of naming and classifying nature. And, as the serpent tells Eve, if she and Adam will eat of the fruit of the Tree of Knowledge, they will become as gods, knowing (*scientes*) good and evil. There is an essential difference, however. Whereas Prometheus was venerated for his scientific achievements, Adam was lamented. From the sixth century B.C. the quest for scientific knowledge provided one of the most powerful motivations for Greek culture. The Hebrews had an entirely different conception. "In much wisdom is much grief; and he that increaseth knowledge [the Vulgate uses the term *scientia*] increaseth sorrow" (Eccl. i:18). The ambivalence regarding science that we encounter in *Frankenstein* results from a conflation of these two opposing views. In both cultures we encounter the paradigm of the scientist who seeks to increase knowledge by probing hitherto forbidden secrets; in both cases new consciousness is brought to the human race as a result of the scientific discovery; and both scientists receive typically political punishment for their transgressions: Prometheus is imprisoned and Adam is sent into exile. But the difference between their reactions to their fates produces the ambivalence toward science in our modern society, which arises from the dual traditions of Judeo-Christian and Greco-Roman culture: Adam skulks out of Eden, ashamed of his knowledge and deplored by all posterity for his Fall; Prometheus remains defiant in his attitude, cheered by the gratitude of the human race, until he is ultimately liberated by a tyrannical Zeus.

The analogy between the two myths has been recognized by theologians and poets since the Renaissance—especially the parallel between the temptresses Eve and Pandora. Milton, for instance, speaks of Eve "in naked beauty more adorned, / More lovely than Pandora, whom the gods / Endowed with all their gifts" (*Paradise Lost*, 4.713-15). Dora and Erwin Panofsky have shown, in their iconographical study of *Pandora's Box*, how fruitful the association became for post-Renaissance art. In the nineteenth century the interest shifted to the analogy between Adam and Prometheus, who were seen to exemplify the differences between Nazarene and Hellene that had been made popular by Heinrich Heine and Matthew Arnold, among others. This tradition culminates in Nietzsche, who argues in *The Birth of Tragedy* (Ch. 9) that the myth of Prometheus has the same characteristic significance for Aryan man as does the myth of the Fall for Semitic man. In both cases, Nietzsche suggests, mankind achieves its highest goal, cognition, through an act of sacrilege. In the Greek myth the sacrilege is perpetrated consciously in the interest of human achievement and dignity; in the Hebrew myth, in contrast, it is prompted by idle curiosity and the reaction is shame.

We can now see that Mary Shelley's novel represents a surprisingly early conflation of the two representative myths. It is well-known that during the composition of the novel Mary Shelley and her husband studied *Paradise Lost* and *Prometheus Bound*—that the Bible and Aeschylus' drama were therefore very much in her mind as she worked. But is has not been sufficiently stressed that her inability to reconcile the conflict inherent in her two sources—between pride and shame in cognition—produced for the first time that ambivalence toward scientific knowledge that we have come to regard as characteristically modern.

We can go a step further in our analysis. The myths of the Fall and of Prometheus, while they stand close to the beginning of their respective mythological traditions, at the crucial juncture between cosmology and human history, are in fact relatively late interpolations that go back to earlier Oriental sources. Homer was aware of various legends attached to Prometheus, but he did not bother to include them in his mythology.[16] Hesiod was the first of the Greeks to tell the story, but his version, related in his *Theogony* (ll. 517-616) and again in *Works and Days* (ll. 42-105), is patchy and inconsistent. We read of Prometheus' attempt to deceive Zeus at the feast of gods and men and Zeus' decision to punish mankind by withholding fire from them; we hear of the theft of fire; we are told about the displeasure of the gods, who send Pandora to marry Prometheus' brother, Epimetheus. But there is no symbolic interpretation of the events: the fire is still specifically alimentary in function and not symbolic of knowledge in general. The first consistent version of the legend was written by Aeschylus shortly before the middle of the fifth century B.C. In *Prometheus Bound* Aeschylus strips the archetype of all non-essentials: notably, the motif of Pandora and Epimetheus. Moreover, the detail concerning Prometheus as the creator of men—the feature that particularly appealed to the romantic poets—was a late addition, inspired by conflation of Prometheus with a local Attic god of pottery, that had not yet entered the legend. For Aeschylus, Prometheus is first and foremost a culture-hero: the Titan who, out of his love for mankind, brought knowledge—that is, science and the arts—to man symbolically through the gift of fire (ll. 436-506). Before Prometheus gave them "understanding and a portion of reason," men lived like children. "Seeing they saw not, and hearing they understood not." Prometheus did not simply steal fire for them: he taught them to build houses and to weave fabrics, to understand the seasons, and to know the stars; to count and to write; to tame beasts and to build ships. "All human arts are from Prometheus." (The image of fire that we associate with Prometheus became so central to the archetype of the scientist that we can trace it through the crackling electrical instruments and lightning flashes that dominate every Frankenstein film right down to Robert Oppenheimer at Los Alamos, who allegedly reacted to the first explosion of the atomic bomb by reciting to himself the words from the *Bhagavad-Gita* that describe the "radiance of a thousand suns"—a clear instance of the extent to which our imagination is shaped by cultural images or, to put it more crudely, life imitates art.) For Aeschylus science and knowledge may bring suffering; but the acquisition of knowledge stems from a decision consciously made, with dignity and with the full acceptance of ethical responsibility for the act.

The legend of the Fall also occurs relatively late in the formation of Hebrew thought.[17] It is generally agreed that its author, the so-called Yahwist, was writing after the time of Solomon—that is, following the events depicted in the Old Testament down to the times of Chronicles II. Most of the elements of the story—including a garden of paradise with its serpent, a tree of knowledge, and a temptress—had long been present in a variety of Near Eastern sources, such as the Gilgamesh Epic. The Hebrews were no doubt aware of these tales, but it was not until the tenth century B.C., well after the ethical system of Judaism was firmly established and the race already had a long history, that it seemed desirable or useful to include the story of the Fall as the background of human history. When the narrator of Genesis did incorporate those ancient legends, he shifted their emphasis in a manner that stamps them unmistakably as Hebrew. In Genesis, as opposed to the Gilgamesh Epic, it is sin, not fate, that causes man's "Fall." In Sumero-Akkadian mythology it was perfectly acceptable for man to have divine understanding; Enkidu achieves godlike wisdom through his union with the priestess of love. It was eternal life that the gods prohibited; Gilgamesh seeks the herb of immortality, not the Tree of Knowledge. In Genesis the circumstances are reversed; God is content for Adam and Eve to eat of the Tree of Life—at least, until they have sinned by tasting the fruit from the forbidden Tree of Knowledge.

What I am suggesting is this: the two great myths of knowledge and responsibility, of science and ethics, are "relatively simultaneous" in Spengler's sense and therefore analogous in their cultural function. Although the constitutive elements of both myths had long been present in both cultures, the myths themselves received their authoritative form—in Genesis and in Aeschylus' *Prometheus Bound*—at that moment in the history of their peoples when consciousness had developed to a point at which man had become aware of its problematic nature. It has often been pointed out that myths of paradise or a Golden Age arise from an urban nostalgia for the lost joys of rural life—more or less the conditions in the sophistication of Solomon's Jerusalem or the so-called Greek Enlightenment of fifth-century Athens. At a certain point, in any case, the myths were introduced retrospectively into the existing mythological systems in order to explain etiologically each society's attitude toward scientific advances.

If this model is correct, we can see it verified at other points in history. We have already noted that *Frankenstein*, to the extent that it was a response to an unrestrained commitment to "pure" science, fulfilled precisely the same function for romanticism. If we glance for a moment at the other great modern myth of the scientist—the legend of Faust, who signs a pact with the Devil to obtain knowledge not accessible by ordinary scientific means—we see that precisely the same analogy obtains. I am speaking, of course, not of Goethe's *Faust*, a late treatment of the theme that expresses the romantic ambivalence toward science and knowledge, but of the sixteenth-century chapbook in which *The Historie of the damnable life, and deserved death of Doctor John Faustus* was first completely recorded.

In its original form of 1587 the chapbook of Faust was a Reformation tract aimed at the untrammeled scientific investigations of the Renaissance that threatened to undermine traditional bourgeois values. For these reasons the Faust of the chapbooks is portrayed in the foulest possible light: he is not merely a charlatan and a magician but also a ruffian and a pederast. The author of the tract wants to make sure that we have absolutely no sympathy for Faust, who is not yet the noble figure— "the branch that might have grown full straight"—that he was to become only a few years later in Marlowe's tragedy. This Faust is a degenerate, and his lust for forbidden knowledge, like his lust for food or women or

young boys, is simply another example of his degeneracy. It is fitting, therefore, that he ends up ignominiously.

> But when it was day, the Students that had taken
> no rest that night, arose and went into the hall in
> which they left Doctor Faustus, where notwith-
> standing they found no Faustus, but all the hall lay
> besprinkled with blood, his brains cleaving to the
> wall: for the Devil had beaten him from one wall
> against another, in one corner lay his eyes, in an-
> other his teeth, a pitiful and fearful sight to behold.
> Then began the Students to bewail and weep for
> him and sought for his body in many places: lastly
> they came into the yard where they found his body
> lying on the horse dung, most monstrously torn,
> and fearful to behold, for his head and all his joints
> were dashed in pieces.[18]

Faust, in short, is the Protestant equivalent of the Hebrew myth of the Fall. In both cases a stern and ascetic
religious attitude vents its abhorrence of the quest for
knowledge that it considers forbidden. When, during the
romantic age, the puritanical Judeo-Christian attitude
was mollified by the introduction of the Greco-Roman
tradition and the story of Prometheus, a new image of
the scientist emerged from that synthesis: Goethe's *Faust*,
in which the scientist, for all his faults, is redeemed; and
Mary Shelley's *Frankenstein*, in which the quest for scientific knowledge attains the classic expression of its
modern ambivalence.

IV

WE CAN DRAW several conclusions from these examples.
First of all, our survey has shown that the details change
in accordance with the currently fashionable science: the
hero may be a stealer of fire like Prometheus, a magician
like Faust, a galvanist like Frankenstein, a physicist like
Einstein, or in some drama yet to be written a biochemist
cloning new homunculi. But the archetypal pattern re-

mains remarkably constant from Adam to Einstein. In every case humanity looks on with wonder and awe as the seeker strives after forbidden knowledge and, following its acquisition, is appalled at the ethical implications of his science. There has been a gradual internalization of the story, from works in which scientists are punished drastically by such external agents as gods or the devil to the other extreme at which the scientist suffers only the pangs of his own conscience. But this archetypal motif, in the various thematic forms it assumes over the ages, provides the exclamation mark that punctuates the prose of the history of science. The legends mark those moments in the growth of human consciousness when mankind, forced to the outer limits by startling new developments in scientific knowledge, must grapple with its conscience to establish the delicate balance between progress and ethics. People are not disturbed by technological advances: the man who reckons his income tax with a pocket calculator can come to terms with the most sophisticated computer; anyone who has flown in a jetliner can cope imaginatively with space flight. It is new ideas that cause the leaps in consciousness: the notion that the earth revolves around the sun and that man is therefore no longer the center of creation; that matter is composed of energy and that therefore the atom can be split; that life can be created *in vitro* or altered by genetic engineering.

We should be alerted, therefore, when the figure of Frankenstein begins to be invoked frequently and almost routinely in public discussions, for his name—as we have seen in the case of the atomic bomb—is one of the code words that signal a profound cultural malaise. Time does not stand still. In the rhetoric of our nightmares the ominous mushroom cloud of Hiroshima has been displaced by the delicate coils of the double helix. In the summer of 1976, when heated debates were taking place on the campuses of many universities concerning recombinant DNA research, Mayor Alfred Vellucci of Cambridge, Massachusetts, voiced his strong opposition to

a so-called P3 facility that Harvard proposed to construct on the fourth floor of its biology laboratory. "We
want to be damned sure the people of Cambridge won't
be affected by anything that could crawl out of that
laboratory. . . . They may come up with a disease that
can't be cured, even a monster. Is this the answer to Dr.
Frankenstein's dream?"[19] With his inspired allusion Mayor
Vellucci seems to have touched an archetypal sore spot.
Ever since, poor Frankenstein has again enjoyed a remarkably bad press—yet a press quite consistent with
his actual function as the creator of new life. The *Washington Star* headlined its report on the Cambridge controversy: "Is Harvard the Proper Place for Frankenstein
Tinkering?" Later that year a correspondent wrote to
Science magazine: "Are we really that much further along
on the path to comprehensive knowledge that we can
forget the overwhelming pride with which Dr. Frankenstein made his monster? . . . Like the physicists before
us, we have entered the realm of the Faustian bargain,
and it behooves all of us biologists to think very carefully
about the conditions of these agreements before we plunge
ahead into the darkness."[20] Michael Rogers entitled a
chapter of his book *Biohazard* (1977) "The Frankenstein
Syndrome." And at the beginning of their study of genetic engineering, *Who Should Play God?* (1977), Ted
Howard and Jeremy Rifkin justified their topic by saying: "Once, all of this could be dismissed as science
fiction, or the mad ravings of a Dr. Frankenstein. No
more" (p. 15). It was no doubt such examples as these
that led William Barrett to conclude in *The Illusion of
Technique* that "the suspicion of technology has become
so widespread that the dominant myth of our time may
become that of Frankenstein's monster."[21]

Donald D. Brown, Director of the Carnegie Institution, completely misses the point when he objects that
"Frankensteinian spectres raised by proponents of re-
striction are mostly emotional, political, rhetorical and
unscientific."[22] Of course they are! Yet to a much greater
extent than reason is often willing to acknowledge, our

thinking—not to mention our voting—is governed by emotion and rhetoric, no matter how unscientific they may be.

It behooves us, therefore, to ponder these ancient myths and their underlying patterns. Science has provided us with a number of images that have been applied more or less illuminatingly to human affairs: we speak of relativity in morals, entropy in business, a quantum leap in political relations, or the uncertainty principle in human psychology. Conversely men seem to need myth in order to cope with the human implications of scientific discovery: the biochemists talk of Frankenstein and Oppenheimer chants Vedic poetry. In the beginning science *was* the science of ethics: Adam came away from the Tree of Knowledge knowing precious little about physics or biochemistry but a great deal about Good and Evil. Down to the eighteenth century science was largely subordinated to theology. During the Age of Reason science gradually liberated itself from that domination until, in the nineteenth century, it attained the romantic goal of a value-free science. Frankenstein, anticipating the physicists of the German dramas, stresses the initially playful and, in the loftiest sense, ethically irresponsible aspect of his research.

But doubts—perhaps a nagging theological conscience—have clouded "pure" scientific inquiry from its romantic beginnings. Since Hiroshima science has become increasingly public, social, and hence explicitly ethical again. Its issues are a matter of urgent concern not just to theologians and philosophers but also to the general public.[23] Citizens want to know whether or not they are exposed to biological danger from the laboratory next door, to radiation from the nuclear power reactor down the road, or to falling fragments from a disintegrating Skylab. The scientists themselves participate in the controversy. The epoch-making Asilomar Conference on the ethics of genetic manipulation in 1975 produced the NIH guidelines that catalyzed the public debates in 1976. The records of almost any hearings on biohazards—e.g. the Academy Forum of March 7-9, 1977, sponsored by the National Academy of Sciences—attest to the scientists' own perplexity and ambivalence regarding the proper relationship between the ideal of absolute freedom of inquiry and their responsibility to society. (So far the discussion has been liveliest in the United States. But in Germany recently the debate has been complicated by references to the "absolute freedom of inquiry" enjoyed and perpetrated by scientists in the Nazi concentration camps.) Concerned groups have established such forums as the Hastings Institute of Society, Ethics, and the Life Sciences and the Center for Bioethics in Washington. The National Endowment for the Humanities has sponsored a series of seminars in which scientists meet representatives of various disciplines in order to explore the social and ethical implications of their research. Frankenstein, in short, has emerged from his laboratory to attend the town meetings. Faust has swapped his flying wine keg for the Concorde that spirits him from conference to conference. The question concerning the ethics of science once again enjoys the urgency that it did in the misty beginnings of Western civilization. It may well turn out that the conclusions of these conferences on the most timely scientific advances will produce little more than variations and elaborations on the ancient myths of Adam and Prometheus, on the legends of Faust and Frankenstein. We would therefore do well to look again and again at those tales in the light of present experience, if we wish to understand the public response to scientific discovery. Science may change, but man remains constant, and myth is the record of that constant, eternal humanity. In the last analysis nothing is more modern than myth.

APPENDIX

Appendix

A PRACTICAL GUIDE
TO LITERARY THEMATICS

I

THIS APPENDIX has evolved by accretion from a bibliography I prepared some years ago for students of comparative literature at Princeton University who participated in my seminar on thematic research. Despite an abundance of books and articles dealing with the history, theory, and terminology of *Stoffgeschichte*, or thematology (to mention that unfortunate term), there was no bibliographical or methodological guide directed to the practical needs of students wishing to pursue research on thematic topics. Over the years I added new titles to the list, and I have now provided a running commentary describing the usefulness of each work and the sequence according to which, in my experience, each might be most profitably consulted. This excursus does not aspire to be a systematic bibliography. For their own valid reasons bibliographers present materials in a sequence— alphabetically, or chronologically, or by some other system—unlike that followed by the practicing scholar working his way through the library in pursuit of a specific topic. This vade-mecum purports to be nothing more than an informal and, inevitably, idiosyncratic guide to the research tools and procedures I have found most productive in my own work. I hope that my remarks and comments will be useful to students who have not already become acquainted, through trial and error, with the sources cited here. The experienced scholar of lit-

erary thematics may choose to skip this section altogether. Yet perhaps curiosity will prompt some to eaves-
drop on what amounts to shoptalk among colleagues
interested in a common field of endeavor.

For the purposes of this excursus I understand under
"literary thematics" nothing more and nothing less than
studies like the ones represented in the preceding chapters. I have addressed myself elsewhere—in the Introduction to *Disenchanted Images: A Literary Iconology*
(Princeton, N.J.: Princeton Univ. Press, 1977)—to problems of definition regarding such central and disputed
terms as image, theme, motif, and symbol. I would be
reluctant to distract from the pragmatic concerns of this
manual by entering that interminable debate again at
this point. For the benefit of those who wish to inform
themselves, I append at the end of the chapter a list of
works concerning the theory and terminology of literary
thematics.

This essay assumes a disposition toward literary thematics on the part of the reader. I cannot imagine why
anyone without prior interest should have picked up a
book with this title in the first place or, having done so
by mistake, should have read it through to this point.
All theoretical reasons aside, why does anyone undertake research on a topic of literary thematics? Possibly
the student has been assigned a topic for a class report—
say, the history of the Faust theme for a course on Goethe
or Marlowe, or the motif of the man between two women
as a pattern in eighteenth-century literature, or the image
of the nightingale in romantic poetry. Indeed, during
certain periods in Germany and France thematic topics
were routinely handed out for dissertations: e.g., the
sixteen volumes in the series "Stoff- und Motivgeschichte
der deutschen Literatur," edited by Paul Merker and
Gerhardt Lüdtke (1929-1937). It was rumored in Leipzig at the time that sheer professorial caprice allotted to
Hansgeorg Kind the topic: *Das Kind in der Ideologie
und der Dichtung der deutschen Romantik* (Dresden:
Dittert, 1936). Assuming, however, that the topic has

not been assigned—to a student by a professor or to a teacher by the demands of a course-syllabus—I would imagine that whimsy and chance play a role more often than people sometimes assume about scholarship. I can only guess what impelled Moritz Steinschneider to write his essay on the cultural history of lapidaries (cited in Chapter Two). A play on the authors' forename and nickname is hidden in the title of Dora and Erwin Panofsky's classic iconographical study, *Pandora's Box* (New York: Bollingen, 1956). Jürgen Einhorn, in a concluding digression on names, frankly acknowledges the onomastic curiosity that informed his study *Spiritalis unicornis: Das Einhorn als Bedeutungsträger in Literatur und Kunst des Mittelalters* (cited in Chapter Two). Most of us do not have names that so charmingly elicit a thematic interpretation, but that lack does not rule out the personal element. I had just celebrated my thirtieth birthday when I happened to read in quick succession— for course preparation—three novels with a thirty-year-old hero, and that conjunction prompted me to pursue more systematically "The Crisis of the Thirty-Year-Old in Modern Fiction," which eventually became a chapter in my *Dimensions of the Modern Novel* (Princeton, N.J.: Princeton Univ. Press, 1968). Walther Rehm's beautifully evocative thematic monograph on *Europäische Romdichtung* (1939; rpt. Munich: Hueber, 1960) was stimulated, as he graciously acknowledged in both prefaces, by happy days and weeks spent in that unforgettable city. Cases of this sort exemplify the spirit of playfulness that underlies much thematic research.

In every instance I can recall vividly the reasons underlying my own fascination with the topics that make up the chapters of this book. It stemmed inevitably from an accident of simultaneous or closely sequential reading of two or more works in which the same image or theme or motif occurs strikingly, often coupled with some external stimulus. My curiosity about carbuncles, for instance, dates back to a period during my graduate studies at Yale University when I happened to read Novalis'

Heinrich von Ofterdingen and Wolfram von Eschen-bach's *Parzival* at the same time and wondered how the magical stone acquired its reputation for luminosity in the first place and then retained its glow for the six hundred years between the Middle High German courtly romance and the romantic novel. The talking dogs started gnawing at my imagination when, for a freshman course on European Short Fiction, I drew up a syllabus includ-ing tales by Cervantes, Hoffmann, and Gogol and no-ticed through that conjunction of texts that all of them included the figure of the garrulous canine that, during the seventies, was also showing up frequently in tele-vision commercials advertising dog food. The observa-tion, which first produced nothing more than a two-page feature for TV GUIDE, would not let go until I had worked it out more fully in the form presented here. Thomas Mann's obsession with teeth as a means of char-acterization is a critical commonplace. While I was pe-rusing Koestler's *Darkness at Noon* and Greene's *The Power and the Glory* for a wholly different purpose, it struck me that those two writers also made extensive use of the same image. Then when I encountered Günther Grass's *Local Anaesthetic* a short time later, I began to think that I had stumbled onto a topic worth boring into.

The point is this: unless the topic has been assigned, then you are often well along with your own thinking and collecting before you realize that you are already engaged on a bit of literary thematics. I tend to jot down the first few occurrences of a potential topic on a sheet of paper that I toss into a folder containing many other topics. When the examples for any given topic reach what I think of as a certain *density* or specific gravity, I make a separate folder and begin to think about it more systematically. Many topics never mature; my files are filled with topics waiting for further examples—or with examples waiting for a motivating idea. Density is a matter of judgment. I started thinking systematically about talking dogs when I had only three or four ex-amples because the examples all came from powerful writers—Cervantes, Hoffmann, Gogol, Kafka—and anything that won their attention certainly deserved mine. The carbuncles had to pile up for several years before I was convinced that their sheer frequency justified more careful consideration.

Other factors also count in the process of consideration. It is not enough simply to fill in a gap in the bibliography of thematic studies. I must convince myself that the study will contribute something to my understanding of both the literary texts and their cultural background—that the labor, in other words, will be worth the effort. For several years after I had completed my essay on "The Crisis of the Thirty-Year-Old" I collected—and, in fact, still do collect—literary examples illustrating other generational crises: my file is teeming with forty-year-old heroes, and I have started on the fifty-year-olds. But I finally decided that the topic would not teach me anything that I had not already learned from the thirty-year-old. The examples are different, and each crisis involves different implications. But from the standpoint of literary scholarship, and even existentially, I would be forced to cover much of the same ground; the returns would not justify the investment of time. Yet that does not mean that the topic is not a valid one. Finally, the topic needs to be sufficiently compelling— and, if you are lucky, amusing—to sustain interest for a long period of time. Thematic studies cannot be rushed; the period of collection often lasts for years. In fact, one test of a topic is that the memory remains lively enough to remind me to add ever new examples to the file. There are specific stages, however, through which any study ought to proceed once it reaches a certain point. The reference works I cite in the sections that follow are selective; but I believe that the stages of research are valid in every case.

II

As SOON as I begin to believe that a topic deserves a closer look, I take the first step: a quick preliminary bibliographical scan to find out whether or not the work has already been done and, if so, how well. The bibliographical scan is reasonably simple if you are interested in a theme or figure—from mythology, history, culture, or literature—that is identifiable by a specific name: e.g., Faust, Don Juan, Odysseus, Shakespeare, Raphael, Beethoven. I always reach first for a volume that I keep at hand on my desk: Elisabeth Frenzel's *Stoffe der Weltliteratur: Ein Lexikon dichtungsgeschichtlicher Längsschnitte* (1962; 4th ed. Stuttgart: Kröner, 1976). Frenzel's lexicon comprises some three hundred topics or themes arranged alphabetically from Abelard to Niklas Zrinyi. Each entry identifies the subject and outlines the historical or literary background; it goes on to discuss the principal treatments of each theme in world literature; and it concludes with a concise bibliography of the most important secondary studies in various languages. Thus the rubric "Odysseus" directs the reader to W. B. Stanford's standard work on *The Ulysses Theme*; the section on Don Juan refers to Leo Weinstein's *The Metamorphoses of Don Juan*; and so forth.

Frenzel can be supplemented by several other works that, though overlapping in certain respects, provide additional information. Erwin Heinzel's two works—*Lexikon historischer Ereignisse und Personen in Kunst, Literatur und Musik* (Vienna: Hollinek, 1956) and *Lexikon der Kulturgeschichte in Literatur, Kunst und Musik* (Vienna: Hollinek, 1962)—concentrate, as the titles suggest, not on mythological or literary subjects but on figures and events from history and cultural life, many of which are not included in Frenzel (e.g., Dreyfus, Schubert, the French Revolution); they also include references to paintings and musical works depicting the theme as well as literary treatments. Herbert Hunger's *Lexikon der griechischen und römischen Mythologie* (1953; 6th ed. Vienna: Hollinek, 1969) cites studies dealing with themes and motifs from classical antiquity in the art, literature, and music of the West down to the present. All these works are comparative in scope.

If the topic involves not a specific theme or figure that can be identified by name but a more general motif or type or situation, other bibliographical sources are available. The most general one is again by Elisabeth Frenzel: *Motive der Weltliteratur: Ein Lexikon dichtungsge-schichtlicher Längsschnitte* (Stuttgart: Kröner, 1976). The organization is similar to that of *Stoffe der Weltliteratur*. But since the entries deal with general motifs—like Arcadia, *Doppelgänger*, incest, father-son conflict—rather than specific themes, they tend to be considerably longer. (In *Stoffe der Weltliteratur*, for instance, Wilhelm Tell has a separate three-page entry for himself; in *Motive der Weltliteratur*, in contrast, he merits only one paragraph in a fifteen-page discussion of the "Rebell.") Often the user must browse around among the fifty entries in order to find the appropriate heading for the motif that interests him, but it is well worth the time required to familiarize himself with this valuable tool. Similar to Frenzel is the *Dictionnaire des types et caractères litté-raires*, ed. Claude Aziza, Claude Olivieri, and Robert Sctrick (Paris: Fernand Nathan, 1978), which lists figures and types from *actant, acteur*, and *amant* to *voleur* and *voyageur*, as they occur in important works of world literature, as well as representative secondary studies dealing with each. (I know of no similar work in English; but Greenwood Press has announced the preparation of a *Dictionary of Literary Themes and Motifs* explicitly patterned after the lexicons of Frenzel and Aziza.)

In addition to the lexicons cited above an exceedingly useful bibliography of themes and motifs in German literature includes many references to studies dealing with world literature: Franz Anselm Schmitt's *Stoff- und Motivgeschichte der deutschen Literatur: Eine Biblio-graphie* (1959; 3rd ed. Berlin: De Gruyter, 1976), which contains 8,000 bibliographical listings for more than 1,500 topics—themes as well as motifs—listed alphabetically from Abelard, Abel, *Abend*, and *Abenteuer* to *Zwilling* and Zwingli.

A vast bibliographical apparatus is available, finally,

for works dealing with such non-human objects as symbols, images and icons. Any thorough search ought to begin with Manfred Lurker's three-volume *Bibliographie zur Symbolkunde* (Baden-Baden: Heitz, 1964-66), which includes a detailed index of subjects that enables quick reference to bibliographical items on specific symbols and images. For specifically Christian iconography there are many works, of which I have found most useful the eight-volume *Lexikon der christlichen Ikonographie*, ed. Engelbert Kirschbaum (Freiburg im Breisgau: Herder, 1968-1976).

Only at this point, if the specific lexicons of themes, motifs, and symbols have failed, is it feasible to turn to the more general bibliographies, which are often less convenient to use because they indiscriminately list themes, motifs, symbols, images, figures, types, and everything else that might conceivably fall into this category. The basic work here is the *Bibliography of Comparative Literature* by Fernand Baldensperger and Werner P. Friederich (1950; rpt. New York: Russell & Russell, 1960), which includes as Part Six a major bibliography of "Literary Themes *(Stoffgeschichte)*" (pp. 70-178). The bibliography is cumbersome because it heaps everything together unselectively in an alphabetical list. But if the works in Round 1 have failed to turn up anything, Baldensperger/Friederich should be the first step in the more tedious Round 2 of bibliographical combing since it subsumes all earlier bibliographies and provides the basis for all subsequent ones. Beginning in 1952 Baldensperger/Friederich was updated by the bibliographies published periodically in the *Yearbook of Comparative and General Literature*. After 1969 that bibliography was replaced by the annual *MLA International Bibliography*, which lists themes and motifs in world literature under the heading "General Literature." A systematic search for secondary studies dealing with a thematic topic would therefore begin with the *Bibliography of Comparative Literature*, continue to 1969 with the *Yearbook of Com-*

parative and General Literature, and come down to the present with the annual bibliographies of the MLA.

In addition to the general bibliographies you should also consult the excellent bibliographies of national literature that often contain citations for thematic studies. For instance, the *MLA International Bibliography* contains additional themes and motifs under the heading "General and Miscellaneous" within the various national literatures—items not included in the general section. Otto Klapp's annual *Bibliographie der französischen Literaturwissenschaft* includes a section on "Thèmes et motifs." The bibliographical works for German literary scholarship almost always contain references pertinent to comparative literature. The basis is provided by two bibliographies that appeared at mid-century and therefore supplement Baldensperger/Friederich: Josef Körner's standard *Bibliographisches Handbuch des deutschen Schrifttums* (3rd ed. Bern: Francke, 1949), which includes an entire section on themes and motifs (pp. 40-56); and Vol. XI/2 of Karl Goedeke's *Grundriß zur Geschichte der deutschen Dichtung* (2nd ed. Düsseldorf: Ehlemann, 1951), pp. 122-42. For the years 1945 to 1969 Clemens Köttelwesch's *Bibliographisches Handbuch der deutschen Literaturwissenschaft* (Frankfurt am Main: Vittorio Klostermann, 1973) contains a long section on "Stoffe, Motive, Themen, Gestalten, Topoi" (I, 744-826) and makes further information handily accessible through a detailed index in Vol. III. These listings are updated annually in the *Bibliographie der deutschen Literaturwissenschaft,* ed. Clemens Köttelwesch and Heinz-Georg Halbe, which covers "Stoff- und Motivgeschichte" in the section labeled "Deutsche Literaturgeschichte." These references may be supplemented by the section on "Stoffe und Motive" in the semi-annual critical bibliography *Germanistik: Internationales Referatenorgan mit bibliographischen Hinweisen,* as well as the *Jahrbuch für Internationale Germanistik,* where *Stoffgeschichte* is listed under the general heading "Komparatistik."

Anyone who has made these various bibliographical searches—first through the bibliographies of specific themes, motifs, and symbols; then through the bibliographies of comparative literature; and finally through the bibliographies of the various national literatures—may feel reasonably confident that he has not missed any conspicuous article or book dealing with his thematic topic in its literary context. The scholar familiar with his library—who knows, that is to say, where the various books are located and does not need to look them up in the card catalogue—should be able to carry out such a search in a few hours. It goes without saying that any adequate research library should own all of the works mentioned above.

For the most recent publications, of course, the student should regularly scan the reviews and lists of Books Received as well as the publishers' announcements in the appropriate journals. For thematic studies these would include not only such literary journals as *Comparative Literature, Arcadia, Revue de Littérature Comparée, Germanisch-Romanische Monatsschrift, Modern Language Review*, and the important journals of national literatures; but also such periodicals as *Journal of the History of Ideas, Archiv für Begriffsgeschichte, Symbolon: Jahrbuch für Symbolforschung*, and other similar ones. As thematic research again becomes popular, the constant check on new publications becomes increasingly important because of the significant lag between publication and bibliographical citation.

III

IF THE preliminary bibliographical survey has produced no satisfactory studies of the topic that interests you, you may decide to proceed with your own investigation. If so, the next step should be the systematic collection of primary material—that is, the most important literary works in which the theme, motif, or image plays a significant role. In thematic studies no realistic scholar ever expects to collect every example or—if, God forbid, he should happen to do so—to exhaust his reader by using them all. But we all live with the nightmare of bringing out a study that has managed to overlook an obvious major example. When I published "The Telltale Teeth" in *PMLA*, I omitted Frank Norris's *McTeague*, reasoning that the novel is about greed and gold rather than teeth. A barrage of letters from indignant Americanists persuaded me that I had made an error of judgment in the interests of economy. I have included that work in the revised version here.

Normally you already have several important examples at this point—the ones that initially alerted you to the topic. Some material comes to you through chance, as you browse through the library or read on wholly unrelated subjects; some can come from the suggestions of friends and colleagues aware that you are working on a given topic. However, there are also several more systematic procedures that help to generate new items for your list. I want to stress again that the following suggestions are selective and describe the works and procedures I have found useful for my own purposes— notably Western European literature from about 1750 to the present. Students working in other periods will no doubt turn up reference works germane to their own fields of specialization. Robert F. Arnold's *Allgemeine Bücherkunde zur neueren deutschen Literaturgeschichte*, 4th edition revised by Herbert Jacob (Berlin: De Gruyter, 1966) cites bibliographies of "Stoff- und Motivgeschichte" in a variety of national literatures and older periods (pp. 90-94). But I believe that the basic stages of research are applicable, *mutatis mutandis*, in most circumstances.

If you are interested in a theme or motif (in contrast to a non-human image), then the first scan may well have produced some primary material even if it did not turn up a thorough secondary study: notably Frenzel, Heinzel, Aziza, and Hunger. At this point it would be useful to consult another group of works that list primary texts by theme and motif but no secondary studies. One of the most fruitful sources is Bompiani's great nine-volume lexicon of world literature: *Dizionario letterario delle opere e dei personaggi di tutti i tempi e di tutte le letterature* (Milan: Bompiani, 1947-1950; with a two-volume supplement in 1964-66). Bompiani's exhaustive articles on specific works and (in vol. IX) on specific literary characters often contain references to other works in which the same character or theme reappears. Bompiani provided the model for two other useful works: Kindler's seven-volume *Literatur Lexikon* (Zürich: Kindler, 1965-72) and the Laffont-Bompiani *Dictionnaire des personnages littéraires et dramatiques de tous les temps et de tous les pays* (Paris: Société d'Édition de dictionnaires et encyclopédies, 1960). In addition to the above, Ernest A. Baker's *Guide to Historical Fiction* (New York: Macmillan, 1914) cites hundreds of works based on historical figures and events from classical antiquity to the present and organized according to a simple system.

If you are concerned with a general motif rather than a specific personage or theme, then another set of works provide useful leads, although they are restricted almost wholly to prose fiction. Elbert Lenrow's *Reader's Guide to Prose Fiction* (New York: Appleton-Century, 1940) is an annotated list of novels from world literature classified according to a wide variety of topics. Zella Allen Dixson's old but still useful *Comprehensive Subject Index to Universal Prose Fiction* (New York: Dodd, Mead, 1897) lists fiction under headings ranging from Abbeys and Acadia to Wycliffe, Yosemite, and Zoology. Much more limited, because it refers primarily to English and American literature of the nineteenth and early twentieth centuries, is Mary Rebecca Lingenfelter's *Vocations in Literature: An Annotated Bibliography* (2nd ed. Chicago: American Library Association, 1938), which analyzes 463 novels by some one hundred vocations ranging from actor, advertiser, and antique dealer to textile worker and trapper. This is also the place to mention Franz

Anselm Schmitt's earlier work, *Beruf und Arbeit in deutscher Erzählung: Ein literarisches Lexikon* (Stuttgart: Hiersemann, 1952), which lists more than twelve thousand literary works featuring some four hundred professions ranging from abbot and alchemist to *Zollbeamter* and zoologist. In this connection, finally, it is worth mentioning the unusual file of "Motive des Romans von 1800 bis 1850," which analyzes 2927 novels of the specified period by theme and motif. This unpublished collection of material by Dietrich Naumann may be consulted at the Institut für Deutsche Sprache und Literatur II at the Johann Wolfgang Goethe Universität in Frankfurt am Main. (See Naumann's report on his collection in *Germanisch-Romanische Monatsschrift*, N.F. 31 [1981], 304-317.) These (with the exception of Naumann) are some of the works I consulted, for instance, when I was collecting material for a study of mining and the miner as image and figure in romantic and post-romantic literature.

If you are interested in a non-human object (as symbol, image, icon), the first survey probably did not turn up much new material. (Indirectly, of course, bibliographies like Schmitt or Baldensperger/Friederich sometimes alert us to works in which a given image appears.) In these cases I have found it productive to turn first of all to the great historical dictionaries that cite passages exemplifying the usage of a given word—say "carbuncle" or "teeth"—at various periods. In addition to the *Oxford English Dictionary* I have found the following to be especially fruitful for my purposes: Grimms' *Deutsches Wörterbuch*, Littré's *Dictionnaire de la langue française*, Battaglia's *Grande Dizionario della Lingua Italiana*, and Du Cange's *Glossarium mediae et infimae latinitatis*. It is also stimulating to consult contemporary dictionaries used by writers during the period of interest: since my own work frequently involves, or indeed usually begins with, texts from the period of German romanticism, I routinely consult Adelung's standard five-volume *Gram-*

matisch-kritisches Wörterbuch. But each topic demands its own lexical references.

A second source of information is provided by the great encyclopedias. Here you should not content yourself with the standard modern works: *Britannica*, Larousse, Brockhaus, and others. The great eighteenth-century encyclopedias—notably the *Encyclopédie* and Chambers' *Cyclopaedia*—are valuable. For cultural topics the sixty-four volumes of Zedler's *Großes vollständiges Universal-Lexikon* provide an incomparable and almost inexhaustible repository of knowledge, legend, myth, and lore from classical antiquity and the Middle Ages. Through quotation or citation Zedler usually directs the reader to relevant passages in older lexicons, from Isidore's *Etymologiae* down to the vast seventeenth-century compendia. In the process you will usually collect a good number of examples in addition to much useful background information on specific images and symbols. Zedler was one of the most productive sources, for instance, for the essay on "The Mystic Carbuncle."

Whether you are concerned with personal themes and motifs or non-human images, you can often find additional references in another group of sources. Critical editions of the works already on your list frequently annotate interesting or unusual topics: e.g., Kinzel's edition of *Lamprechts Alexander* cites a dozen passages from other Middle High German and medieval Latin texts in the note to one line in which the carbuncle occurs. Word indices cite occurrences of the same topic in other works by the same author: e.g., Goethe's use of the word "Karfunkel." Biographies of the writer often cite the writer's sources for particular works or topics and contain other useful information: e.g., concerning Novalis' study of mineralogy or Hans Christian Andersen's agonies with toothache. Interpretations of specific works often note parallels in works by other writers: e.g., S. S. Prawer's essay on Hoffmann and Cervantes. Finally, the great influence studies can provide valuable information: J.-J. A. Bertrand's *Cervantes et le Roman- tisme allemand* discusses the impact of Cervantes' "Col- loquy of the Dogs" on Hoffmann and other writers; Charles Passage's *The Russian Hoffmannists* pursues the influence of Hoffmann's "Berganza" on Gogol and other Russian writers; Werner Vordtriede's *Novalis und die französischen Symbolisten* investigates the transmission of lapidary imagery from German romanticism to French symbolism.

IV

AFTER you have collected your literary examples, the third stage involves an exploration of the sources of your topic as well as its extensions into other fields. In prac- tice, this is not so much a stage as an aspect: I start this phase of the research while I am still reading the primary works produced by my preliminary bibliographical combings. Indeed, the exploration of the sources will often turn up other primary texts. It needs to be stressed again that at each stage the procedures become less and less orderly. The initial bibliographical scan for second- ary studies can be methodical and reasonably thorough. The search for additional literary examples can be fur- thered in a number of ways by a variety of reference tools, but it also involves a great deal more serendipity than we sometimes like to admit. And at the third stage ingenuity and resourcefulness begin to play a very sig- nificant role.

In my own experience the search for sources often leads back to the Bible and classical antiquity. (In all the preceding essays except "Figures on Loan" my path led back at one point or another to the Bible.) In addition to the dictionaries and encyclopedias, therefore, I rou- tinely consult a good concordance of the Bible to de- termine whether or not an image (teeth, carbuncles, dogs) shows up there. (We already know from other reference works, of course, whether or not the theme or motif is biblical.) Determining that a theme, motif, or image occurs in the Bible is only the first step. If the Bible turns out to be relevant, then you should consult a handbook that clarifies the biblical reference and cites other passages and sources and dimensions. I have found three works most useful for my own purposes: the four-volume *Interpreter's Dictionary of the Bible: An Illustrated Encyclopedia* (New York-Nashville: Abingdon, 1962; with a 1976 supplement); the twelve-volume *Encyclopedia of Religion and Ethics*, ed. James Hastings (New York: Scribner, 1908-1927); and the still incomplete *Reallexikon für Antike und Christentum*, ed. Theodor Klauser (Stuttgart: Hiersemann, 1950ff.).

If a topic leads back to the Bible, then it almost certainly goes back by parallel paths to classical antiquity, for which there is no finer reference tool than Pauly-Wissowa's multi-volume *Real-Enzyklopädie der classischen Altertumswissenschaft*. For quick reference I often prefer to consult the so-called *Kleine Pauly* in five volumes (Stuttgart: Druckenmüller, 1964-75) or the handy *Oxford Companion to Classical Literature*, ed. Paul Harvey (first published in 1937 and frequently revised since then).

Themes, motifs, and images that show up in the Bible and classical antiquity often have a broader base in folklore and myth, which can be traced by means of Stith Thompson's six-volume *Motif-Index of Folk-Literature*, rev. ed. (Bloomington: Indiana Univ. Press, 1955), whose index directs the user to bibliographical citations cataloguing hundreds of motifs and images in folk literature from the entire world. Another invaluable reference tool for primitive myth, magic, and religion is James Frazer's *The Golden Bough* (1890), which I usually consult initially in the updated abridgment by Theodor H. Gaster: *The New Golden Bough* (New York: New American Library, 1964). In the preceding chapters, for instance, Frazer produced useful material in connection with dogs, teeth, and resurrection. I also routinely consult the ten-volume *Handwörterbuch des deutschen Aberglaubens*, ed. Hanns Bächtold-Stäubli (Berlin and Leipzig: De Gruyter, 1931-32), which goes well beyond German superstitions in its various rubrics. (It provided material that I often found nowhere else for teeth, carbuncles, and dogs.) Useful though less comprehensive is the two-volume *Standard Dictionary of Folklore, Mythology, and Legend*, ed. Maria Leach (New York: Funk and Wagnall, 1949-1950).

At a certain point the search for sources leads to an awareness of the topic's extension into other fields. When you are looking systematically for the prolongation of themes, motifs, and images into other areas, you can consult various works. We have already noted that Herbert Hunger's *Lexikon der griechischen und römischen Mythologie* as well as Erwin Heinzel's two lexicons of historical themes record treatments in art and music of their subject matter. Another useful source for musical treatments of a given theme (e.g., Don Giovanni, Don Quixote, Faust, or Orpheus) is one of the older editions of *Grove's Dictionary of Music and Musicians* (the five-volume third edition; New York: Macmillan, 1935). The so-called *New Grove*, ed. Stanley Sadie (London: Macmillan, 1980) has unfortunately done away with such entries. For the general bibliography of subjects, themes, and motifs in Western art I know of no single work comparable to Henri Van de Waal's *ICONCLASS: An Iconographic Classification System*, completed and edited by L. D. Couprie (Amsterdam: North-Holland Publishing Co., 1974-1980). This work, explicitly patterned after Stith Thompson's *Motif-Index of Folk-Literature*, is divided into two parts, each consisting of five volumes. Part I simply introduces the system of iconographic classification that the author advocates; Part II consists of a bibliography of works dealing with themes and motifs in art, organized in an easily accessible manner. The volume devoted to "Literature, Classical Mythology, and Ancient History" (Part II, Vols. 8-9), for instance, provides references to studies on such topics as Don Quixote or Faust in art. In addition to the works cited above, the resourceful student will wish from time to time to consult such works as James Hall's *Dictionary of Subjects and Symbols in Art* (New York: Harper & Row, 1974); the handy *Herder Lexikon: Symbole*, ed. Marianne Oesterreicher-Mollwo (Freiburg im Breisgau: Herder, 1978); or Karl Künstle's two-volume *Ikonographie der christlichen Kunst* (Freiburg im Breisgau: Herder, 1926-28). A variety of such handbooks is available in reasonable editions. And highly specialized resources are accessible for other purposes: e.g., the Index of Christian Art at Princeton University, which lists all iconographical representations of Christian themes, motifs, and images in art down to 1400.

At some point in this process, finally, you should analyze your topic to decide to which larger genus or class it belongs. The study of any single stone like the carbuncle leads at an early stage, for instance, to the rich library of works on precious stones, lapidaries, and geology in general. The figure of the talking dog points, on the one hand, to the large body of works about dogs altogether and, on the other, to the substantial category of studies on animal literature, including fables, bestiaries, beast epics, and fairy tales. The topic of teeth leads beyond folklore and myth to the history of dentistry as well as to organismic theories of society. You must find these implications through your analysis of the topic; they would rarely be listed in the bibliographies under the specific topic of investigation. But they often contain paragraphs or even pages of extremely useful information; they provide the larger cultural context within which the specific topic should be seen and comprehended; and they invariably supply additional references to primary and secondary sources. To a certain extent every topic has its unique bibliography which only the researcher's imagination and originality can assemble. But that is precisely the point where the drudgery ends and the exhilaration of thematic study beings.

V

AT THIS POINT—when you have collected a satisfactory amount of material and evaluated the available secondary studies; when you think that you understand the sources of your theme, motif, or image as well as the course of its transmission from the source to the literary point that originally kindled your interest; when you have explored its various extensions into music, art, and the appropriate intellectual and cultural backgrounds—it is time to decide how to present the topic. On very rare occasions the obvious organization may emerge smoothly in the course of the research, but in my experience it is usually not so simple. It is tempting, in the excitement and fun of the hunt, to become obsessed with the material in itself, with the result that you lose sight of the reason for your original interest and collect far more material than you can possibly use. At this point it is usually necessary to sit back and assess your material, to decide what you want to demonstrate, and then to be ruthlessly selective in organizing your material for the specific purposes of the demonstration.

If *Stoffgeschichte* had fallen by mid-century to a position of such low esteem that Wellek and Warren in their *Theory of Literature* (1949) were able to call it "the least literary of histories" (Ch. 19), it was because of the perception that scholars of the German positivistic school and their followers in France and the United States were interested in nothing but the mindless accumulation of material, which they then served up without selectivity or focus—or literary purpose. Susanne Schröder has portrayed the early history of *Stoffgeschichte* in her book *Deutsche Komparatistik im Wilhelminischen Zeitalter*, 1871-1918 (Bonn: Bouvier, 1979). And Major Gerald McGough has outlined the entire history in his (unpublished) dissertation "*Stoffgeschichte*/Thematology: A Historical Survey, Synthesis, and Practical Application" (Vanderbilt, 1975). It is certainly possible to find examples of poor *Stoffgeschichte*, the sort of scholarship that provided the model for Robert K. Merton's hilarious spoof of thematic research *On the Shoulders of Giants: A Shandean Postscript* (New York: The Free Press, 1965), which ought to be required reading for every aspiring thematologist. Yet, all in all, the early scholars of literary thematics were no worse than advocates of any other approach, from *Geistesgeschichte* to New Criticism—not to mention such contemporary trends as deconstruction or reader-response theory.

As I have sought to suggest through the title and organization of this book, literary thematics offers many possible varieties. In fact, the only unacceptable approach is the unselective listing of material, though even such a listing would have its proper function in a bibliography or lexicon. In general, however, the scholar must always make choices concerning the focus and emphasis of his presentation. I have often found it useful— as in the essays on talking dogs and figures on loan— to include the reasons for my decisions in the discussion itself. It not only helps the reader to understand certain omissions; it also helps to define more sharply the area of particular concern and to set it off against areas that you choose not to discuss.

I would begin by emphasizing my conviction that there is no conflict between thematic study and critical interpretation. Indeed, I would go so far as to argue that the critic unaware of the background and implications of any theme, motif, or image that plays an important role in a literary text cannot do justice to the work. I believe that our appreciation of the meaning of one group of texts is enhanced by an understanding of the author's use of teeth as an image and that our interpretation of another group is deepened by an understanding of the different ways in which the motif of resurrection is handled within the same general theme. Similarly, my appreciation of Mary Shelley's novel is affected by my awareness of the tensions between two different thematic traditions—a tension expressed not just in the characters themselves but in the very rhetoric of the fiction. Too often, I believe, we are seduced by our own ignorance into believing that the author of a literary work did not know something—a theme, a motif, an image—simply because *we* do not know it. It is our responsibility as scholars and critics to inform ourselves.

Although the understanding and appreciation of the individual literary work is usually the starting point of my studies, research in literary thematics can and should have other implications. It is clear, for instance, that certain themes and motifs display a pronounced genre-affinity: e.g., Odysseus shows up more often in narrative contexts whereas Don Juan prefers a dramatic (or operatic) setting. Genre affinity is not always a relevant consideration, especially with smaller elements like symbols and images: the mystic carbuncle shows up in every conceivable literary context. But it is a question that the student of literary thematics should keep constantly in mind as he sifts and analyzes the material. For reasons I have attempted to adumbrate, figures on loan are almost inevitably borrowed from one fictional narrative to be used in another: they almost never appear in dramatic or lyrical settings. Similarly, the situations that produce talking dogs have tended, for two thousand years, to be so similar that we can properly speak of an affinity between that canine figure and the dramatic dialogue.

Though themes and motifs sometimes display an affinity for certain genres, periods and epochs in turn display a pronounced affinity for certain themes, motifs, and images. Indeed, in all six of the preceding essays I found it appropriate to deal at some point with the reasons for the revival of interest in a given topic at a given time. Sometimes it is relevant to consider the transformations that a particular image (e.g., the carbuncle) undergoes in the course of the centuries. Sometimes we find that a particular concern—e.g., the ethics of science—attracts a variety of themes (from Prometheus and Adam to Faust and Frankenstein) in order to express itself in different cultures and at different periods.

VI

THE THEORETICAL JUSTIFICATION and the role of thematic studies within literary studies in general have been discussed frequently during the past two decades as part of the process of rehabilitation of *Stoffgeschichte,* or *thématologie,* or literary thematics. The two basic monographs are those by Elisabeth Frenzel: *Stoff-, Motif- und Symbolforschung* (Stuttgart: Metzler, 1963) and *Stoff- und Motivgeschichte* (Berlin: Schmidt, 1966), which outline respectively in historical and systematic succession the various applications of *Stoffgeschichte* to literary analysis and criticism. But important contributions have also been made by three groups of scholars concerned with literary thematics.

First, a significant group of thematologists—theoretical advocates of literary thematics—have contributed to the justification and terminological clarification of the discipline: Raymond Trousson, "Plaidoyer pour la Stoffgeschichte," *Revue de Littérature Comparée,* 38 (1964), 101-114; and *Un Problème de littérature comparée: les études de thèmes* (Paris: Minard, 1965); Harry Levin, "Thematics and Criticism," in *The Disciplines of Criticism: Essays in Literary Theory, Interpretation, and History,* ed. Peter Demetz, Thomas Greene, and Lowry Nelson, Jr. (New Haven: Yale Univ. Press, 1968), pp. 125-45; Manfred Beller, "Von der Stoffgeschichte zur Thematologie: Ein Beitrag zur komparatistischen Methodenlehre," *Arcadia,* 5 (1970), 1-38; Adam John Bisanz, "Zwischen Stoffgeschichte und Thematologie: Betrachtungen zu einem literaturtheoretischen Dilemma," *Deutsche Vierteljahrsschrift,* 47 (1973), 148-66; François Jost, "Grundbegriffe der Thematologie," *Theorie und Kritik: Zur vergleichenden und neueren deutschen Literatur,* ed. Stefan Grunwald and Bruce A. Beatie (Bern and Munich: Francke, 1974), pp. 15-46; Adam J. Bisanz, "Stoff, Thema, Motiv: Zur Problematik des Transfers von Begriffsbestimmungen zwischen der englischen und deutschen Literaturwissenschaft," *Neo-*

philologus, 59 (1975), 317-23; and Joachim Schulze, "Geschichte oder Systematik: Zu einem Problem der Themen- und Motivgeschichte," *Arcadia*, 10 (1975), 76-82.

Second, most recent authors of thematic studies have felt obliged to justify their undertaking with a chapter on theory and definition: Raymond Trousson, *Le Thème de Promethée dans la littérature européenne* (Geneva: Droz, 1964); Anne Marie Musschoot, *Het Judith-Thema in de Nederlandse Letterkunde* (Gent: Koninklijke Academie voor Nederlandse Taal- en Letterkunde, 1972), pp. 13-41; Horst S. and Ingrid Daemmrich, *Wiederholte Spiegelungen: Themen und Motive in der Literatur* (Bern und München: Francke, 1978), pp. 5-23; Ernst Osterkamp, *Lucifer: Stationen eines Motivs* (Berlin: De Gruyter, 1979), pp. 1-5. Even volumes of essays by others require their theoretical justification: e.g., Margot Kruse, "Literaturgeschichte als Themengeschichte" in: Hellmuth Petriconi, *Metamorphosen der Traüme: Fünf Beispiele zu einer Literaturgeschichte als Themengeschichte* (Frankfurt am Main: Athenäum, 1971), pp. 195-208; and Raymond Trousson, "Les Études de thèmes: Questions de méthode" in the two-volume *Festschrift* for Elisabeth Frenzel: *Elemente der Literatur: Beiträge zur Stoff-, Motiv- und Themenforschung*, ed. Adam Bisanz and Raymond Trousson (Stuttgart: Kröner, 1980), I, 1-10.

Finally, most major introductions to the study of comparative literature during the past fifteen years have included a chapter assessing the role of *Stoffgeschichte/thématologie* within the field of literary study as a whole: Claude Pichois and A.-M. Rousseau, *La Littérature comparée* (Paris: Armand Colin, 1967), pp. 145-54; Jan Brandt Corstius, *Introduction to the Comparative Study of Literature* (New York: Random House, 1968), pp. 115-27; Simon Jeune, *Littérature générale et littérature comparée: essai d'orientation* (Paris: Minard, 1968), pp. 61-71; Ulrich Weisstein, *Einführung in die vergleichende Literaturwissenschaft* (Stuttgart: Kohlhammer, 1968), pp. 125-45; English trans. William Riggan *Comparative Literature and Literary Theory* (Bloomington: Indiana Univ. Press, 1973), pp. 124-49; Frank C. Maatje, *Literatuurwetenschap: Grondslagen van een theorie van het literaire werk* (Utrecht: Oosthoek, 1970), pp. 203-213; S. S. Prawer, *Comparative Literary Studies: An Introduction* (London: Duckworth, 1973), pp. 99-113; François Jost, *Introduction to Comparative Literature* (Indianapolis: Bobbs-Merrill, 1974), pp. 175-87; Hugo Dyserinck, *Komparatistik: Eine Einführung* (Bonn: Bouvier, 1977), pp. 102-113; Robert J. Clements, *Comparative Literature as Academic Discipline: A Statement of Principles, Praxis, Standards* (New York: MLA, 1978), pp. 165-79; Joseph Strelka, *Methodologie der Literaturwissenschaft* (Tübingen: Niemeyer, 1978), pp. 124-45; Gerhard R. Kaiser, *Einführung in die vergleichende Literaturwissenschaft: Forschungsstand, Kritik, Aufgaben* (Darmstadt: Wissenschaftliche Buchgesellschaft, 1980), pp. 80-92; and Manfred Beller, "Thematologie," in *Vergleichende Literaturwissenschaft: Theorie und Praxis*, ed. Manfred Schmeling (Wiesbaden: Akademische Verlagsgesellschaft Athenaion, 1981), pp. 73-97.

VII

THERE REMAINS, finally, the question of organization. Having collected and analyzed the material, how do you present it most persuasively? In her *Stoff- und Motivgeschichte* (pp. 142-53) Elisabeth Frenzel briefly discusses six basic strategies for thematic studies: linear development (e.g., the Ulysses theme in Western literature); the epochal cross-section (e.g., the nightingale as a motif in romantic poetry); studies limited to national literatures (e.g., the figure of Napoleon in English literature); anthropologically extended studies (e.g., the divine child in mythology, literature, and psychology); studies focused on individual writers (e.g., the image of teeth in the works of Thomas Mann); and poetological studies (e.g., the treatment of the Nibelungen theme in epic, drama, and opera). Her bibliography cites representative examples of each type.

The material dictates the approach up to a point. If you are interested in the Odysseus theme in the postwar German novel, or the Aeolian harp as an image in the European romantic imagination, the choice of texts and emphasis are predetermined to a certain extent. In general, however, I prefer a synthesis incorporating several approaches. More specifically, I believe that the organization should make explicit the critical or interpretive impulse that initially prompted the investigation. In other words, I like for the product to exemplify the process. Accordingly, the preceding essays begin in every case with questions generated by a specific text, or group of texts, from the period of my own specialization. That *terminus a quo* necessitates, in turn, a more or less circular organization since it is necessary to loop back into the past in order to discover the sources of the topic. At this stage of the proceedings the approach is frequently what Frenzel would call "anthropologically extended" as we explore the sources in myth, religion, and folklore of the world. From the source a linear development leads us forward again (the carbuncles, the talking dogs, the teeth); but at certain points it is necessary to pause for an epochal cross-section (carbuncles in the Middle Ages, teeth in the twentieth century). Indeed, any concentration of examples in a given period should be the grateful occasion for inquiry into the reasons underlying the popularity or revival of any theme, motif, or symbol; and the same applies in the case of individual writers. In most cases, finally—having gone through most of the approaches suggested by Frenzel—we return to the starting-point to determine what new light may be cast on the original text, or group of texts, by the thematic study. Often the conclusion leads past the initial text and opens new dimensions of the theme.

Every topic requires its own organization, with the selection of examples, investigation of sources, and emphasis of period and author appropriate to the subject.

Organization should never be mindless and mechanical. It should respond to the questions that we put to our material. What is the meaning of a theme, motif, or image in a given literary work? What are the deepest ascertainable sources of the theme, motif, or image? How does it aid our apprehension of the work and our appreciation of its aesthetic qualities? How does it enable the readers at various points in history to respond to the work or works employing the same thematic material? Why does the material thrust itself upon certain writers and certain periods and not upon others? Why does it lend itself to treatment in one genre and not in another?

You should never relax into the illusion that you have exhausted the material until you determine—or at least speculate—why a given theme, motif, or image assumes importance, or suffers neglect, in our own time. The preoccupation with teeth turned out to reveal the writers' obsession with the health of modern society. The reluminescence of the mystic carbuncle signaled among certain writers a longing for spiritual reintegration in a fragmented world. When dogs begin to talk in any age, we have learned to be prepared for their cynical analysis of a world that has gone to the dogs. The figures on loan expose an anxiety regarding the frangibility of the world both in fictional and nonfictional reality. The attempts to rationalize the resurrection betray the need of believers and non-believers alike in a rational age to come to terms with a clearly irrational feature that lies at the center of Christian faith. "Frankenstein" functions as a code-word in a world that has come to distrust the science that has brought us so much destruction along with so much light.

In his introductory essay to the recent *Festschrift* for Elisabeth Frenzel, Raymond Trousson suggested that *Stoffgeschichte*, or *thématologie*, might accomplish a "Synthèse historico-esthétique" for the fragmented literary scholarship of our time. But at its best, I believe, the study of literary thematics can go well beyond that narrowly focused goal to expose unexpected dimensions of the literary work. By emphasizing their continuity through time it alerts us to the urgent modernity of mankind's oldest myths and images. At the same time, by drawing on a variety of disciplines to explain their permutations it shows us how those themes and motifs reflect in all their breadth, and in turn are shaped by, the societies captivated by their perennial allure.

NOTES

Chapter One

1. *örtlich betäubt* (Neuwied: Luchterhand, 1969); hereafter cited from the English trans. by Ralph Manheim: *Local Anaesthetic* (1970; rpt. Greenwich, Conn.: Fawcett, 1971). The pathological philosophy of history is not original with Grass, of course. In the nineteenth century it was so widespread that in *War and Peace* (Bk. X, Ch. 28) Tolstoy challenged the notion that the French suffered such heavy losses in the battle of Borodino because Napoleon had a cold. In support he cites Voltaire's cynical quip that the Massacre of St. Bartholomew's Day occurred because Charles IX had an upset stomach.

2. Grass has used tooth images in many of his works to represent professional incompetence, artistic sterility, suppressed aggressiveness, and sexual impotence. See Carl O. Enderstein, "Zahnsymbolik und ihre Bedeutung in Günter Grass' Werken," *Monatshefte*, 66 (1974), 5-18. But in no other work is the image developed with such consistency and so centrally as in this novel. Heinrich Böll frequently uses rotting teeth to symbolize the ravages of poverty in the individual: cf. Fred Bogner in *Acquainted with the Night* (*Und sagte kein einziges Wort*, 1953) and Wilma Brielach in *Tomorrow and Yesterday* (*Haus ohne Hüter*, 1954). But he does not use the image more generally to characterize society as a whole.

3. This confident assessment of dentistry is not quite so parodistic as Grass might have intended it. In 1936 Lewis Mumford wrote the following statement to be enclosed in a time capsule: "The best you can do to represent our age of concrete, subway-excavating, scientific skill, fine measurements and physiological knowl-

edge is to enclose a human tooth with the root canal filled and the crown anatomically restored with a gold inlay." Quoted by Israel Shenker in "Words Intended for Next Millenium [sic] on View," *New York Times*, 2 March 1973, p. 33, col. 6.

4. See the Norton Critical Edition of *McTeague*, ed. Donald Pizer (New York: Norton, 1977), pp. 284-89; for further comments on teeth as an image in the novel see William B. Stone's response to the original publication of this chapter in "Forum," *PMLA*, 91 (1976), 463.

5. Thomas W. Ross, *Chaucer's Bawdy* (New York: Dutton, 1972), pp. 60-61.

6. *The New Golden Bough*, a new abridgment of the classic work by Sir James George Frazer, ed. Theodor H. Gaster (1959; rpt. New York; NAL, 1964), pp. 278-79; Pt. III, Par. 190: "Death and Resurrection."

7. Sigmund Freud, *Die Traumdeutung*, 5th ed. (Leipzig: Franz Deuticke, 1919), pp. 263-64: "Zahn-reizträume."

8. See Leo Kanner, *Folklore of the Teeth* (1928; rpt. Detroit: Singing Tree Press, 1968).

9. Charles I. Stoloff, "The Fashionable Tooth," *Natural History*, 81 (1972), 12-21.

10. Vincenzo Guerini, *A History of Dentistry* (Philadelphia: Lea & Febiger, 1909), p. 33.

11. *The Portrait in the Renaissance*, The A. W. Mellon Lecture in the Fine Arts, 1963 (New York: Pantheon, 1966). This observation is borne out by Lavater, who states in the introduction to his *Physiognomic Fragments* (1775-78) that the focal point of all physiognomy is "the closed mouth at the moment of perfect tranquillity." See J. C. Lavater, *Physiognomik: Zur Beförderung der Menschenkenntnis und Menschenliebe*, rev. ed. (Vienna: Sollinger, 1829), I, 10. Lavater concedes that an entire volume could be written on teeth alone; but he restricts himself to a single page since he finds so little evidence in the visual arts (III, 83-84).

12. "Notes," in *The Sense of the Past* (New York: Scribners, 1922), p. 296.

13. *The Oxford Book of Medieval Latin Verse*, ed. F.J.E. Raby (Oxford: Clarendon, 1959), p. 110.

14. Kaufringer, *Werke*, ed. Paul Sappler (Tübingen: Max Niemeyer, 1972), No. 5 ("Der zurückgebliebene Minnelohn").

15. See Timothy C. Blackburn's informative response to the original publication of this chapter in "Forum," *PMLA*, 91 (1976), 461-62.

16. "Berenice," in *The Selected Poetry and Prose of Edgar Allan Poe*, ed. T. O. Mabbott (New York: Random, 1951), pp. 83-90.

17. See Marie Bonaparte, *The Life and Works of Edgar Allan Poe: A Psychoanalytic Interpretation*, trans. John Rodker (London: Imago, 1949), p. 218; and Daniel Hoffman, *Poe Poe Poe Poe Poe Poe Poe* (Garden City: Doubleday, 1972), p. 240.

18. Phyllis McGinley, "Reflections Dental," in *The Love Letters of Phyllis McGinley* (New York: Viking, 1954), p. 98.

19. *Teeth, Dying, and Other Matters* (New York: Harper, 1964), pp. 13-30.

20. See J. J. Pindborg and L. Marvitz, *The Dentist in Art*, trans. Gillian Hartz (Copenhagen: Ejnar Munksgaard, 1960); and Sydney Garfield, *Teeth, Teeth, Teeth: A Treatise on Teeth and Related Parts of Man, Land and Water Animals from Earth's Beginning to the Future of Time* (New York: Simon, 1969).

21. "Der hohle Zahn," in Wilhelm Busch, *Gesamtausgabe*, ed. Otto Nöldeke (Munich: Braun & Schneider, 1943), I, 314-26.

22. "Tante Tandpine"; I have translated from the German ed. of Andersen's *Märchen und Geschichten* (Weimar: Kiepenheuer, n.d.), III, 560-71.

23. *Darkness at Noon*, trans. Daphne Hardy (New York: Random, n.d.).

24. *The Power and the Glory*, Compass ed. (New York: Viking, 1958).

25. "This Is Going to Hurt Just a Little Bit," in *Bed Riddance: A Posy for the Indisposed* (Boston: Little, 1969), pp. 86-87.

26. Preface to *The Shewing-Up of Blanco Posnet*, in *The Complete Prefaces of Bernard Shaw* (London: Hamlyn, 1965), p. 436. Shaw continues: "Prevent dentists and dramatists from giving pain, and not only will our morals become as carious as our teeth, but toothache and the plagues that follow neglected morality will presently cause more agony than all the dentists and dramatists at their worst have caused since the world began."

27. "Hugh Selwyn Mauberley" (1920), in Ezra Pound, *Personae* ([New York]: New Directions, [1950]), p. 191.

28. *Fantasia of the Unconscious and Psychoanalysis and the Unconscious* (London: Heinemann, 1961), pp. 57-58.

29. Brunold Springer, *Die genialen Syphilitiker*, 2nd-4th enl. ed. (Berlin-Nicolassee: Verlag der Neuen Generation, 1926), p. 2.

30. Lewis J. Moorman, *Tuberculosis and Genius* (Chicago: Univ. of Chicago Press, 1940); Saul Nathaniel Brody, *The Disease of the Soul: Leprosy in Medieval Literature* (Ithaca: Cornell Univ. Press, 1974); Peter L. Hays, *The Limping Hero: Grotesques in Literature* (New York: New York Univ. Press, 1971); Michel Foucault, *Madness and Civilization: A History of Insanity in the Age of Reason*, trans. Richard Howard (New York: Random, 1965); Patrick Trevor-Roper, *The World through Blunted Sight: An Inquiry into the Influence of Defective Vision on Art and Character* (Indianapolis: Bobbs-Merrill, 1970). See Theodore Ziolkowski, "Medicine and Literature," *Sewanee Review*, 89 (1981), 652-59.

31. See Ernst Cassirer, *The Myth of the State* (1946; rpt. New Haven: Yale Univ. Press, 1966), esp. pp. 163-86.

32. Francis W. Coker, *Organismic Theories of the State*, Studies in History, Economics, and Public Law, 38 (1910; rpt. New York: AMS, 1967), esp. pp. 11-22;

Volker Stanslowski, "Bürgerliche Gesellschaft als Organismus: Zum Verhältnis von Staats- und Naturwissenschaften in der 'Politischen Romantik,' " in *Romantik in Deutschland: Ein interdisziplinäres Symposion*, ed. Richard Brinkmann (Stuttgart: Metzler, 1978), pp. 90-101.

33. Edgar B. Schick, *Metaphorical Organicism in Herder's Early Works: A Study of the Relation of Herder's Literary Idiom to His Worldview* (The Hague: Mouton, 1971).

34. G. P. Gooch, *History and Historians in the Nineteenth Century* (1913; rpt. Boston: Beacon, 1959), pp. 39-49.

35. Richard P. Appelbaum, *Theories of Social Change* (Chicago: Markham, 1970), pp. 18-23, 30-35.

36. *Entartung* (Berlin: Carl Duncker, n.d.), I, vii.

37. Coker, *Organismic Theories*, pp. 191-204; see also D. C. Phillips, "Organicism in the Late Nineteenth and Early Twentieth Centuries," *Journal of the History of Ideas*, 31 (1970), 413-32.

38. Oswald Spengler, *Der Untergang des Abendlandes: Umrisse einer Morphologie der Weltgeschichte* (1918-22; rpt. Munich: Beck, 1963), p. 35: introd., Par. 9.

CHAPTER TWO

1. See Mario Praz, *The Romantic Agony*, trans. Angus Davidson (1933; rpt. New York: Meridian, 1956), pp. 187-286 (Chap. IV: "La Belle Dame Sans Merci"); Werner Vordtriede, *Novalis und die französischen Symbolisten: Zur Entstehungsgeschichte des dichterischen Symbols* (Stuttgart: Kohlhammer, 1963), pp. 43-97 (Chap. V: "Das Unterreich"); and Heide Eilert, "Die Vorliebe für kostbar-erlesene Materialien und ihre Funktion in der Lyrik des Fin de siècle," in *Fin de Siècle: Zu Literatur und Kunst der Jahrhundertwende*, ed. Roger Bauer (Frankfurt am Main: Klostermann, 1977), pp. 421-41.

2. Cited by Eilert, p. 421.

3. J.-K. Huysmans, "Préface écrite vingt ans après le

roman," in À *Rebours,* ed. Marc Fumaroli (Paris: Gallimard, 1977), p. 63.

4. See Earle R. Caley and John F. C. Richards, *Theophrastus on Stones: Introduction, Greek Text, English Translation, and Commentary* (Columbus: Ohio State Univ. Press, 1956); and *Theophrastus De Lapidibus,* ed. with Introduction, Translation and Commentary by D. E. Eichholz (Oxford: Clarendon, 1965).

5. Max Wellmann, "Die Stein- und Gemmenbücher der Antike," in *Quellen und Studien zur Geschichte der Naturwissenschaften und der Medizin,* ed. P. Diepgen and J. Ruska, vol. IV, no. 4 (Berlin: Springer, 1935), pp. 86-149; and Frank Dawson Adams, *The Birth and Development of the Geological Sciences* (1938; rpt. New York: Dover, 1954), pp. 8-32.

6. Cited according to vol. X of the Loeb Classical edition by D. E. Eichholz (Cambridge: Harvard Univ. Press, 1962), pp. 283-43 (XXXVII, xxv. 92-xxvi. 98).

7. Most of these texts are cited in Fernand de Mély, *Les Lapidaires de l'Antiquité et du Moyen Age* (Paris, 1896-1902), vol. II and vol. III/1 (*Les Lapidaires grecs*).

8. See Adams, pp. 103-112 ("Stones Growing in the Bodies of Animals").

9. De Mély, vol. III/1, pp. v-xxiv; and *Das Steinbuch des Aristoteles,* ed. and trans. by Julius Ruska (Heidelberg, 1912), pp. 9-23.

10. Harry Emanuel, *Diamonds and Precious Stones,* 2nd ed. (London, 1867), p. 39 and p. 107.

11. In vol. IV of the Loeb Classical edition of *Works,* ed. A. M. Harmon (New York: Putnam's, 1925), pp. 386-87 ("The Goddesse of Surrye," § 32).

12. M. Berthelot, *Collection des anciens Alchimistes Grecs* (Paris, 1888), Texte Grec, p. 351.

13. *Opera Omnia,* ed. Auguste Borgnet (Paris, 1890), V, 32.

14. Cf. Eusebius' *De laudibus Constantini* (Migne, *Patrologia Graeca,* XX, 1337), which ridicules those who persist in this childish delusion.

15. The textual history of this writing is complicated.

Only two short excerpts from the Greek original are extant; a somewhat longer Latin translation from the fifth century is fragmentary (both in Migne, *Patrologia Graeca*, XLIII, 322-66). The text in its entirety is known only in the Georgian version of a tenth-century Armenian translation. See Robert P. Blake, *Epiphanius De Gemmis: The Old Georgian Version and the Fragments of the Armenian Version* (London: Christophers, 1934).

16. Blake, p. 129; here the term has been translated as jacinth.

17. See Moritz Steinschneider, "Lapidarien: ein culturgeschichtlicher Versuch," in *Semitic Studies in Memory of Alexander Kohut*, ed. George A. Kohut (Berlin, 1897), pp. 42-72; and Julius Ruska, *Griechische Planetendarstellungen in arabischen Steinbüchern*, Sitzungsberichte der Heidelberger Akademie der Wissenschaften: Phil.-Hist. Klasse, X/3 (1919), 1-50.

18. See in this connection the exhaustive study by Christel Meier, *Gemma Spiritalis: Methode und Gebrauch der Edelsteinallegorese vom frühen Christentum bis ins 18. Jahrhundert*, Part I (Munich: Fink, 1977), esp. pp. 27-55.

19. Adams, pp. 474-49; Meier, pp. 246-53.

20. Migne, *Patrologia Latina*, LXXXII, 578 (= XVI, xiv, 1).

21. Meier, pp. 12-15.

22. See Adams, pp. 149-55; and Joan Evans, *Magical Jewels of the Middle Ages and the Renaissance, particularly in England* (Oxford: Clarendon, 1922), pp. 33-35.

23. Migne, *Patrologia Latina*, CLXXI, 1754.

24. Valentin Rose, "Aristoteles de lapidibus und Arnoldus Saxo," *Zeitschrift für deutsches Altertum*, 18, N. F. 6 (1875), 431-32.

25. Cf. Léopold Pannier, *Les Lapidaires français du moyen age* (Paris, 1882); Paul Studer and Joan Evans, *Anglo-Norman Lapidaries* (Paris: Champion, 1924); Joan Evans and Mary S. Sergeantson, *English Medieval Lapidaries* (London: Oxford Univ. Press, 1933); Léon Bai-

sier, *The Lapidaire Chrétien, Its Composition, Its Influence, Its Sources* (Washington, D.C.: Catholic Univ. of America, 1936).

26. *Opera Omnia*, ed. Auguste Borgnet (Paris, 1890), V, 32.

27. Der Stricker, *Kleine Gedichte*, ed. Karl August Hahn (Quedlinburg & Leipzig, 1839), p. 51.

28. See Littré, *Dictionnaire de la Langue Française*; Kluge-Götze, *Etymologisches Wörterbuch der deutschen Sprache*; and Du Cange, *Glossarium mediae et infimae Latinitatis*.

29. Urban T. Holmes, "Medieval Gem Stones," *Speculum*, 9 (1934), 200. Many of the trade names for certain stones, including *granatus* and *rubinus*, seem to occur for the first time in Thomas Cantimpratensis' late thirteenth-century *De Natura Rerum*; see Adams, p. 141.

30. Konrad von Megenburg, *Das Buch der Natur*, ed. Franz Pfeiffer (Stuttgart, 1861), p. 437. For a discussion of Mariological interpretations of the carbuncle, popular especially in Germany, see Ulrich Engelen, *Die Edelsteine in der deutschen Dichtung des 12. und 13. Jahrhunderts* (München: Wilhelm Fink, 1978), pp. 324-31.

31. See Adams, pp. 155-59; the text itself is now available in the Readex Microprint Edition: Landmarks of Science.

32. I quote from the third edition of 1647, p. 140.

33. Pp. 957-61 (Landmarks of Science).

34. *A Lapidary: or, The History of Pretious Stones* (Cambridge, 1652), pp. 54-58 (Landmarks of Science).

35. Pp. 227-36 (Landmarks of Science).

36. Johann Heinrich Zedler, *Großes vollständiges Universal Lexikon aller Wissenschaften und Künste* (Halle & Leipzig, 1733), V, 780.

37. A. Levavasseur, "Les pierres précieuses dans *La Divine Comédie*," *Revue des Etudes Italiennes*, N. S. IV (1957), 31-100, esp. p. 34.

38. *Reinke de Vos*, ed. Friedrich Prien (Halle, 1887), vv. 4897-4922.

39. *Deutsche Barocklyrik*, ed. Max Wehrli (Basel, 1945), p. 75.

40. Migne, *Patrologia Latina*, XIV, 281.

41. *Itinerario de Ludovico de Varthema* (Rome, 1510), ed. Alberto Bacchi della Lega (Bologna, 1885), p. 195; trans. John Winter Jones and ed. Lincoln Davis Hammond (Cambridge: Harvard Univ. Press, 1963), p. 180.

42. The mistake in translation has been handed down to the twentieth century, where we still find it in the otherwise excellent article "Karfunkelstein" in the *Handwörterbuch des deutschen Aberglaubens*, ed. Hanns Bächtold-Stäubli (Berlin & Leipzig: De Gruyter, 1931-1932), IV, 1004-1006, as well as various popular articles on precious stones.

43. *Ruolandes Liet*, ed. Wilhelm Grimm (Göttingen, 1838), p. 238.

44. *Ruolandes Liet*, p. 196.

45. See Charles Norton Elvin, *A Dictionary of Heraldry* (London, 1889), p. 56.

46. Facsimile edition with unnumbered pages.

47. Théodore de Renesse, *Dictionnaire des figures héraldiques* (Bruxelles, 1899), IV, 277-79.

48. W. Gundel, "Alchemie," in *Reallexikon für Antike und Christentum* (Stuttgart: Hiersemann, 1950 ff.) I, 239-60; and *Alchimia: Ideologie und Technologie*, ed. Emil Ernst Ploss (Munich: Moos, 1970).

49. See C. G. Jung, *Psychology and Alchemy*, trans. R.F.C. Hull, 2nd rev. ed. (Princeton, N.J.: Princeton Univ. Press, 1968), pp. 475-83.

50. Cited by M.-L. von Franz in her commentary to *Aurora consurgens* in the supplemental volume of: C. G. Jung, *Mysterium Coniunctionis: Untersuchung über die Trennung und Zusammensetzung der seelischen Gegensätze in der Alchemie* (Olten & Freiburg im Breisgau: Walter-Verlag, 1971) (=C. G. Jung, *Gesammelte Werke*, XIV/3), p. 298.

51. From Lilius in *Rosarium Philosophorum*; cited by C. G. Jung, *Psychology and Alchemy*, p. 469.

52. *Alchimia*, ed. E. E. Ploss, p. 146.

53. Cited by F. Freudenberg, *Paracelsus und Fludd* (Berlin, 1918), p. 82.

54. See Vlesvolod Slessarev, *Prester John: The Letter and the Legend* (Minneapolis: Univ. of Minnesota Press, 1959); and Friedrich Zarncke, *Der Priester Johannes*, 2 vols. (Leipzig, 1876-79), which contains all relevant texts in the original.

55. Zarncke, I, 91.

56. Zarncke, I, 95.

57. *La Chanson de Roland*, ed. Theodor Müller (Göttingen, 1878), vv. 2632-35.

58. See Arthur Robert Harden, "The Carbuncle in Medieval Literature," *Romance Notes*, II/1 (1960), 58-62, from which the following examples are taken.

59. Zarncke, II, 125-26.

60. Zarncke, I, 158-66.

61. Albrecht von Scharfenberg, *Jüngerer Titurel*, ed. Werner Wolf, vol. I (Berlin 1955), strophes 430-31.

62. In the edition by Félix Lecoy (Paris: Champion, 1965-70), III, 115-16.

63. *Gesta Romanorum*, trans. Charles Swan, rev. ed. Wynnard Hooper (1876; rpt. New York: Dover, 1959), p. 187.

64. See "Karfunkelstein" in *Handwörterbuch des deutschen Aberglaubens*.

65. Georg Graber, *Sagen aus Kärnten*, 6th ed. (Graz, 1944), p. 40ff.

66. Josef Müller, *Sagen aus Uri*, ed. Hanns Bächtold-Stäubli (Basel, 1926), I, 269-71.

67. Zarncke, *Der Priester Johannes*, II, 125.

68. Migne, *Patrologia Graeca*, XLIII, 338-39.

69. Adams, p. 104.

70. Ernest Ingersoll, *Dragons and Dragon Lore* (New York: Payson and Clarke, 1928), esp. Chap. 10: "The Dragon's Precious Pearl."

71. De Mély, II, p. 169.

72. De Mély, III/1, p. 27.

73. Studer and Evans, *Anglo-Norman Lapidaries*, p. 229.

74. *Les Merveilles de l'Asie par le père Jourdain Catalani de Sévérac*, ed. Henri Cordier (Paris: Librairie Orientaliste Paul Geuthner, 1925), p. 119.

75. De Mély, II, p. 36 and p. 71.

76. Odell Shepard, *Lore of the Unicorn* (Boston: Houghton, 1930); Liselotte Wehrhand-Stauch, "Einhorn," in *Reallexikon zur deutschen Kunstgeschichte*, IV, 1504-1544; Rüdiger Robert Beer, *Einhorn: Fabel und Wirklichkeit* (Munich: Callwey, 1972); Jürgen W. Einhorn, *Spiritalis Unicornis: Das Einhorn als Bedeutungsträger in Literatur und Kunst des Mittelalters* (Munich: Fink, 1976). It is clear from many texts that the ambivalence in classical antiquity between μονοκέρως and ῥινοκέρως was continued in the Middle Ages, which glossed *Rhinoceros* as *unicornis* or *Ainhurn*.

77. *Lamprechts Alexander*, ed. Karl Kinzel (Halle, 1884), vv. 5578-584.

78. For a fuller discussion of the medieval German association of carbuncle and unicorn see Theodore Ziolkowski, "Der Karfunkelstein," *Euphorion*, 55 (1961), 297-326; and Einhorn, *Spiritalis Unicornis*, pp. 154-60.

79. *Werke* (Weimar Ausgabe), XVI, 443-52.

80. *Werke* (Hamburger Ausgabe), V, 217.

81. *Werke* (Hamburger Ausgabe), II, 63.

82. *Werke* (Hamburger Ausgabe), VIII, 361.

83. *Werke* (Hamburger Ausgabe), III, 209 (= ll. 6823-6827).

84. Novalis, *Schriften*, ed. Paul Kluckhohn and Richard Samuel, 2nd ed. (Darmstadt: Wissenschaftliche Buchgesellschaft, 1960), I, 106.

85. Novalis, *Schriften*, I, 218-19.

86. Novalis, *Schriften*, I, 368.

87. *Ausgewählte Schriften* (Grimma, 1840), VI, viii.

88. *Ausgewählte Schriften*, VI, 166-68.

89. *Schriften*, (Berlin, 1828), I, 141: "mit blitzenden Karfunkel-Augen, / So roth wie Blut, so brennend wie ein Feuer."

90. *Der Schwan* (Leipzig: Göschen, 1816), p. 162.

91. *Gedichte*, ed. Erich Schmidt and Julius Hartmann (Stuttgart, 1898), I, 263-70.

92. *Poetische Werke* (Berlin: Aufbau, 1958), I, 297.

93. *Poetische Werke*, III, 245.

94. Johann Peter Hebel, *Poetische Werke* (Munich: Winckler, 1961), pp. 569-77.

95. *Werke und Schriften*, ed. Gerhart Baumann (Stuttgart: Cotta, [1957]), II, 132.

96. *Antisymbolik* (Stuttgart, 1826), II, 252: "Wilhelm Schlegels edle Geheimbündner zur Herstellung der hildebrandischen Domherrnzeit, von welchen ein Klupp im Jahre 1805 sich bei uns eingenistet, übten zumeist nur Sang und Klang für die geahnten Anschauungen des karfunkelnden Orients und des südlichen Sonnenlichtes."

97. *Der Karfunkel oder Klingklingel-Almanach: Ein Taschenbuch für vollendete Romantiker und angehende Mystiker* (Tübingen: Cotta, 1810), p. iv.

98. *Die Karfunkel-Weihe: Romantisches Trauerspiel von Till Ballistarius* ([n.p.], 1818), p. 61.

99. In Paul Claudel, *L'Oeil écoute* (Paris: Gallimard, 1946), pp. 215-27.

100. First published in an unpaginated facsimile edition (Frankfurt am Main: Suhrkamp, 1954); a facsimile edition of a different holograph was published as Insel Taschenbuch 122 (Frankfurt am Main, 1976); this second facsimile has been reproduced as a photographic inset in Hesse, *Pictor's Metamorphoses and Other Fantasies*, ed. Theodore Ziolkowski and trans. Rika Lesser (New York: Farrar, Straus & Giroux, 1982).

101. C. G. Jung, *Memories, Dreams, Reflections*, ed. Aniela Jaffé and trans. Richard and Clara Winston (New York: Random House-Vintage Books, 1963), p. 175. Photographs of Jung's various stone carvings are available in: C. G. Jung, *Word and Image*, ed. Aniela Jaffé and trans. Krishna Winston (Princeton, N.J.: Princeton Univ. Press, 1979), pp. 193-205.

102. *Memories, Dreams, Reflections*, p. 228.

103. C. G. Jung, *Aion: Researches into the Phenom-*

enology of the Self, trans. R.F.C. Hull, 2nd ed. (Princeton, N.J.: Princeton Univ. Press, 1968), p. 170.

104. *Aion*, p. 268.

105. *Aion*, pp. 170-71: *Transmutemini de lapidibus mortuis in vivos lapides philosophicos!*

CHAPTER THREE

1. "Forschungen eines Hundes," *Sämtliche Erzählungen*, ed. Paul Raabe (Frankfurt am Main: Fischer Taschenbuch Verlag, 1970), pp. 323-54; cited according to Willa and Edwin Muir's translation of *Selected Short Stories of Franz Kafka* (New York: Random House-Modern Library, 1952), pp. 202-55.

2. See Howard M. Chapin, *The Peter Chapin Collection of Books on Dogs: A Short-Title List*. Bulletin of the College of William and Mary, vol. 32, no. 7 (Williamsburg, Va., 1938).

3. Kafka may have had other specific sources as well. For instance, his vision of the dancing dogs may have been inspired by a scene from Dickens, one of his favorite writers: there are conspicuous similarities between Kafka's scene and the description of Jerry's dismal troop of dancing dogs in *The Old Curiosity Shop* (Chap. xviii). It seems likely, in turn, that Kafka's fragment, first published in 1931, provided the source for the dog-fairies dancing on a silvery meadow in Karel Čapek's "The Dog's Tale" (1932; in Čapek's *Fairy Tales*).

4. For the following paragraphs I am indebted especially to: "Dog," in *Encyclopaedia of Superstitions, Folklore, and the Occult Sciences of the World*, ed. C. L. Daniels and C. M. Stevans (Chicago: Yewdale, 1903), II, 613-21; "Hund," in *Handwörterbuch des deutschen Aberglaubens*, ed. Hanns Bächtold-Stäubli (Berlin and Leipzig: De Gruyter, 1931-32), IV, 470-90; Herbert Scholz, *Der Hund in der griechisch-römischen Magie und Religion* (Diss. Berlin: Triltsch und Huther, 1937); "Cynotherapy," in *Encyclopaedia Britannica*, 1957 ed., VI, 928-29; "Dogs," in E. and M. A. Radford, *Ency-*

clopaedia of Superstitions, rev. Christina Hole (London: Huchinson, 1961), pp. 135-37; and M. O. Howey, *The Cults of the Dog* (Ashington, Essex, England: Daniel, 1972).

5. For many other examples see Carolyn Boyce Johnes, *Please Don't Call Me Fido* (New York: Berkley Medallion Books, 1977).

6. See Robert Bishop, *The All-American Dog: Man's Best Friend in Folk Art* (New York: Avon Books, 1977), the catalogue for an exhibition at the Museum of American Folk Art. In conjunction with the 1978 Westminster Kennel Club Show there was also a Canine Art Exhibition in the Madison Square Garden Art Center.

7. See Thomas Whiteside, "On and Upward with the Arts (Pet Food)," *The New Yorker*, 1 November 1976, pp. 51-98.

8. These examples of dog-humanization are by no means a cultural manifestation exclusive to the contemporary United States. See Dorothy Dunbar Bromley, "A Dog's Life in Paris," *Harper's Magazine*, October 1932, pp. 625-31.

9. *The Golden Legend of Jacobus de Voragine*, trans. and adapted by Granger Ryan and Helmut Ripperger (1941; rpt. New York: Arno Press, 1969), p. 465 (entry for August 20).

10. See Manfred Lurker, "Hund und Wolf in ihrer Beziehung zum Tode," *Antaios*, 10 (July 1968), 199-216.

11. Barbara Allen Woods, *The Devil in Dog Form: A Partial Type-Index of Devil Legends*. Folklore Studies, 11 (Berkeley and Los Angeles: Univ. of California Press, 1959).

12. William Empson, "The English Dog," in *The Structure of Complex Words* (1967; Ann Arbor: Univ. of Michigan Press, 1967), pp. 158-74.

13. John Galsworthy, *Memories* (New York: Scribner's, 1927).

14. W. Kühlhorn, "Tierdichtung," in *Reallexikon der deutschen Literaturgeschichte*, ed. Paul Merker and

Wolfgang Stammler (Berlin: De Gruyter, 1928-29), III, 360-70, differentiates according to degrees of "relative" and "absolute"; Frank X. Braun, "Das Tier in der modernen Dichtung und Kritik," *Michigan Germanic Studies*, I (1975), 316-27, speaks of "anthropocentric" and "biocentric."

15. In the translation by Paul Shorey, rpt. in *The Collected Dialogues of Plato*, ed. Edith Hamilton and Huntingdon Cairns, Bollingen Series LXXI (Princeton, N.J.: Princeton Univ. Press, 1961) pp. 621-23.

16. K. A. Neuhausen, "Platons philosophischer Hund bei Sextus Empiricus," *Rheinisches Museum für Philologie*, 118 (1975), 240-64.

17. *The Works of Lucian of Samosata*, trans. H. W. Fowler and F. G. Fowler (Oxford: Clarendon, 1905), I, 142-43.

18. Francis G. Allinson, *Lucian: The Satirist and Artist* (Boston: Marshall Jones, 1926), pp. 121-87 ("Lucian's Creditors and Debtors"); and Christopher Robinson, *Lucian and His Influence in Europe* (London: Duckworth, 1979).

19. Bonaventure des Périers, *Cymbalum Mundi*. Texte établi et presenté par Peter H. Nurse (Manchester: Univ. Press, 1958); cited here according to *Cymbalum Mundi: Four Very Ancient Joyous and Facetious Poetic Dialogues*, trans. Bettina L. Knapp (New York: Bookman, 1965), pp. 65-74.

20. See Dorothea Neidhart, *Das "Cymbalum Mundi" des Bonaventure des Périers. Forschungslage und Deutung*. Kölner Romanistische Arbeiten, 16 (Paris: Minard, 1959).

21. Antonio Olivier, "La Filosofía Cínica y el 'Coloquio de los Perros,' " *Anales Cervantinos*, 3 (1953), 291-307.

22. Agustín G. De Amezúa y Mayo, *El Casamiento engañosa y El Coloquio de los Perros: Novelas ejemplares de Miguel de Cervantes Saavedra*. Edición crítica con introducción y notas (Madrid: Bailly-Baillière, 1912); cited according to *The Deceitful Marriage and Other*

Exemplary Novels, trans. Walter Starkie (New York: New American Library-Signet, 1963).

23. Cervantes provides the literary analogy for a device Kenneth Clark has pointed out in contemporary painting. In his study *Animals and Men* (London: Thames & Hudson, 1977) Clark argues that the dogs that so frequently gaze out at us in portraits by Titian and Velásquez seem to make through their very presence an ironic comment on the human subjects.

24. See the analysis by Ruth S. El Saffar, *Novel to Romance: A Study of Cervantes's "Novelas ejemplares"* (Baltimore and London: The Johns Hopkins Univ. Press, 1974), pp. 62-85.

25. Cervantes, Lucian, and the dialogue of the dogs seem to have had no influence on the many dog epicedia, satirical or other, written in various European languages during the seventeenth century. See Blake Lee Spahr, "Dogs and Doggerel in the German Baroque," *Journal of English and Germanic Philology*, 54 (1955), 380-86.

26. See Robert Adam Day's Introduction to his edition of *Pompey the Little* (London: Oxford Univ. Press, 1974), p. xviii.

27. See J.-J.A. Bertrand, *Cervantes et le Romantisme allemand* (Paris: Félix Alcan, 1914). The enthusiasm lasted, by the way. When Sigmund Freud and his friend Eduard Silberstein were studying Spanish together during their schooldays, they used as code names the dogs from Cervantes' colloquy. Silbermann was Berganza, and Freud himself assumed the name of Cipion. See Ronald W. Clark, *Freud: The Man and the Cause* (London: Jonathan Cape, 1980), p. 21.

28. I know of no translation; I refer to the text as published in E.T.A. Hoffmann, *Poetische Werke* (Berlin: Aufbau, 1958), I, 147-225. For a comparison of Hoffmann and Cervantes, see Siegbert S. Prawer, " 'Ein poetischer Hund': E.T.A. Hoffmann's *Nachrichten von den neuesten Schicksalen des Hundes Berganza* and its Antecedents in European Literature," in *Aspekte der Goethezeit*, ed. S. A. Corngold, M. Curschmann, T.

Ziolkowski (Göttingen: Vandenhoeck & Ruprecht, 1977), pp. 273-92.

29. It is fitting that Hoffmann has provided the model for a contemporary author in much the same way as Cervantes provided him with a model. Christa Wolf's story, "Neue Lebensansichten eines Katers" (1970), is a reworking of Hoffmann's *Kater Murr*; see C. Wolf, *Unter den Linden: Drei unwahrscheinliche Geschichten* (Darmstadt: Luchterhand, 1974), pp. 77-121.

30. See Vsevolod Setchkarev, *Gogol: His Life and Works*, trans. Robert Kramer (New York: N.Y.U. Press, 1965), p. 133; and M. Gorlin, *N. V. Gogol und E.T.A. Hoffmann.* Veröffentlichungen des Slavischen Instituts, 9 (Leipzig, 1933), pp. 62-78.

31. Cited according to *The Diary of a Madman and Other Stories*, trans. Andrew R. MacAndrew (New York: New American Library-Signet, 1960).

32. I know of no translation; I cite the text according to Benavente's *Obras Completas* (Madrid: Aguilar, 1942), VI, 857-97.

33. For references see Peter U. Beicken, *Franz Kafka: Eine kritische Einführung in die Forschung* (Frankfurt am Main; Athenäum Fischer Taschenbuch Verlag, 1974), pp. 307-309 and *passim.*

34. *The Heart of a Dog*, trans. Michael Glenny (London: Collins and Harvill, 1968). The Russian text was first published in 1969 by the YMCA Press in Paris.

35. His name, in fact, has etymological associations with "transformation" and even "transfiguration." As a figure, Preobrazhensky would seem to be based on Sergei Voronoff, the Russian-born French surgeon who in the 1920's achieved considerable fame for his experiments with gland-grafting in animals.

36. See Helen Howard Partridge, "Comedy in the Early Works of Mikhail Bulgakov" (Diss. Georgetown Univ., 1968).

37. *City* cited here according to Sphere Books edition (London, 1971).

38. New York: M. Evans and Co., 1974.

39. *Cuor di Padrone* (Padova: Edizioni del Ruzante, 1977).

CHAPTER FOUR

1. *Die Versuche und Hindernisse Karls: Eine deutsche Geschichte aus neuerer Zeit*; facsimile edition reprinted in *Der Doppelroman der Berliner Romantik*, ed. Helmuth Rogge (Leipzig: Klinkhardt & Biermann, 1926), II, 1-406 and II, 1-30.

2. All quotations in this paragraph are taken from the critical apparatus in Vol. II of Rogge's edition; here, p. 312.

3. See Georg Lukács, *The Historical Novel* (1937), trans. Hannah and Stanley Mitchell (Boston: Beacon, 1963), esp. Chap. 1: "The Classical Form of the Historical Novel."

4. *Chimera* (New York: Random House, 1972), p. 8.

5. Herman Meyer, *The Poetics of Quotation in the European Novel*, trans. Theodore and Yetta Ziolkowski (Princeton, N.J.: Princeton Univ. Press, 1968), p. 6.

6. E. M. Butler, *The Fortunes of Faust* (Cambridge: Cambridge Univ. Press, 1952); Leo Weinstein, *The Metamorphoses of Don Juan* (Stanford, Cal.: Stanford Univ. Press, 1959); Raymond Trousson, *Le Thème de Prométhée dans la littérature européenne* (Geneva: Droz, 1964); W. B. Stanford, *The Ulysses Theme: A Study in the Adaptability of a Traditional Hero* (Oxford: Blackwell, 1954).

7. Johann Wilhelm Friedrich Pustkuchen-Glanzow, *Wilhelm Meisters Meisterjahre* (1824) and *Wilhelm Meisters Tagebuch* (1824).

8. "Kressler," *Artiste*, I (20 février 1831), 42-44; cited by Elizabeth Teichmann, *La Fortune d'Hoffmann en France* (Paris: Minard, 1961), pp. 69-70.

9. "Ein Bild," in *Münchner Dichterbuch*, ed. Emanuel Geibel, 3rd ed. (Stuttgart: A. Kröner, 1863), pp. 170-72.

10. *Leporello fällt aus der Rolle: Zeitgenössische Au-*

toren erzählen das Leben von Figuren der Weltliteratur weiter, ed. Peter Härtling (Frankfurt am Main: Fischer, 1971).

11. E.T.A. Hoffmann, *Poetische Werke* (Berlin: Aufbau, 1958), I, 381-86 ("Die Gesellschaft im Keller").

12. For a fuller discussion see pp. 104-108 above.

13. *Der Doppelroman der Berliner Romantik*, II, 22-30.

14. Joseph Freiherr von Eichendorff, *Werke und Schriften in vier Bänden*, ed. Gerhart Baumann (Stuttgart: Cotta, 1957), II, 462.

15. Théophile Gautier, *Les Jeunes France: Romans Goguenards*, in *Oeuvres*, vol. XVI (Paris: G. Charpentier, 1883), pp. 25-70.

16. Tzvetan Todorov, *The Fantastic: A Structural Approach to a Literary Genre*, trans. Richard Howard (Ithaca, N.Y.: Cornell Univ. Press, 1975).

17. *Gesammelte Dichtungen* (Frankfurt am Main: Suhrkamp, 1952), VI, 23-27.

18. *Henry Brocken: His Travels & Adventures in the Rich, Strange, Scarce-Imaginable Regions of Romance* (New York: Knopf, 1924), p. 20.

19. See Theodore Ziolkowski, "Otherworlds: Fantasy and the Fantastic," *Sewanee Review*, 86 (1978), 121-29.

20. Miguel de Unamuno, *Novela/Nivola*, trans. Anthony Kerrigan, Bollingen Series LXXXV, 6 (Princeton, N.J.: Princeton Univ. Press, 1976), p. 219.

21. *Breakfast of Champions* (New York: Delacorte, 1973), p. 291.

22. Hella S. Haasse, *Ein gevaarlijke verhouding of Daal-en-Bergse brieven* (Amsterdam: Querido, 1976), p. 138.

23. *Letters* (New York: Putnam's, 1979), p. 189.

24. Ingrid Strohschneider-Kohrs, *Die romantische Ironie in Theorie und Gestaltung* (Tübingen: Niemeyer, 1960); and Bernhard Heimrich, *Fiktion und Fiktions-*

ironie in Theorie und Dichtung der deutschen Romantik (Tübingen: Niemeyer, 1968).

25. Karl Konrad Polheim, *Die Arabeske: Ansichten und Ideen aus Friedrich Schlegels Poetik* (München: Schöningh, 1966), esp. pp. 198-234; and Walter Bausch, *Theorien des epischen Erzählens in der deutschen Frühromantik* (Bonn: Bouvier, 1964).

26. René Wellek, *A History of Modern Criticism*. Vol. I, *The Later Eighteenth Century* (New Haven: Yale Univ. Press, 1955), pp. 12-30 ("Neoclassicism"); also Dieter Kafitz, *Figurenkonstellation als Mittel der Wirklichkeitsauffassung* (Kronberg: Athenäum, 1978), pp. 31-36.

27. "Zum Shakespeares-Tag," in *Goethes Werke* (Hamburger-Ausgabe), XII, 225-26.

28. Wellek, *History of Modern Criticism*, I, 117-18.

29. Wellek, *History of Modern Criticism*, II, 182.

30. Faksimiledruck der Originalausgabe von 1774, ed. Eberhart Lämmert (Stuttgart: Metzler, 1965), p. 77.

31. Jean Paul, *Werke*, ed. Norbert Miller (München: Hanser, 1962), V, 211-12.

32. *The Selected Poetry and Prose of Edgar Allan Poe*, ed. T. O. Mabbott (New York: Modern Library, 1951), p. 361.

33. *Fiction and the Reading Public* (London: Chatto & Windus, 1932), p. 58.

34. Theodor W. Adorno, *Ästhetische Theorie*, ed. Gretel Adorno and Rolf Tiedemann (Frankfurt am Main: Suhrkamp, 1970), p. 514.

35. Miguel de Unamuno, *Our Lord Don Quixote: The Life of Don Quixote and Sancho with Related Essays*, trans. Anthony Kerrigan, Bollingen Series LXXXV, 3 (Princeton, N.J.: Princeton Univ. Press, 1967), p. 323.

36. Luigi Pirandello, *Naked Masks: Five Plays*, ed. Eric Bentley (New York: Dutton, 1952), p. 364.

37. Cited by Morris Weitz, *Hamlet and the Philosophy of Literary Criticism* (Chicago: Univ. of Chicago Press, 1964), pp. 19-26.

38. T. S. Eliot, *Selected Essays 1917-1932* (New York: Harcourt, Brace, 1932), p. 121.

39. *Aspects of the Novel* (1927; rpt. New York: Harcourt, Brace-Harvest, 1954), p. 62-63.

40. *How Many Children Had Lady Macbeth?* (1933; rpt. New York: Haskell House, 1973), p. 27.

41. Hélène Cixous, "The Character of 'Character,' " *New Literary History*, 5 (1974), 387. The fascination of character has by no means vanished completely. See the anthology *Romanfiguren*, ed. Walter Helmut Fritz (Mainz: Hase und Koehler, 1971), in which thirteen writers talk about literary figures who have meant a great deal to them—who are, in short, as real as life.

42. Paul Ernst, *Erdachte Gespräche* (Munich: Georg Müller, 1921), p. 109. This dialogue is unusual to the extent that it involves two literary figures. Most works of the genre—e.g., Walter Savage Landor's *Imaginary Conversations* (1824-29)—involve historical personages. See, for instance, Anna Seghers' story "Die Reisebegegnung" (in *Sonderbare Begegnungen* [Berlin: Aufbau, 1973], pp. 107-148), in which E.T.A. Hoffmann, on his way to Dresden to visit Anselmus and Lindhorst (characters from *The Golden Pot*), stops off in Prague, where he spends an evening in a cafe with Gogol and Kafka. The same applies to the genre of *Totengespräche* that was so popular in eighteenth-century Germany. See John Rutledge, *The Dialogue of the Dead in Eighteenth-Century Germany* (Bern and Frankfurt am Main: Herbert Lang, 1974).

43. See especially Willard V. Quine, "On What There Is," *The Review of Metaphysics*, 2 (1948), 21-38; John R. Searle, "The Logical Status of Fictional Discourse," *New Literary History*, 6 (1975), 319-32; Charles Crittenden, "Fictional Existence," *American Philosophical Quarterly*, 3 (1966), 317-21; Gottfried Gabriel, *Fiktion und Wahrheit: Eine semantische Theorie der Literatur* (Stuttgart-Bad Cannstatt: Friedrich Frommann, 1975).

44. Jorge Luis Borges, "Partial Magic in the *Quixote*," in *Labyrinths: Selected Stories and Other Writings*, ed.

Donald A. Yates and James E. Irby (New York: New Directions, 1964), p. 196.

CHAPTER FIVE

1. George Moore, *The Apostle. A Drama in Three Acts* (Dublin: Maunsel, 1911).
2. George Moore, *The Brook Kerith: A Syrian Story.* New Edition with a Preface (New York: Macmillan, 1917).
3. David Friedrich Strauss, *The Life of Jesus Critically Examined*, trans. George Eliot; edited and with an Introduction by Peter C. Hodgson (London: SCM Press, 1973), pp. 709-744 (esp. paragraph 140 on Resurrection).
4. Ferdinand Christian Baur, *The Church History of the First Three Centuries*, trans. Allan Menzies; 3rd edition (London: Williams and Norgate, 1878), I, 43.
5. See Albert Schweitzer, *The Quest of the Historical Jesus: A Study of Its Progress from Reimarus to Wrede*, trans. from 1st ed. by W. Montgomery (1910; rpt. New York: Macmillan, 1968).
6. The following paragraphs recapitulate in brief the argument advanced in my book *Disenchanted Images: A Literary Iconology* (Princeton, N.J.: Princeton Univ. Press, 1977), esp. pp. 18-77 ("Image as Theme: Venus and the Ring").
7. See Alexander Gode von Aesch, *Natural Science in German Romanticism* (New York: Columbia Univ. Press, 1941); and Walter D. Wetzels, "Aspects of Natural Science in German Romanticism," *Studies in Romanticism*, 10 (1971), 44-59.
8. See Hodgson's Introduction to Strauss, *The Life of Jesus*, p. xx.
9. Giovanni Papini, *Life of Christ*, trans. Dorothy Canfield Fisher (New York: Harcourt, Brace, 1923).
10. Lloyd C. Douglas, *The Big Fisherman* (Boston: Houghton Mifflin, 1948).

11. D. H. Lawrence, *St. Mawr and The Man Who Died* (New York: Random House-Vintage Books, n.d.).

12. Ernest Renan, *The Life of Jesus*, translator not named (1864; rpt. Garden City, N.Y.: Doubleday-Dolphin, n.d.), p. 302.

13. Emil Ludwig, *The Son of Man*, translator not named (1928; rpt. New York: Fawcett World Library-Premier Books, 1957), p. vii.

14. Edzard Schaper, *Das Leben Jesu* (1936; rpt. Frankfurt am Main: Fischer Bücherei, 1957).

15. Frank G. Slaughter, *The Crown and the Cross: The Life of Christ* (Cleveland and New York: World, 1959).

16. Sholem Asch, *The Nazarene*, trans. Maurice Samuel (New York: Putnam's, 1939).

17. Robert Graves, *King Jesus* (1946; rpt. New York: Funk & Wagnalls-Minerva Press, n.d.).

18. Pär Lagerkvist, *Barabbas*, trans. Alan Blair; with a Preface by Lucien Maury and a Letter by André Gide (1951; rpt. New York: Random House-Bantam, 1968).

CHAPTER SIX

1. Ernst Schumacher, *Brecht: Theater und Gesellschaft im 20. Jahrhundert* (Berlin: Henschel, 1973), p. 198. Schumacher himself attempted to carry out Brecht's plan in his Einstein drama, *Die Versuchung des Forschers oder Visionen aus der Realität. Ein Biophysikal.* I have not seen the text, but the play is discussed by Jim Elliott, Bruce Little, and Carol Poore in their chapter "Naturwissenschaftlerdramen und Kalter Krieg," in *Geschichte im Gegenwartsdrama*, ed. Reinhold Grimm and Jost Hermand (Stuttgart: Kohlhammer, 1976), pp. 54-65.

2. Karl Mickel, *Einstein/Nausikaa: Die Schrecken des Humanismus in zwei Stücken* (Berlin: Rotbuch, 1974), pp. 5-39.

3. *Das kalte Licht* (Frankfurt am Main: Fischer, 1955), p. 162: "Krise des Vertrauens."

4. *In der Sache J. Robert Oppenheimer* (Frankfurt am Main: Suhrkamp, 1964); trans. Ruth Speirs, *In the Matter of J. Robert Oppenheimer* (London: Methuen, 1967), p. 71.

5. *Die Physiker* (Zurich: Die Arche, 1962); trans. James Kirkup, *The Physicists* (New York: Grove, 1964), p. 96.

6. *The Journals of David E. Lilienthal* (New York: Harper & Row, 1964), p. 581; cited in R. W. Reid, *Tongues of Conscience: Weapons Research and the Scientists' Dilemma* (New York: Walker, 1969), p. 272.

7. Quoted in Ralph E. Lapp, *The New Priesthood: The Scientific Elite and The Uses of Power* (New York: Harper & Row, 1965), p. 17.

8. On the Frankenstein theme, its background, and its popularizations see D. F. Glut, *The Frankenstein Legend* (Metuchen, N.J.: Scarecrow, 1973); and Radu Florescu, *In Search of Frankenstein* (Boston: New York Graphic Society, 1975).

9. I cite the third edition of 1831 in the Signet Classics edition of *Frankenstein, or The Modern Prometheus* (New York: New American Library, 1965). For studies of the novel see W. H. Lyles, *Mary Shelley: An Annotated Bibliography* (New York: Garland, 1975); and David Ketterer, "Mary Shelley and Science Fiction: A Select Bibliography Selectively Annotated," *Science-Fiction Studies*, 5 (1978), 172-78.

10. Quoted in Ted Howard and Jeremy Rifkin, *Who Should Play God?* (New York: Delacorte, 1977), p. 225.

11. In this connection see M. A. Goldberg, "Moral and Myth in Mrs. Shelley's *Frankenstein*," *Keats-Shelley Journal*, 8 (1959), 27-28.

12. Wilfred Cude, "Mary Shelley's Modern Prometheus: A Study in the Ethics of Scientific Creativity," *Dalhousie Review*, 52 (1972), 212-25.

13. George Basalla, "Pop Science: The Depiction of Science in Popular Culture," in *Science and its Public*, ed. G. Holton and W. A. Blanpied (Dordrecht: Reidel, 1976), pp. 261-78.

14. *Le Thème de Prométhée dans la littérature européenne*, 2 vols. (Geneva: Droz, 1964).

15. *The Complete Works of Percy Bysshe Shelley*, ed. Roger Ingpen and Walter E. Peck (New York: Scribner, 1927), II, 171-72.

16. In addition to Trousson, *Le Thème de Prométhée*, see Jacqueline Duchemin, *Prométhée: Histoire du mythe, de ses origines orientales à ses incarnations modernes* (Paris: Les Belles Lettres, 1974); and Hans-Georg Gadamer, "Prometheus und die Tragödie der Kultur," in *Kleine Schriften II: Interpretationen* (Tübingen: Mohr, 1967), pp. 64-74.

17. See "The Fall" in *The Interpreter's Dictionary of the Bible* (New York and Nashville: Abingdon, 1962), II, 235-37; Robert Graves and Raphael Patai, *Hebrew Myths: The Book of Genesis* (Garden City, N.Y.: Doubleday, 1964), esp. pp. 78-81; and Oswald Loretz, *Schöpfung und Mythos: Mensch und Welt nach den Anfangskapiteln der Genesis*, Stuttgarter Bibelstudien 32 (Stuttgart: Katholisches Bibelwerk, 1968).

18. Chap. 63 of the English translation of 1592, ed. William Rose (New York: Dutton, 1925; rpt. South Bend, Indiana: Univ. of Notre Dame Press, 1963).

19. Quoted in John Langone, *Human Engineering: Marvel or Menace* (Boston: Little, Brown, 1978), p. 110.

20. *Science*, 194 (15 October 1976), 256-57.

21. *The Illusion of Technique: A Search for Meaning in a Technological Civilization* (Garden City, N.Y.: Doubleday-Anchor, 1978), p. 20.

22. Quoted in John Langone, *Human Engineering*, p. 113.

23. See John Egerton, "The Issues Medical Schools Have Ignored," *Chronicle of Higher Education*, XVII/7 (16 October 1978), p. 11; and Jane Stein, "The Bioethicists: Facing Matters of Life and Death," *Smithsonian*, IX/10 (January 1979), 107-115; and the essays in *Science and the Public Interest: Recombinant DNA Research*, ed. Robert P. Bareikis (Indianapolis: Indiana Committee for the Humanities, 1978).

INDEX

Abelson, Philip, 179
Adam, myth of, 187-92
Adams, Frank Dawson, 233n5, 233n8, 234n19, 234n22, 235n31,
  237n69
Adams, Richard, *The Plague Dogs*, 95
Adorno, Theodor W., 148
Aesch, Alexander Gode von, 249n7
Aeschylus, 189, 190, 191
Agréda, Maria d', 36
Agricola, Georgius, 39, 52
Aimeri de Narbonne, 61
Albertus Magnus, 42, 48, 49, 50, 51, 57, 81, 182
alchemy, 42, 57-58, 72, 74, 79, 83-84
Aldrovandi, Ulisse, 51, 52
Alexander the Great, 34, 80; *Lay of*, 68-69
Alexis, Willibald, 127
allegoresis, Christian, 43-48
Allinson, Francis G., 242n18
Alphabetical Lapidary, 67
Alphonso, *Disciplina clericalis*, 34
Ambrose, Saint, 54, 65
Amezuá y Majo, Agustín de, 242n22
Andersen, Hans Christian, 23, 28, 32, 214; "Auntie Toothache,"
  20-21
Apollonia, Saint, 5, 18
Appelbaum, Richard P., 232n35
Aquinas, Thomas, 57-58
arabesque, 143-44
Arabian Nights, 65, 129
Aristotle, 38, 40, 41, 65, 144
Arnold, Matthew, 189
Arnold, Robert F., 211
Arnoldus Saxo, 47-48
Asch, Sholem, *The Nazarene*, 171-72, 173
Aucassin et Nicolette, 13
Audry, Colette, 94
Augustine, Saint, 13, 44-45

253

Library of Congress Cataloging in Publication Data

Ziolkowski, Theodore.
Varieties of literary thematics.

Includes index.
Contents: The telltale teeth—The mystic carbuncle
—Talking dogs—[etc.]
1. Literature, Comparative—Themes, motives—Addresses,
essays, lectures.   I. Title.
PN45.Z487   1983   809'.933   83-42585
ISBN 0-691-06577-2